MY HUS
MY KILLER

MY HUSBAND
MY KILLER

The murder of
Megan Kalajzich

Lindsay Simpson and Sandra Harvey

ALLEN & UNWIN

First published in 1992
Allen & Unwin Pty Ltd
8 Napier Street, North Sydney, NSW 2059 Australia

National Library of Australia
Cataloguing-in-Publication entry:

Harvey, Sandra.
My husband my killer.

ISBN 1 86373 175 X.

1. Kalajzich, Andrew. 2. Kalajzich, Megan, d. 1986—Assassination.
3. Murder—New South Wales—Manly. 4. Millionaires—New South
Wales—Manly. 5. Murderers—New South Wales—Manly. I. Simpson,
Lindsay. II. Title.

364.1523099441

Set in 10½/12 pt Goudy Old Style, by Adtype Graphics
Printed by The Book Printer, Maryborough Victoria

Back cover photo taken by Paul Matthews for
The Sydney Morning Herald

CONTENTS

THE AUTHORS

Sandra Harvey and Lindsay Simpson are two investigative crime writers who first collaborated in 1984 to write their best-selling book, *Brothers in Arms*, the story of the 1984 Milperra bikie massacre. *My Husband, My Killer*, their second book, is also a true murder story, filled with suspense and intrigue.

Harvey and Simpson are journalists for *The Sydney Morning Herald*. Both women live in Sydney. Simpson is married to a press photographer and has three children. The authors are working on their third crime book on another contemporary Australian murder.

ACKNOWLEDGEMENTS

My Husband, My Killer is non-fiction, written in a style pioneered by Truman Capote in his book, *In Cold Blood*. Although the book reads like a novel, the authors have at all times attempted to be accurate in their portrayals of characters and events.

All the material in this book is either from official court records, original correspondence, or is the result of extensive interviews with many people conducted over 18 months.

Many of those who assisted the authors have asked not to be publicly acknowledged. Our sincere thanks is extended to you all.

Among those we would like to publicly thank are the New South Wales police who gave their time and assistance; in particular Inspectors Bob Inkster, Bob Richardson and Mike Hagan; Sergeant John Radalj, Detective Stephen Nicholas and Senior Constable Geoff Bell.

We would also like to thank Jill Cash, from the office of the New South Wales Director of Public Prosecutions, and Ron Woodham and Dave Farrell from the New South Wales Department of Corrective Services.

We are grateful, too, for the help we received at *The Manly Daily*, particularly from Chris Davies, and for the co-operation of the following: Steve Barrett and Channel Nine News, Max Blenkin, the New South Wales Ambulance Service, Cate Carrigan, Jonathan Chancellor, Jon Cleary, Jenny Cooke, Jo Cronin, Terry Cutcliffe, the John Fairfax Group, Margaret McDonald, Nick Papadopoulos, Larry Schwartz, John Hilzinger and Amanda Smith. Finally, our thanks to those who helped us gain an insight into Andrew Kalajzich and without whose help our book could not have been written. For your encouragement and support, we thank you.

ONE

BLOOD ON HIS HANDS

It was his first murder. He felt the blood sticky on his hands. It was drying and had already worked its way under his fingernails. He looked at his watch. It was 1.40 am, 27 January 1986. Matthew Davis picked up the radio handset and held it to his mouth.

'Ambulance 534 to Control.'

'Go ahead 34.'

'Paramedics are not required, Control. Patient is Code 4.'

'Thanks 34, I'll call them off.'

The young ambulance officer put the radio back and inspected his arms. His van was well stocked with sterile strips and alcohol swabs but he knew that hot running water was the best way to clean off blood.

Davis left the van and walked back inside the house. More police had arrived and he noticed security guards out the front. It seemed like hours since he and his partner, Ottmar Nouak, had arrived at the house. It had been so still and quiet then, they wondered whether they had found the right address.

Both ambulance officers had been dozing in front of the

1

television at Manly Ambulance Station when the emergency alert, a high-pitched signal, sounded. Then came the message over the radio: 'Report of female shot.'

Calls to shootings were rare in this Sydney seaside suburb; more than one a year was unusual. Davis and Nouak were in their primary-care van within seconds. Nouak drove while Davis double-checked the address they had been given, 31 Fairlight Crescent, in the street directory. Davis had driven along Lauderdale Avenue—the nearest cross street—hundreds of times, but he needed to be certain that he had Fairlight Crescent and not Fairlight Street.

The siren pierced the sleeping neighbourhood, the pulsing glow from their red lights bouncing off garden fences and garage walls. Davis felt a surge of adrenalin.

The street was deserted. Not even a police car had arrived when they pulled up. Nouak jumped down from the front seat and ran to the garage doors.

'This is the place,' he called to his partner when his torch-light picked out a pair of brass numerals, 31, on the wall between the carport and the garage.

Davis picked up the radio. '534 on scene at 0122, Control,' he said.

'Thanks, 534. 0122.' The radio operator repeated the time out loud.

Three minutes later, the first of the police, two constables in a Frenchs Forest patrol car, arrived.

Constable First-Class David Christie and Constable Delores Lassen had been returning to their station from another job in Manly when they heard the high-pitched alert over their car radio, followed by the report of a shooting. Lassen, behind the wheel, turned on the siren and lights, did a U-turn on the Wakehurst Parkway and drove to Fairlight Crescent faster than she had ever driven. The radio operator had warned that the offender might still be on the premises. With guns drawn they approached the ambulance officers.

'You been called to a shooting?' Davis asked Constable Christie.

'Yeah, do you know what's going on?' Christie asked.

'No, we don't know, mate. We just got here ourselves.'

'We'd better go down and take a look,' Christie said. He and Lassen began walking down the steps leading to the house. It was a three-storey brick and timber building which fronted onto the Esplanade. Steep steps led down from the carport through tiered gardens to the back of the house. Davis, equipped with an Oxy-viva resuscitator and a first-aid kit, descended the steps carefully towards a sliding glass door which was the back entrance.

An elderly woman dressed in a nightgown was sitting on a lounge chair just inside. She stood up and pulled the door open. Christie and Lassen lowered their guns.

'She's through there,' said the woman, pointing down the hallway, 'but I think she's gone.'

Christie headed along the hall, almost running, into a bedroom opposite. Lassen and the two ambulance officers followed.

The first thing they noticed in the soft golden light from the bedside lamps was the blood. There was so much of it. A woman was lying on one side of a bed facing the door. A dark-haired man was kneeling beside the bed, his head nuzzling into the hips of the inanimate body, his arm draped over her knees. He appeared to be crying. The top of the woman's body was almost completely red.

As Christie approached the bed he noticed two small bullet holes on the side of her face, just below her ear. He put his hand on her throat to feel for a pulse.

'Excuse me, mate, but can you move back a bit so the ambulance officers can take a look?' the constable said quietly.

Andrew Kalajzich hardly responded, moving only slightly towards the end of the bed.

Davis came forward with his first-aid kit. He, too, saw the bullet holes. He expected to find more wounds on the woman's chest, because of the amount of blood that had soaked the front of her orange, sleeveless nightgown. At first glance, he was almost certain she was dead. He put his fingers on the woman's forearm. Still warm. He put his hand firmly on the shoulder of the man, still kneeling by the bed.

'Excuse me, mate, can you just move up here to the other end of the bed?'

Kalajzich lifted his head. The face was middle-aged, with strong European features: a large nose, dark eyes and thick black hair, peppered grey. He was tall and slim, his long legs stretched out behind as he knelt on the floor. Davis was immediately struck by the doleful look in the reddened eyes staring up at him. He was mourning, but his grief seemed distant. Odd he thought. But then, in his six years as an ambulance officer, he had never attended a shooting as serious as this.

Kalajzich said nothing but moved a little further towards the foot of the bed, where he sat watching the ambulance officer. Constable Lassen stepped in. Lassen, a tall, well built New Zealander, put her hand firmly on Kalajzich's shoulder.

'Come on, sir. Let's just go and wait outside while the ambulance officers take a look.' She had a strong physical presence and authoritative voice. 'There's nothing we can do in here. We'll go and wait outside,' she said. Kalajzich stood up, and Lassen ushered him out of the bedroom. He was reluctant to leave and strained to watch what Davis was doing as she led him out of the bedroom door.

Davis pulled back the purple-patterned cotton sheet and a light blanket which covered the woman to her waist. He guessed she was in her late forties. She was lying on her right side and angled slightly, face down into the pillow. Blood had formed around her face and stained the pillowslip beneath her head.

Because of the angle at which she lay, Davis found it difficult to find the carotid pulse in her neck or to check her pupil reaction—both basic 'life sign' tests.

He removed the pillow from under her head and noted that the blood had already begun to coagulate. Rolling her body back several degrees so it was properly on its side, he moved her leg up into a coma position to support its weight. He noticed faint, old bruising around her ankles and left knee.

There was no pulse; her pupils were fixed and dilated. She was dead.

Mopping the blood from her chest, Davis looked for further injuries but could find none. He surmised that the woman had haemorrhaged to death. The bullets had struck a major artery. Blood would have spurted out for several seconds after she was shot. The blood collecting under her skin had already begun to disfigure and bloat her strong features. Using dressings from his first-aid kit, Davis wiped away the blood from her head. There was little else he could do.

Satisfied there were no more wounds, he stood up and looked down at the corpse. Before he had moved her, she looked almost serene, curled up in foetal-like sleep, her right hand slipped innocently under the pillow. The woman had a healthy-looking, robust body and an attractive, kind face with a dusting of light brown freckles across the bridge of her nose. Davis was struck by her beautiful hair: thick and shiny brown. He had no idea who she was. He assumed the man had been her husband. He looked around the room.

Despite the salubrious waterfront address overlooking Manly Esplanade and the Bay of Forty Baskets Beach, the house was not furnished extravagantly. The furniture was outdated and a little tired, more fashionable in the 1970s. Tube-like bedside lampshades in orange shot silk stood on ornate cream wooden tables with curved Italian-style legs. The bedhead was cream quilted leather. The walls were busy with elaborate, embossed gold wallpaper.

The room was small, big enough only for the double bed and a large built-in wardrobe along one wall. Above the bed was a long, narrow rectangular window. On a dark velvet Florentine stool beside the bed lay a woman's red sweatshirt with a furry koala bear motif on the front. Its store labels were still attached.

In a simple gold frame on the wall opposite, a younger version of the dead woman smiled from a formal wedding photograph. She was dressed in a long, straight bridal gown and clutched a bunch of flowers.

Davis' eyes travelled back to the bed again, to the woman's bedside table. There was a bottle of French perfume, the lightly floral-scented Anäis Anäis, and a few jewellery boxes. A clock radio occupied the husband's bedside table.

Davis moved away so Nouak could double-check the woman's vital signs—again, standard practice. Kalajzich had reappeared in the bedroom.

Davis whispered to Christie: 'There's nothing we can do, I'm afraid. She's dead. There's two bullet wounds on the left-hand side of her face.'

Two more constables in a Mosman division patrol car arrived. Christie got them to check the grounds and foreshore. The only sound outside was the occasional tinkling from yachts as they bobbed on their moorings. Davis felt the need for fresh air. He followed Christie through a sliding glass door which led to a balcony off the bedroom. The door was slightly ajar.

A half moon lit up a clear sky and light danced on the water below. A soft night breeze ruffled the water's surface.

Inside, Kalajzich had once again been ushered from the bedroom by Constable Lassen. He now sat in the family room with his head in his hands. 'What bastard would have wanted to shoot her?' he asked, staring at the floor. 'What bastard would have wanted to do this to her?' It was a question to which no-one else in the room had an answer.

Kalajzich's mother-in-law, May Carmichael, who had met them at the door, sat opposite, oddly composed in her shock. Andrew junior, his nineteen-year-old son, sat on a chair next to him. He, too, seemed calm and controlled.

Lassen watched as Kalajzich appeared to sob, but no tears fell from his eyes. She noticed him rubbing his eyes, making them redder.

Christie brought out his police notebook and pen and began asking Kalajzich what had happened. Kalajzich had already told him the killer had fired at him as well, the bullets narrowly missing him.

'The detectives will probably want to take a statement later,' Christie told him, 'but let's just go through the basic details of what happened.' He sat down opposite Kalajzich. 'Can you start by giving me your details and those of your wife . . .'

Lassen nodded to Christie and positioned herself as a guard at the bedroom doorway. No-one else would enter the room until the detectives arrived.

As Christie finished taking details from Kalajzich, Davis came back inside the house. After reporting to ambulance control, Davis's official duties were over. Now all he wanted to do was find a tap to wash his hands and then go. Walking into the family room, Davis noticed some blood smeared on the front of Kalajzich's summer dressing-gown and blue-striped pyjamas.

'Could I wash my hands somewhere?' Davis asked him quietly. There was no reply, but Kalajzich stood up, and, trance-like, led him to a bathroom to the left of the hallway and opened the door.

Warren Elkins started closing up the bar at the Manly Pacific hotel's Dalleys nightclub about 1.30 am. It had been a busy Sunday night—Australia Day and a long weekend. He was at the cash register when he noticed James Taylor, a security guard, coming into the empty nightclub.

'Do you know where Mr Kalajzich lives, Warren?' Taylor asked.

'Somewhere in Fairlight Crescent, I think. Why? What's up?' Elkins asked quickly.

'There's been some trouble around there. I've got a message from the boss on my pager. He wants us down there as soon as possible.'

Elkins almost ran towards the two barmen stacking away the glasses behind the bar. 'There's been a spot of trouble down at the boss's house,' he said breathlessly. 'I'm closing up shop and I want you to come with me. We're leaving now.'

As he walked outside to the lifts, Taylor's words kept replaying in his mind. Taylor, Elkins, and the barmen—Christopher Stear and David Packer—took the lift down to the basement carpark.

Elkins noticed the marked police car parked in the middle of the road as soon as they turned into Fairlight Crescent. He did not even see the ambulance. He led the way down the steep steps to the house. Neil Southerby, the hotel duty manager, had arrived at the same time.

Mrs Carmichael was standing at the sliding door where the police had entered thirty minutes earlier. Her face was a sickly, chalk colour. 'It's Megan,' she addressed the men standing on the porch. 'They tried to get her a couple of weeks ago and now they finished it.' She began to sob.

Elkins stopped Stear and Packer from entering. 'There's no need for us to go inside,' he said.

Southerby entered the house. He could see his boss sitting on a lounge chair behind the old lady. Kalajzich acknowledged him briefly.

'Is there anything I can do?' Southerby asked Kalajzich. Kalajzich was sitting with his head in his hands. He shook his head. 'No ... oh, yes—ring Tony.' Tony was Kalajzich's older brother. Southerby nodded.

'Who would have done something like that?' Stear asked Elkins in the car as they headed back to the Manly Pacific.

Elkins didn't answer. As they pulled up outside the hotel, the lights were still on in the nightclub. Some of the staff had stayed behind. Elkins turned to his passengers: 'I don't think we should say anything about this to anyone. Don't tell any of the staff.'

When Detective-Sergeant Bob Inkster arrived at Fairlight Crescent at 1.50 am, he was pleased. The two young constables had done their jobs well. They had 'kept their hands in their pockets', the most vital requirement for the first police to a crime scene.

As he entered the house, Inkster recognised the man sitting in the family room. Andrew Kalajzich seemed so calm. Here was a man who had just seen his wife die, and probably just escaped being killed himself. Perhaps it was deep shock—at the moment he could give him the benefit of the doubt.

At 39, Robert Bruce Inkster was fit and taller than average at 189 cm. His shiny balding crown made him appear older than his years. His big blue eyes were wide-set underneath thick eyebrows which had already settled into a frown of concentration. Inkster was not prone to smiling. He was a hard-working, matter-of-fact cop. One of his biggest breaks to date had been interviewing a man then considered a key informant for the Hilton Hotel bomb task force in 1978.

Inkster had been out for the evening at the Manly Fishermen's Club celebrating a victory over the Yass Soldiers Memorial Club cricket team. He had not long been home when the phone rang with news of the murder. He drove down to the police station to pick up the police Commodore in his old yellow and white Land Rover. Although he had spent most of his life in plain clothes, he had never before headed a murder investigation.

Inkster was the '2IC', the acting sergeant-in-charge of detectives at Manly police station. As the senior detective, he had been called out to take control of the crime scene. He would have the help of some of the district's best detectives and others from the Criminal Investigation Branch (CIB) which had also been informed. Bob Worthington, his boss, was on leave. Inkster knew there was a chance he could see the whole inquiry through. The prospect excited him but at the same time the responsibility was daunting. His frown deepened.

A stickler for propriety, he arrived dressed in a jacket, tie and trousers. 'If you're going to act like a detective,' he would lecture, 'you might as well look like one too.'

Inkster was a second-generation resident of Sydney's northern beaches. Like most locals, he knew of Kalajzich but he had never met him.

He searched his mind for any details of the deceased . . .

Megan Kalajzich. She had been attacked recently, assaulted at her home, about a fortnight ago. Possibly cat burglars, but there was something about the husband, he had behaved strangely; he wouldn't help the police at all.

Inkster was ready to see the body. It was not the first bloodied corpse he had seen, but the sight of Megan Kalajzich somehow chilled him, lying helplessly in the privacy of her own home. He glanced around the room.

Inkster, whose motto was 'Don't tell me—show me', did not tolerate fools. Nor would he tolerate shoddy or slothful investigative work. He knew that what counted were facts. He was never flamboyant, but thorough and even pedantic—skills he had honed while working as an insurance claims clerk and accident underwriter before joining the force in 1966.

Only the ambulance officers had been allowed in to the bedroom the young constables told him. Inkster asked them some brief questions about what they had done and seen.

'We examined the balcony door,' said Lassen.

'The flyscreen door was closed, Sergeant, but the glass door was open, wide enough to let a person fit through,' Christie continued.

'And,' said Lassen, 'Mr Kalajzich told me that he forgot to lock the downstairs door before he went to bed, but May, his mother-in-law, said she had checked and locked it before she retired.'

'I see,' said Inkster. 'You've done very well. A good job.'

Constables Christie and Lassen appreciated Inkster's compliment. They knew of the nickname he had been give twenty years ago, not long after joining the force—'The Snake'. It suited him: long and lean with his ear close to the ground. But Inkster also had a reputation for sinking his fangs in, refusing to relinquish his prey until he was satisfied all of the evidence had been extracted.

'When you've finished taking any other details from the family,' Inkster continued, 'I want you to go straight back to Manly police station and record everything you heard and saw and did. We'll take over from here.'

The atmosphere was solemn and quiet. Everyone was talking in hushed tones. Detective-Sergeant John Barber, a scientific officer, arrived and went straight through to the bedroom. Other officers arrived and joined the police who were congregating in the kitchen.

Inkster met the Manly district Inspector, Jim Rope, in the hallway and walked with him out of earshot of the family room. Rope was the most senior officer on the northern peninsula. Inkster gave him an update.

Rope nodded. 'I've called out Bob Richardson from Dee Why to come down and give us a hand,' he said. 'He can talk to the husband and take him down to Manly and get a statement from him.'

'OK, boss,' said Inkster. He knew Richardson, who was in charge of detectives at Dee Why. They had worked together before. He was a good operator.

Using his portable radio, Inkster contacted the Sydney duty operations inspector—the DOI in police jargon—and asked him to call out Dr Godfrey Oettle, the government pathologist, to examine the corpse.

Inkster had to make sure the crime scene remained intact and liaise with the CIB and ballistics.

Tony Kalajzich arrived. As he stood looking at Megan's body, and formally identified it, he wept openly. Constable Lassen comforted him.

With a few moments' respite, Inkster began asking himself the obvious questions. Why would anyone want to kill Andrew Kalajzich and his wife? And, the killer must have been standing no more than one metre from the bed when Megan was shot. How on earth could he or she have missed the husband? It didn't make sense—at first glance, anyway. But Inkster had to get things moving. If they caught someone, every step tonight would be examined and re-examined in the cold, clinical atmosphere of a courtroom. He wanted everything to be done meticulously.

More scientific officers arrived and began coating the doors and furniture with fine hodinite powder, looking for finger-prints.

Inkster contacted the duty officer again to ask for the police divers to do a dawn search for the weapon along the foreshore. He organised a door-to-door canvass of the area. A team of fourteen detectives would door-knock every house in the area the next day to see if anyone had heard or seen anything suspicious during the night. The supervising sergeant from Manly station, Colin Alterator, arranged for twenty uniformed police and rescue squad officers to search the grounds with a metal detector at first light.

Inkster checked the security of the house then, and again at dawn. After his second inspection of all the doorways and windows, he confirmed his initial conclusion that there had been no forced entry.

About 8 am, Lassen and Christie returned to the house after having completed their paperwork at Manly. They had to wait for the government contractors who would take the body to the morgue. As the first officers on the scene that night, they had to accompany the body.

Lassen went into the bedroom to assist the ballistics officers. They were using string and measuring tools to try to calculate the trajectory of the bullets. That would help determine the type of weapon used. They had already found spent cartridge cases hidden in the folds of the bedspread and blanket.

'That's odd,' said Detective Barber. 'You wouldn't think you'd need a blanket on a night like this.'

Meanwhile, the news had begun to filter through to the media. Most newspapers and television stations monitored the police radios, although the story did not break until a 6 am radio bulletin. It threw the rest of the pack into a flurry, too late for the daily newspapers but a bonus for the radio stations.

It was a quiet public holiday Monday morning, and the police reporters who began their shifts at police headquarters in College Street had expected little more than a game of cards. Instead, they had a story that would carry them through the whole week. Radio reporters sweated over the best lead, looking for new angles and updates as the next half-hourly deadline loomed. Television crews and newspaper reporters pocketed notebooks and arrived by car. It would be front page tomorrow, for sure.

The local paper, *The Manly Daily*, had a few good stock photos of Megan Kalajzich. The best was one taken at the December 1982 opening of her husband's hotel, the Manly Pacific. She was smiling, flanked by her husband and the Premier of New South Wales, Neville Wran.

By the time news of her death became public, her body was being identified to a pathologist at the city morgue. An identification tag was tied around her wrist and the body given a number. In the presence of the government doctor, the Coroner and Detective Barber, Constable Christie formally identified the body as that of Megan Kalajzich. Then he filled out the standard P79A form, a report of a death to the Coroner.

As he left the Kalajzich house, the Snake was besieged by reporters. He knew he would have to say something to the media. He wanted to. After all, he knew they could be useful, especially in the early stages of a murder like this, with no obvious leads or clues. But he wasn't used to dealing with reporters, especially in packs. He wanted to get it right—and on his terms. He told several reporters at the house that he would give them a proper statement back at the station. By the time he got back there, word had spread. A crowd of reporters was waiting outside.

'Sorry,' he told them as he moved towards the front steps of the police station. 'We've got nothing to tell you at the moment but we will prepare a statement and have a brief press conference as soon as it's ready.'

Once inside the station, Inkster chaired a conference of twelve detectives. They decided how much information they should broadcast and Inkster typed a statement for the press. An hour later, clutching fifteen copies of the press release, Inkster cleared his throat and went outside.

Camera flashes exploded as he appeared at the top of the steps, highlighting the beads of perspiration on his head and face. He felt the early morning January heat. He started reading, slowly and carefully:

> Shortly after 1 am this morning, Mrs Megan Kalajzich of Fairlight Crescent, Fairlight, was fatally wounded whilst asleep in bed with her husband. She was shot twice in the head by a .22 calibre weapon and died instantly. Two further shots were fired in the direction of her husband, Andrew. However, he was not hit or injured.
>
> At this stage, police are investigating an intruder, entering the bedroom of Mrs Kalajzich through an open balcony door and committing the offence. It would then appear that the offender ... left through the same balcony door. No apparent motive for this killing is to hand at this stage.
>
> We are also investigating an assault upon Mrs Kalajzich about 12.15 am on Saturday the 11th January, 1986, when she was confronted by a person at the front of her home and struck about the head with an unknown object. At the time of this assault, the offender was wearing dark clothing and a black balaclava ... No further description of this offender is available.
>
> There is every possibility that the assault upon Mrs Kalajzich and this morning's shooting are connected.
>
> We are now seeking the assistance of the public who may have seen any person, either in Fairlight Crescent, Fairlight, or on the public walkway alongside the harbour, between Manly and Forty Baskets Beach about 1 am or shortly after this morning. Such information should be passed on to the Manly detectives on 20966 or 977 2144.

As soon as he had finished, the questions started. But Inkster, always sure and careful, wasn't having any of it. He'd done what he had to do. The reporters began heading off to their phones and radios.

'Hey, mate.' Inkster recognised Norm Lipson, an old-school police reporter now working for one of the television stations. 'What's the real mail?' Lipson asked.

'I'm sorry, Norm, but I can't say a thing,' Inkster said. Then, against his better judgement, he added, 'This thing is political dynamite, that's all I can say. It's big—very big.'

It had been a long night. As with most of the other reporters, Lipson was annoyed at the lack of information they had been given. The TV reporters were doubly cursed, with little in the way of footage, other than shots of the house. Lipson had managed to get a colour photo of Megan, at least. It was a few years old, but it wasn't bad: it showed her smiling at the races. As he prepared to do his stand-up to the cameras outside 31 Fairlight Crescent, he kept remembering what Inkster had said. Political dynamite. What the hell did that mean?

It was Judy Mellowes, Manly's Lord Mayor, who coined the phrase that morning that was picked up by the media—'The day that Manly lost its innocence'. A killer was in their midst and Manly did not like it.

George Canellis was approaching the driveway of his central coast home at Kurri Kurri when news of the murder crackled over his car radio. It was the lead item on the 11 am bulletin:

> The cold-blooded killing has baffled detectives, who are seeking the assistance of the public and calling on anyone who may have seen any person, either in Fairlight Crescent, Fairlight, or on the public walkway, to come forward ... Craig Middleton, Macquarie National News, Manly.

'Those fuckin' cunts,' Canellis said out loud. He hit the brakes then reversed quickly back onto the road, his tyres squealing in the process.

They had used his gun, the bastards. He was sure of it.

TWO

THE IMMIGRANT

'Date of birth?' Detective-Sergeant Bob Richardson peered at Andrew Kalajzich over the top of his bifocals as he dispensed with the preliminaries.

Even though it was 5 am, Richardson still managed to look spruce. He was wearing a navy blue jacket, light-coloured trousers, a shirt and tie. By contrast, the man sitting opposite him was dressed in grey track pants and sweatshirt. It gave Richardson the edge.

Richardson liked to be organised. Even his home life was geared to his job and efficiency. He had had a telephone installed in his bedhead so he did not have to fumble in the dark when emergency calls disturbed his sleep.

When it rang early that morning on 27 January, he realised within seconds of waking it was a high-profile murder. Megan Kalajzich was the wife of a local millionaire. That would mean a lot of media—television cameras, photographers. In his wardrobe, suits, jackets, shirts and ties hung neatly. It took Richardson exactly ten minutes from the time the telephone rang until he was sitting in his unmarked blue Holden Commodore.

Richardson was a tall, distinguished-looking man with silvery grey hair, dark eyebrows, and the healthy, unruffled complexion of a long-time resident of Sydney's northern peninsula.

He was one of the first senior detectives to be called out that night. Inspector Rope briefed him at the house and asked him to take a statement from Andrew Kalajzich.

When Richardson met Kalajzich there had been no handshake, merely a nod between the two men, a gesture Richardson considered more appropriate under the circumstances. It allowed him to observe as much as possible without getting involved in irrelevant conversation. Silence helped him think.

Now, four hours after the murder, Kalajzich sat across from him at a laminated table in the interview room of the Manly police station. Richardson, in his familiar environment, was in control. There was one door and no windows. The room was soundproof.

By 5 am, Manly station was abuzz. People were moving in and out constantly, phones were ringing and there was a continuous throng of activity. But behind the closed door of the spartan interview room, Richardson did not so much as toy with his ballpoint pen. At the typewriter, Detective Bob Monk fed in the standard two sheets of A4 paper and one of carbon. He turned back the roller to the top of the page. Both detectives had coffee cups in front of them. Kalajzich's deep voice sounded hollow.

'I was born on the 28th May 1940. Andrew Peter Kalajzich, company director of 31 Fairlight Crescent, Fairlight . . .'

Bob Monk typed steadily, the typewriter's clatter echoing Kalajzich's answers.

I am a married man with two children, a married daughter, Michele Economides, and a son who is 19 years old, Andrew Kenneth, and he resides with us in the family home. Also residing at these premises is my mother-in-law, Mrs May Carmichael. I've owned and resided at the present address for the past ten years. I have business interests including ownership of the Manly

Pacific International Hotel. In the past, I've owned restaurants in Manly in conjunction with my family.

I married Megan in 1962. Her involvement in my business was recently decreased following settlement of the family business ...

With all my activities I am virtually working perhaps 90 hours a week ... About six months ago, I purchased a small fibro weekender at 36 Cowan Drive, Cottage Point, where my wife and I have been endeavouring to spend as much time as possible with other members of the family as relaxation ... About 12.15 am on Saturday, 11th of January 1986, an incident involving my wife occurred at the carport entrance to our home ... She was hit over the head by an assailant dressed with a balaclava over his head ...

Richardson listened dispassionately. He remembered how Kalajzich had seemed upset at the house. Now, he felt it had been an act. He appeared to show no genuine emotion. Some things bothered Richardson already: how could Kalajzich have been lying, barely asleep, next to his wife while an armed intruder came in, walked past him and fired off two shots before Kalajzich reacted? Why hadn't he seen or heard anything? How could the killer have mistaken the wife for Kalajzich?

Surely Kalajzich, the millionaire businessman, would have been more likely to have had enemies? Not much was adding up so far. But suspicions, as Richardson also knew, proved nothing. He brought his attention back to Kalajzich, who was still talking.

'... At this stage I cannot think of any reason for this offence to have taken place apart from an attempt to frighten me for some reason.'

Richardson cleared his throat and began asking questions. Kalajzich answered in short sentences.

'Did you consider locking the sliding door leading from the bedroom to the balcony?'

'No.'

'How many shots did you hear?'

'Only two. I only recall two thuds.'

'Is your wife the holder of a life insurance policy?'

'No.'

About 6.30 am, after ninety minutes of interviewing, the three men had a short break. As they walked out of the interview room Richardson saw several people waiting to see Kalajzich. There was John Humphrey, who owned one of Sydney's biggest newsagencies in the Corso in Manly. His pale blue eyes brimming with tears, he hugged Kalajzich, shaking his head in disbelief.

And John Webb, a prominent and popular Manly solicitor, also consoled his friend and client. 'If there is anything I can do, Andrew, just let me know,' he said, putting an arm around Kalajzich's shoulder and shaking his hand.

David Hay, a local Liberal Party alderman, former Manly mayor and soon-to-be state minister, was also there. By the end of the week, Kalajzich had also received a telegram of commiseration from the Prime Minister, Bob Hawke.

Richardson watched the impressive show of support. When his visitors left, the interview resumed for a further forty-five minutes. About 7.30 am, Kalajzich read over the typed statement and signed the bottom of each page. Formalities over, Richardson tried another tack: man-to-man. He looked directly into Kalajzich's eyes.

'I want you to give a lot of thought as to who may be responsible for this murder,' he said in a steady, measured tone. 'Think about your business dealings and anything else that may be relevant. If you have any skeletons in the cupboard, either of a business or a personal nature, it's best that they come out now.'

'We run an impeccable operation and I have a happy married life. What else can I say?' Kalajzich answered evenly.

Richardson countered: 'At a later stage I'd like you to be hypnotised. I feel it would be beneficial to our inquiries.'

'I can't think about anything like that now,' said Kalajzich.

'Well, I'll be in touch with you and, likewise, I want you to contact me if you think of anything else.'

'I will,' Kalajzich said. He stood up and left the room.

Detective Monk followed Kalajzich out to the front desk and for several minutes Richardson sat alone with his thoughts. He read over the statement. Who was this man Kalajzich? He picked up the detailed running sheets compiled by Constable Christie. He was intrigued by the young man's observations halfway down the first page: '... Mr Kalajzich's grief did not appear to be genuine ...'

There was something strange here. Richardson knew that uncovering the motive would be their hardest task but he also knew, and feared, that if they didn't find it soon, they might well find themselves floundering in the dark. The next few days brought no further clues. The police divers had found nothing in their search of the harbour, nor had a search of the foreshore turned up anything. And none of the neighbours had reported anything strange.

Richardson began checking out Kalajzich's financial status. He organised an interview with John Thomas, Kalajzich's accountant and financial adviser for the past fifteen years. During the next few days, Kalajzich peppered Richardson with all sorts of information—stories of his background, possible Yugoslav conspiracy theories behind the attack, all piecemeal offerings and tidbits.

Richardson was forever answering the phone from callers wishing to ingratiate themselves, saying they had information about the murder. One man, who claimed he had lived near Kalajzich's brother, Tony, for many years, said that Megan Kalajzich had refused to contribute to a Yugoslav terrorist agency. He said that although Kalajzich was happy to contribute, Megan had been opposed to the idea.

'The murder would have been committed by an overseas assassin,' the man said. 'He would have left the country just after the murder. Oh, and you should make a careful check of Kalajzich's banking transactions. I reckon there'll be a substantial withdrawal fairly soon.'

'I see,' Richardson said slowly. 'And what proof do you have, sir, for this theory?'

Another caller said, 'Take a look at the big blond bloke—George—at the Manly hotel.'

'Where does he live?' Richardson asked.

'I don't know and I don't know his other name either, but he went back to Junee after the murder.'

It was all a great waste of time, thought Richardson. Kalajzich appeared to have some critics and Richardson concluded he was something of a political chameleon. One article he found in a Yugoslav magazine said:

> It is interesting to note . . . the road to progress of this hotelier of ours who, by working hard . . . selling 'fish and chips' and through the 'capital gains tax' against which he . . . voted at the last election, built a beautiful hotel, in which he entertains and flatters people whom he should not.
>
> First he was a nobody, like most of us, then he was a Yugoslav, then he was a Titoist, then he cursed Tito, then he was a supporter of the Cominform, then he became a Titoist . . . and he will die a Titoist, how appalling.

One week after his wife's murder, Kalajzich sent Richardson typed notes outlining his family's history and arrival in Australia. It began:

> My father, Andrew Kalajzich Snr, was active during the war years in the Yugoslav community, having come to Australia before the war. He came because two of his older brothers came some years before him . . .

At the age of 40, Andrew Kalajzich had visited his parents' birthplace, Omis (pronounced Ormish), a small fishing village on the Dalmatian coast of Yugoslavia, several times. His parents, who had emigrated to Australia in 1938, returned as often as they could. With their newfound wealth, they bought property there to renew their relationship with the land of their birth. In almost forty years, Omis had hardly changed.

The Kalajzich ancestors had settled in the Adriatic coastal village. One of their clan, Anthony Kalajzich, is remembered by a small stone plaque erected at the entrance to one of the tunnels that cut into the moss-covered limestone cliffs at the northern entrance to the town. It reads: 'Podize Supru I djeca'— a memorial to Anthony Kalajzich, a member of the family, who died in September 1936 and was survived by his wife and several children.

The Kalajzichs were a poor family of vine growers. For decades they worked every inch of red soil between the crumbly granite rocks of their land to produce grapes, olives, olive oil, red and white wines and liqueur. They were lucky: the soil was good for the area and their vines faced east, soaking up the sun's rays most of the day.

From every point in Omis, the forbidding Biokovo Mountains can be seen as they rise, almost perpendicular, from the coastline. They tower above all, their hostile outline softened only by a gentle cloak of white sea haze. In parts of the town, which dates back to the tenth century, cobbled streets wind up to the hillsides. Chimes ring out from the old church in the village centre and in the mornings, fishing boats bob along the waterfront, their reflections shimmering in the sun.

On most days, the old peasants, faces hardened from the rigours of life in the open fields, make their way to the village markets. The old women wear black and the men, with traditional caps, stroll past the water en route to the marketplace. There, they sell bright yellow daffodils and the hard-earned produce of their stony land—apples, potatoes, nuts and olives.

The Cetina River cuts through Omis and vanishes underground into the mountains, reappearing several hundreds of kilometres away. In the 1920s the Kalajzich children played by the river, following its course into the mountains where they caught birds—singing birds the size of canaries—shiny red with yellow and black wings, and carefully brought them home for pets.

Andrew Kalajzich's father came from a family of eight boys and three girls. Sometimes in times of poor crops they relied on food from local nuns to survive. Shoes were a luxury. The Kalajzich boys were forced to leave school as young as twelve to start trades and earn money. Andrew Kalajzich left school in fourth class and started carpentry.

The first Kalajzichs to leave Omis for Australia were part of a wave of Dalmatian settlers who sailed into Sydney Harbour in the early 1920s. Frustrated by deteriorating social and economic conditions in Yugoslavia after World War I, and the creation of a new state under the former Serbian monarchy, many Croatians decided to look for a better life elsewhere.

In 1924 Joseph Kalajzich, the oldest brother, a cobbler by trade, stepped off a ship at Circular Quay. He followed a well-worn path up the road to The Rocks, to a boarding house run by a wealthy but benevolent Yugoslav, Mate Slavič. Newly arrived migrants knew by word of mouth that they would find accommodation there for a week while they looked for a job. If they hadn't found anything by then, Slavič believed they weren't trying and would tell them to move on. Those who needed more time headed for Ivan Lenditch's boarding house, a few blocks away near the corner of Kent and Argyle streets, Millers Point.

Most found work. Many moved north across the harbour to Warriewood to try their hand as market gardeners. Land was cheap and arable, particularly for tomatoes. It gave them a chance to employ a skill from their homeland, which helped ease the pain of their separation.

Others moved out west to the mines of Broken Hill. By 1929, there were 300 Yugoslavs, mostly Croatians from the Makarska Riviera and Adriatic islands, in the outback mining town.

Regardless of where they headed, all the Dalmatian migrants in the 1920s were poor. Joe Kalajzich was no exception but he was a proud and honourable man, determined to make a good life for his family in this new land. He headed for Warriewood where the market gardens gave him a foothold in his new home. He would remain a man of the land all his life. Another brother, Peter, a painter, followed Joe to Australia, followed shortly after by the youngest brother, Ivan.

By the mid-1930s, after ten years of hard work, Joe Kalajzich owned some 30 of the 1500 glasshouses in Warriewood in a community where the number of glasshouses was a measure of your worth. He also owned a large tract of land and was a respected citizen in the Dalmatian community.

Peter Kalajzich ran a mixed business at Forest Lodge, south of the Harbour near Glebe. In 1938, the promise of wealth, good fortune and a satisfying life in Australia coaxed Andrew, the second-youngest brother, his wife Olga, and their first son, Tony, from Omis.

Andrew was employed as a carpenter in a furniture factory at Glebe but found himself out of work within a few months when the factory closed in the Depression before World War II. His forced unemployment spurred him to open his own business. Ivan, his closest brother and childhood playmate, joined him and in June 1939 the two brothers opened a fish shop in Victoria Avenue, Chatswood.

It was a bold move: they hardly spoke English and had more determination than money to make their business work. They decided to dress in white, and they kept the shop spotless. They prospered, working seven days a week. Andrew and Olga lived above the shop. During this time Olga gave birth to a second child, Andrew Peter. He was born at the Crown Street Women's Hospital in inner-city Surry Hills on 28 May 1940.

During the war years, Andrew Kalajzich senior became involved in the Yugoslav community, joining a Yugoslav club and attending social functions. He also helped raise money to assist his fellow countrymen back home in Yugoslavia by sending them food and clothing parcels.

As young Andrew grew up, he and his brother Tony helped their parents in the shop, gutting and filleting fish, or peeling potatoes out the back. It was their first taste of working for the family business. They maintained their strong family ideals. If a decision had to be made, they made it as a family, all sitting down to discuss the matter.

The Kalajzichs became leading members of the local Yugoslav community. The clan regularly attended the Yugoslav picnics and dances that helped keep alive the old traditions and develop links with the Anglo-Australians, especially potential brides. The 1950s had brought a new wave of Yugoslav migrants including those fleeing from communism.

Barbecues were often held at Clontarf Reserve. While a pig roasted on a spit, the children played, the women prepared the food and the men enjoyed a game of 'bocce'. The Yugoslav community held dances and encouraged local Australian girls to join in. Often romances began and developed into marriages with eligible young Yugoslav men.

During the early 1950s Olga and Andrew Kalajzich expanded their business. They bought into a small grocery and sandwich shop at Palm Beach with a fellow Yugoslav, Ljubo Franicevic. The shop, near the Barrenjoey lighthouse, did a good trade, selling provisions to the weekend campers who flocked to the beach on hot summer weekends. At Palm Beach, which later blossomed into one of Sydney's more exclusive suburbs, the two young brothers often pitched in to help, unloading soft-drink crates and sometimes serving on weekends. In 1953 Olga gave birth to her third and last child, a daughter, also named Olga.

In the mid-1950s Andrew Kalajzich senior expanded further. He sold his interest at Palm Beach and bought a small but popular fish shop called Murphy's, which he picked up cheaply. It was on the southern side of the Manly Corso, opposite the beachfront.

Andrew and Tony were both good scholars. When they finished their schooling, their father wanted them to continue their education, but they were both determined to work in the family's business.

As young men, the Kalajzich brothers were given more responsibility in running the business. Murphy's continued to thrive. The fish and chips were popular with the crowds of Sydneysiders who headed for the beach on summer weekends. That most arrived by ferry and had to pass Murphy's as they walked to the beach was a bonus.

In 1958 Andrew senior bought another, nearby property

which he turned into a fish shop, Ocean Foods, which is still there today. Murphy's and Ocean Foods were both near the corner, Murphy's on the beach front. Although separated by one shop, they shared a common rear work area. The Kalajzichs installed cool rooms and a filleting area where family and staff gutted and cleaned fish in between serving and running the businesses.

Ocean Foods sold fresh and cooked fish and seafood, while Murphy's kept to the basic fish and chip shop fare. It was an ideal arrangement. The food in both shops was good. If the queues at one were too long, customers moved around the corner to the other.

It was an exciting time for young Andrew. In 1960, at just twenty years of age, he was already becoming known among the Manly local businessmen.

In many ways, Megan Carmichael was Andrew's opposite. Although more than capable, the fresh-faced brunette was shy and softly spoken where he was hungry and ambitious. Her family, too, were migrants—emigrating from England 'with sixpence' when Megan was seven years old. They had settled happily in Australia, and Megan trained as a dental nurse when she finished school. Everybody, it seemed, liked Megan. She was highly regarded by the patients at the local dental surgery on the Corso where she worked. Part of her job was to relax patients, especially when they were facing the drill. One of her tricks was to dip her fingertips into ice-cold water and place them reassuringly on a patient's temples.

Andrew Kalajzich was taken by Megan's kindness, when he visited as a patient, and she was flattered by his attention. They arranged to meet later at a local dance at the North Sydney Police Boys Club.

When Megan, an only child, set off on that first date with Kalajzich, her widowed mother, May, joked, 'Make sure you come home in a Jaguar.'

Megan returned at midnight. 'Guess what I came home in?' she exclaimed excitedly. 'A fish truck!'

Soon Megan and Andrew were dating regularly. She was his first serious girlfriend. They often double-dated with Megan's best friend, Sue, and Andrew's brother Tony. The four often dined out together.

Andrew and Megan married in 1962 at Manly's Mary Immaculate Catholic Church. The young couple moved into the Kalajzichs' family home in Queenscliff, and May Carmichael, Megan's mother, moved to a unit nearby.

Marriage suited Megan. She had never been happier. She adored her new husband and her new life. She felt that the Yugoslav community had accepted her as one of their own and she accepted their traditional family values. She consented to Kalajzich's conservatism: she never bought 'peep-toe' shoes, because he didn't like them. She filled his role model as an ideal wife.

That same year, the Yugal soccer club formed and the Kalajzich brothers joined the club's committee and, in 1969, Andrew became the club secretary.

Four years later, the Kalajzich brothers bought another property. K's Snapper Inn, conveniently and aptly named, was a small seafood restaurant on the beachfront, next to Murphy's. The brothers set to work, eventually turning the tiny ground-floor eatery into one of the most successful seafood restaurants in Sydney.

Megan and Andrew moved out of the family home and into one of the two small flats above the restaurant. By now, Tony and Sue had also married and all four worked together, Sue and Megan working as hostesses, six days and nights a week.

K's fine reputation was not solely based on the quality of the seafood. Much was due to Andrew Kalajzich's tricks of the trade. For instance, K's took no table bookings—first in were first served. So, from Monday to Saturday long queues of hungry diners, ogling at those already inside, formed outside. It was a clever marketing ploy. The restaurant always looked full to overflowing. For many years, K's didn't accept credit cards either, which cut costs for management without deterring diners.

Kalajzich bought a 28-metre wooden fishing trawler, *Vagabond S*, which he ensured appeared regularly off the beach at Manly. All the locals knew it was his and it helped K's reputation that people thought the restaurant caught its own fresh fish and seafood.

The *Vagabond* did trawl a few days a week—about 40 kilometres out to sea off the Continental shelf—but its catches of gemfish, royal red prawns and snapper fell far short of what was consumed each day at K's. Like all Sydney seafood restaurateurs, Tony and Andrew Kalajzich bought most of their fish early in the mornings at the fish markets. Meals at K's were not cheap and the brothers did well—so well that they decided to extend the restaurant by converting the two upstairs flats into dining rooms.

Meanwhile, the Kalajzich family also bought several more shops and offices around the corner of the Corso and South Steyne which was fast becoming theirs.

When work started on the flats, Andrew and Megan moved into a house of their own in Condamine Street, Balgowlah. Soon after, in January 1964, Michele, their first child, was born. Megan stopped work and Kalajzich threw himself into his work with a vengeance.

His business and personal reputation blossomed. Despite his youth, he was respected in the Yugoslav community. Andrew and Tony employed Yugoslavs in their fish shops and migrants often came to see Andrew Kalajzich for advice and to ask him to sponsor migration applications for their relatives to come to Australia. He sometimes translated for migrants having difficulties with the language. To cap his growing reputation, in the late 1960s he was made the youngest-ever Justice of the Peace so that he could witness documents for Yugoslavs.

But he did have some critics. Another rival soccer club was formed and the Yugal players, which included the Kalajzich brothers, found themselves being threatened at matches. Once they received a letter threatening to blow up K's Snapper Inn.

In 1970, the brothers bowed out of the soccer club for good.

Kalajzich started becoming active in the local Chamber of Commerce, and began dipping into local politics. He turned his attention to Manly and found allies in local business and on the Manly Council. He began formulating ideas about the development of the ocean front into a pedestrian mall where Sydney daytrippers could stroll down Manly's main street free of traffic. He believed tourism was the key to transforming Manly from a sluggish seaside village into a cosmopolitan resort.

In June 1966 Megan gave birth to a second child, a boy, named Andrew after his father. He became fondly known as 'Butch' and after he was born Megan continued to work part-time at K's, juggling her time between work and home and the children. She was always well-groomed, her hair immaculately coiffed in the 'beehive' hairstyle that was fashionable then. She had a ready smile and was popular among staff at the fish shops and the restaurant.

Whenever she and Andrew went out at nights, she would always leave something for the babysitter—like her triple-deck raspberry sponge cake—sitting under a tea towel on the tray in the kitchen. She accompanied her husband to business functions, and was photographed smiling at his side. As his reputation grew, they appeared regularly in the social columns of *The Manly Daily*.

On the surface she seemed, to almost everyone who knew her, to be the ideal wife. Despite the wide circle of people she dealt with daily, only two people knew she was having problems—her husband and her doctor, James Clarke. Nothing Dr Clarke had tried seemed to ease the depression she suffered, which at times was debilitating. Searing migraines left her exhausted. And Megan chose not to confide the cause to her doctor. As far as she was concerned, the migraines just happened and all she wanted was Valium to ease them. Dr Clarke knew Megan was proud and stoic. Perhaps, when she was ready, she would talk to him. Until then, he decided not to press her.

THREE

A DRIVE ALONG THE CLIFF

February 16, 1972

I've had to write something to you quickly so that the mail will get to you on time. I hope you sailed away all right and the trip so far is good.

Andrew Kalajzich glanced up at the closed door of his office to reassure himself, but there were no sounds. He was alone as he usually was at this time of the morning. Although married for ten years, and with two children, most of his time was spent away from home. Early each morning he went to his office and sometimes he would make the trip to the fish markets, sharing the task with his brother Tony. He spent the days and the evenings in the shop and the restaurant, and at night he sat alone in his office doing the accounts and paperwork. By the time he returned home at night, his family was usually asleep, the house in darkness.

He continued writing.

I rang Djuro on Monday night because you looked anxious when your sister had still not arrived at the port. He told me that everything was okay, so I felt a lot better. He said to me that he thought you liked me and that we should not have let you go away. I thought to myself if only he knew how much I loved my Indian.

I have been really upset these last few days and every time I think of you, tears come to my eyes and already I miss my Suza very much. I just hope that I have enough energy to do what I must do, because I love you very much.

I was just thinking this morning how lucky we were that the boat sailed on a Monday and that I was able to stay with you and your mother and to get on the boat and finally to be alone together in the cabin.

I really don't know but I think that we do have a guardian angel to look after us. Give my regards to your mother and please tell her I am truly sorry if I caused her any trouble while she was here. Please tell her that I made you make up all the excuses so we could be together. I'm really sorry that I did not see her so often and had to go so quickly on the ship, but I am sure she understands. Maybe one day I will have plenty of time to talk with her. Remind her to look after you for me because that is what I asked her to do.

I have much to write to you but I will save it for another day.

I do miss you and I do love you very much. 'Andrija toof me tade.'

Kalajzich carefully folded the three handwritten pages, addressed the envelope, then looked at his watch. It was time to go to the markets.

He knew Lydia could not read English very well. She had been in Australia only two years when she left. She and her married sister Irma were two of the many migrant hopefuls who turned up at Ocean Foods looking for work. He had taken them on in January 1971.

Marcellina 'Lydia' Iurman was five years younger than Kalajzich. She was a Yugoslav whose family had settled in Brazil and in 1970 they emigrated to Australia, looking for a better life. Lydia and Irma spoke Portuguese as they gutted and filleted fish at Ocean Foods. Later they worked as waitresses as K's Snapper Inn.

Lydia had a quiet innocence, a sexual naivety that stirred Kalajzich. He was usually so immersed in his work that he was oblivious to anyone and anything that played no part in his money-making existence. And yet, he found himself watching her as she worked in the back room, seemingly unaware of the effect she was having on him, stopping occasionally to sweep back a wisp of hair.

That was how it had started—nothing more than an awakening of curiosity. Would a woman like Lydia be interested in him? Kalajzich had slipped into his thirties with such alacrity it disturbed him.

Then he had fallen in love with her. He had never imagined he would ever write anything like this. Here he was, at the age of 32, writing love letters like a schoolboy in the full flush of his first love. Concealing his secret was not easy. He had probably been a fool to go to the ship to see her off. It was difficult to explain such an uncharacteristic absence to the family. Questions had been asked after he returned. He had reacted with mock outrage saying it was 'nobody's business' where he had been. Megan had not asked any questions, but then she rarely did.

Ah, Moja Draja (My darling) Lydia. She had given his life a sense of purpose, a feeling that he had something to look forward to, something apart from the daily grind of the restaurant, the early morning starts, the long days and late nights.

This morning he had come in even earlier than usual to write to his 'little Indian'. He woke long before the sun streamed in through the balcony doors of his bedroom. He dressed and drove with unusual haste to the Corso. He almost ran up the stairs to the office and closed the door before pulling out the sheets of paper he had bought specially. His heart ached like an adolescent's.

On the way to the fish markets he thought again of their parting words in the cabin, her shyness, the awareness of her mother outside, the warmth of her lips in their stolen kiss and the delicious feeling coursing through his veins as he touched the smooth skin of her cheek and her neck.

She had left for Brazil, returned home, despite his entreaties. Lydia had never settled in Australia. She had found it difficult to settle here despite her efforts to learn English by correspondence and at night school. She had worked hard in her first year, finding a job in the Avon cosmetics factory in Frenchs Forest, but she continued to be unhappy. During those first months in Australia, Lydia decided to go back to Brazil, and she found a second job, at Ocean Foods, to help her savings.

Lydia was attractive, but inexperienced with men. The attentions from her new boss flattered her but made her flustered. He remembered her reaction when he first offered her a lift home within weeks of her starting work. She was waiting at the Manly wharf for a bus to her sister's house in Harbord. She had caught the ferry from night school in the city.

'Would you like a lift?' Kalajzich asked, pulling up at the bus stop.

'Um, no, I don't think so,' she stammered. 'I'm waiting for the bus.'

'It's not far out of my way,' he persisted. 'Where are you going? To Harbord—to Irma's place? It's no problem at all, really. I'd like to drive you home.'

Reluctantly, Lydia accepted. She sat next to him, tense and uncomfortable, worried he would make some sort of advance. But he was pleasant and courteous. She thanked him. A few days later, when he turned up at her bus stop outside Irma's house, in Wyadra Avenue, and offered her a lift into the city, she accepted more easily. Lydia was now working at the Bank of Brazil in Martin Place. It was 7.30 am. 'I'm going into the city anyway,' he said, 'to the markets. It's on my way.'

The trip was an hour from Harbord in peak time on public transport—two buses and a 35-minute ride on one of the large blue and white ferries which shuttled commuters from the northern seaside suburbs to the foot of the skyscrapers at Circular Quay.

The lifts to work became a regular Wednesday morning event. Towards the end of 1971, Kalajzich also began picking Lydia up from Manly wharf where she would otherwise queue for the Harbord bus after the two nights she worked at Ocean Foods.

They fell into the habit of stealing an hour together, lingering in the dark in his car outside Irma's house. Their meetings were fraught with Catholic guilt and the thrill of secret excitement. Occasionally, they would even chance a half-hour walk, shoes in hand, along the shore at Curl Curl beach, like teenagers escaping the parental eye.

They saw more and more of each other. It was Lydia who made the first move towards intimacy. One night as they were crossing the Roseville Bridge she leaned towards him: 'Would you mind if I moved a little closer to you?'

They found it easy to talk to one another and she was often surprised that an hour together could pass so quickly. He frequently checked his watch—a reminder that their relationship was clandestine, and that time was rare and precious.

Once, when they pulled up in the carpark at Curl Curl, Lydia asked about Megan. Kalajzich looked out to the vast expanse of darkness that was the ocean.

'I am unhappy in my marriage,' he answered.

'But why? In what way?' she asked.

'There is just no love or understanding between Megan and myself. It's hard to explain, but I just don't feel I love her any more. But, then, I don't hate her either. She is a good wife and a good mother to my children. She works very hard at the shop and she helps the Yugoslav people . . .'

Lydia listened in silence as he took her hand and held it tightly. She realised she was falling in love with this forceful, powerful man who had quietly and persistently pursued her. Lydia had never been wooed before.

One night, Kalajzich confided: 'I feel so sick in my stomach sometimes, from cramps. And I have headaches—I think from sinus. I must be working too hard.'

'No,' Lydia answered and then laughed. 'I think you are pregnant.' It became a private joke. They would often refer to 'the baby'.

Another night, Lydia asked: 'Do you ever sleep with Megan?'

'No,' he replied, but would say no more. He often spoke proudly of his children, Michele and Butch, but rarely of Megan.

Kalajzich and Lydia slipped into a pleasant routine. She would turn up for work, arriving in the kitchen in her white uniform at 6 pm. Kalajzich would watch her from a distance, constantly checking his watch, willing the hands to 9.30 pm when he could drive her home.

Sometimes they would kiss, holding hands, sitting close together, but Kalajzich was always the gentleman. He knew without asking that Lydia would never have become his mistress.

As 1971 drew to a close, Lydia started talking about return- ing to Brazil with her mother. Kalajzich became upset and agitated. One night, he announced abruptly: 'I am going to divorce my wife. I have made up my mind and I would like to seek your hand in marriage.'

But Lydia wasn't swayed. She had also made up her mind. 'I am going to Brazil. I promised my mother. I must go with her.'

'But you are my Indian,' pleaded Kalajzich, 'and we must spend our lives together. It is meant to be.'

Despite his efforts, Lydia stuck to her plan. Her mother came first. Perhaps the separation would decide the future for them, she thought.

Kalajzich drove them to the wharf. 'I'm going to send for you as soon as I sort out this divorce business,' he said. 'Or, I'll come to Brazil to get you. You'll not escape easily, Moja Draja. Then, we will marry.'

Lydia's departure in February 1972 affected Kalajzich more than he had expected. Unused to making decisions based on emotion, he felt unsure, out of his depth. This was not a calculated business deal; there seemed no solution. Lydia was gone. There would be no more stolen hours, no more laugh- ing, no more holding hands, only letters.

As Kalajzich joined the trickle of early morning traffic across the Harbour Bridge following the familiar route to the fish markets, he looked again at the letter lying next to him. For a long time after she left, he had stopped wearing his watch. The hours and minutes meant nothing to him, only the days which he ticked off on a calendar next to his desk. For a while he even stopped going to the fish markets.

One morning, he was interrupted as he sat at his desk.

'I have a card for you.' It was Irma. 'She wanted to know why you hadn't written to her in Wellington. The trip was not so good . . . rough seas.'

Kalajzich took the envelope, Lydia's first reply. His hand shook slightly. 'Thank you,' he said, looking up at her. He was struck by her resemblance to Lydia, not just in the way she looked, but her quiet way of speaking. 'Would you like a lift home?' he asked.

Irma's presence at the restaurant reassured and comforted him. She became his soulmate, his secret link to the woman he loved. She understood. Long after the effect of Lydia's photo faded, he would still have Irma to remind him. He began dropping Irma home after work regularly. They could talk about Lydia and he could collect her letters without anyone knowing. He posted his at the GPO in Martin Place, on his way back from the markets.

Lydia sent back the key to the office where she used to change for work. The office had been 'their' room and Kalajzich still changed his clothes in there. He remembered how she used to leave her pink jeans draped over a chair next to the white pants he wore in the restaurant. It gave him a feeling of domesticity, a secret familiarity they could share. Once he found one of her hairpins on the floor and he kept it in his drawer.

He wrote to her every week, sometimes while he sat in the back of the fish truck. The letters became a release. Sometimes he was moved to try his hand at poetry: 'As I search through life I see I am so minute that I compare with a grain of salt in the vastness and wilderness of the desert . . .'

Other times, he would give her news:

Moja Draja Lydia,
Today the sun was shining for the first time for many
days. We have had so much rain here in Sydney for two
months. The weather is not very important to you or me, we
make our own. I remember being very hot in the middle of
winter at Harbord ... the tropical fish in the tank at the
office had some babies this week, about 200, they are all
very well and growing bigger each day. What about our
baby?

Some letters were more urgent:

Today I received your letter and my stomach began to shake
so much that it took me such a long time to read it I felt
that I just wanted to be with you ... I cannot settle myself
without you. I know now that I live to love you more and
more every day and that I would prefer to be lonely than
pretend to be happy with anyone else. I love you very much.
I wanted very much to write this letter to you and now I
am finding it hard to see the paper in front of me because
of the tears in my eyes ... How I hate going to market on
Wednesdays now, it's just not the same ... My darling
Lydia, I love you so much that it hurts all the time and I
would give anything to have you by my side in the morning.
Write to me as soon as possible.

The days passed slowly. Kalajzich was filled with a restless
longing to be rid of his old life. He had seen a hotel for sale
about 160 kilometres from Sydney and dreamed of running it
with Lydia. He worried about her. Now she had a secretarial
job in São Paulo, would she settle into her old life? What if she
met someone else?

'You don't buy flowers any more,' the man who sold flowers
at the fish markets said to him one Wednesday.

'I don't have anyone to buy for any more,' Kalajzich replied.

A few days later, at his weekly Manly council meeting, the
chairman remarked: 'You stayed to the finish tonight Andrew.'
Kalajzich shrugged in reply. He had no reason to leave early.

In 1972 Australia was poised on the brink of a change of
Federal government. The first Labor government in 23 years
would take office at the end of the year. Kalajzich was hoping
that change would bring about changes in his own life. The

Labor Party promised family law reform, a radical change to the existing divorce laws which, made simple divorce almost impossible. The Labor Party planned to introduce incompatibility after twelve months' separation as grounds for divorce, which had previously been confined to either proof of infidelity or abuse. Everything seemed unsettled around him. New South Wales was riddled with strikes and the Labor Party election slogan, 'It's time', echoed his own feelings.

In your last letter you wrote about sending a petal from the park. Well, would you guess that I thought about that two weeks ago? We still think alike but I wanted some real red rose petals but I could not get any and I did not want to send any other colour but I will try in the market tomorrow morning and put it in this letter and mail it to you.

Lydia had been gone for two months, yet Kalajzich still found himself looking for her at the bus stop near Manly wharf. He remembered the emotions she stirred in him, like the time he walked up to her at the Town Hall and kissed her in full view of the crowd. Some weekends, he occupied his time with soccer. Social commitments bored him. Small things brought him pleasure, such as the morning he managed to talk a police officer out of giving him a parking ticket for parking in a loading zone. The fine was only $15 but Kalajzich considered it a victory.

Sometimes he rang her secretly. Lydia sent him a belt for his birthday and an ornamental fish. When people asked him where he got it he replied: 'I got it from an Indian.'

Despite Kalajzich's almost mechanical attention to business in Lydia's absence, K's continued to do well. One of the Sunday newspapers rated it among Sydney's top ten restaurants. The article praised the food, service and atmosphere.

Three months had passed, and still he felt obsessed with her. He continued writing:

After many years I am going to see the king of soccer. Pele Santos is coming to Australia and they will be playing in Sydney on 17 June. You know it's funny, once Brazil never meant anything to me other than another country but now whenever I hear or read ... the news and hear something about Brazil, I feel something personal ...

Well, on Sat 17, I went to see Pele, it was a wonderful experience. I waited outside the grounds for the teams to arrive from their hotel ... when they arrived they were dressed in very colourful clothes and at one stage I was standing next to Pele as he was ready to run out on to the field. The atmosphere was terrific ... There was a group of Brazilians with flags and drums making a lot of noise but having a really good time. Pele is really a gentleman on the field and Brazil can really be proud of him. So too can Brazil be proud of you, because I am.

By the end of June, Kalajzich had decided to act. He would bring Lydia back. He loved her and he told her he could no longer live with Megan.

No matter how much work or how much fish there is, you're always with me and when I begin to lose my concentration, I go into my office and look at your picture ... Moja, since I love you, I love your mouth and love to kiss you and hold you. You will one day be with me always ... I am listening to the radio, there is a song playing, 'We're Going to Make It Together', we must ...

As I explained (I think) in my last letter to you the time has come for action and I am beginning to do the things that I must do so that we can be together. Now more than ever I need you by my side but I know you are patient with me and it is not only you who is jealous but in many ways I am jealous of you and for you, so let us be happy together.

Kalajzich vented some of his frustration at the local council meetings, disagreeing vehemently with the local town planner, arguing that his plans for Manly were never grand enough. Late in 1972, the Yugoslav Ambassador came to K's for lunch and at the end of the meal, he invited Kalajzich to a private party. Kalajzich saw himself in the role of a diplomat. This was the sort of life he coveted, far away from kitchens and gutting fish. He felt at ease, dressed in a suit, chatting to people of importance. He upgraded his car to a deluxe model Ford, white with rich red upholstery—'like you Lydia' he wrote to her.

By September 1972, Kalajzich had counted 231 days since he had held Lydia in his arms. He kept a bottle of 1954 Chianti for their reunion. Lydia's mother began exerting pressure from Brazil, writing to Irma to ask about Kalajzich's intentions with her daughter. His response was:

If I had only myself to think of, then everything would be easy, but I have my children and I hope you can understand this. It has never been a question of love, but simply responsibility. I hope you can accept my children as though they were also a part of you, but then I ask myself 'Is this fair?' and 'Am I asking too much?'

The Kalajzich family continued to acquire assets. In October 1972 they bought a large silver, lead and zinc mine in Broken Hill, rumoured to hold traces of gold. When they took ownership in November, 150 men were employed there. Kalajzich could see himself as a wealthy man, living in Broken Hill with Lydia. The idea was appealing. He would have independence from his family.

Almost a year had passed since she had left him and Kalajzich's feelings remained unchanged. Every morning, out of habit, he looked up the weather forecasts for Brazil.

The best gift I can send you is the one of love. There is not a parcel big enough to put all my love—me for you.

Lydia must come home. In November 1972, from a park near the fish market, he wrote telling her to prepare her papers for the return trip. If the Australian Embassy in Rio did not approve the extension of her visa, 'I can always bring you here as my wife,' he wrote.

But, on 2 January 1973, he rang her to ask for 'a little more time' to work things out. The 'fire' in his heart was still burning. He would change his life to be with her — but not just yet.

He was confused. Once, while building a new roof on top of

the fish shop, a piece of timber fell on his head. He broke down and wept.

He was also preoccupied with his political aims. That April, he was elected unopposed as President of the Manly Chamber of Commerce. The local newspaper photographed him to mark the event.

'It isn't sufficient to have blanket planning. We want to keep the individuality of Manly at all costs,' Kalajzich told a local journalist, seizing the chance to criticise the retiring President, accusing him of being 'behind the times' in planning. Within two weeks of his election, he announced that plans to improve the wharf were to proceed. Manly needed progress, he said.

He mixed with local influential figures. Alderman David Hay, the Mayor of Manly, and Joan Thorburn, who was campaigning for a seat on the council, were to become friends and allies.

In May he started ringing Lydia regularly, begging her to return. He was feeling strong and powerful in his new role and he wanted her back desperately. He urged her to make travel arrangements and in June she did. In July he wrote:

> I am waiting for your reply by telegram so that I will know definitely when you will come ... All I can say Lydia is that I have been completely unhappy while you have been away and I cannot live like this any longer. I know that there are many problems facing us as to where we will live and all sorts of things but let us not worry too much about that now. I just promise you one thing—when you are here I will be with you all the time.

She returned with her mother on 3 September. She had spent the flight fidgeting nervously. As she walked through the automatic doors of the arrival lounge at Sydney airport, she was sure she could feel his eyes watching her. But no-one called out. She began scanning the eager faces in the crowd but she could not find him anywhere. Irma was there, but with no answers as to where 'he' might be.

Two hours later, as she sat in Irma's house in Harbord, there was a knock on the door. She heard his voice offering apologies to Irma—'My car broke down'—and suddenly he was there, standing in front of her.

She remembered his letters, telling her he used to practise for the moment he would hold her in his arms again.

Within a few days of her arrival, he had asked her officially to marry him. He didn't mention his divorce, so she didn't probe, content that they were together again.

Early one morning the next week, the telephone rang. It was Irma: 'Andrew's had an accident. He's in hospital in a coma. It was in the car—he went over a cliff. That's all I know. They've just come and told us at the restaurant . . .'

Commonwealth Parade, Manly, is a winding road which snakes around the peninsula's harbourside cliffs. A pleasant walkway runs alongside, a favourite route for locals who walk up from the esplanade to take in the sea breeze, past the Fairlight Pool in Manly Cove. The view from the benches on either side of the path stretches out over Manly wharf and the harbour to North Head.

It was along this stretch of the road that Kalajzich, Megan and Butch, now seven, drove late on 9 September 1973 on their way back from Kalajzich's parents' house in nearby Queenscliff. Butch sat quietly in the back seat, not fully understanding the heated discussion in the front.

'And when were you planning to tell the family about your relationship with her?' Megan asked.

Kalajzich took some time to answer. His eyes did not leave the road. When he spoke, his voice was quiet, almost a whisper: 'I hadn't decided yet.'

The white Ford Fairlane was approaching the sharpest bend in the road, just past Manly Marineland. Kalajzich slowed the car. Megan said nothing.

Suddenly the car veered off the road. Kalajzich jumped out of the vehicle, which then smashed through a wooden fence and rolled towards the edge of the embankment. It plunged over the edge, turning several times as it fell ten metres, finally crashing onto a rocky ledge.

When Constable Stephen Nicholas arrived a few minutes later, he found Kalajzich standing at the top of the cliff looking over the edge. Below, he saw Megan, shaken and pale-faced, sitting near the crumpled, overturned wreck of their car. He guessed she had been sick. She was comforting a child who looked confused and scared.

When an ambulance arrived, the officers set up emergency floodlights and helped Megan and Butch to the top of the cliff, but Megan refused to go to hospital. She had escaped with barely a mark and Butch had no more than a few scratches. 'We'll just go home,' was all she would say.

Constable Nicholas noticed she hadn't said a word to her husband. He had clambered down the rock face and sat, head in hands, on a rock near the wreckage.

'Are you all right?' an ambulance officer asked him.

'Not really,' he said. 'I don't feel well. I must have blacked out. What happened?'

The ambulance officers decided to strap him into a stretcher and carry him back up the cliff. A newspaper photographer recorded the rescue for page three of the next day's edition of *The Manly Daily*. Constable Nicholas offered Megan and Butch a lift. She readily accepted.

'Have you any idea what happened?' he asked. He was perplexed about how Kalajzich could have driven the car towards the embankment, blacked out and yet managed to recover and climb out of the car before it crashed over the edge.

'We're experiencing difficulties at the moment,' was all Megan said. 'Andrew said he was feeling ill, so he left the car and then we ran off the road.' Nicholas was even more puzzled.

When they reached the Kalajzich home at Condamine Street, Balgowlah, he asked if there was anything more he could do. Megan still seemed confused, but she politely declined.

'No, we'll be fine, thanks,' she said, fumbling in her handbag for her keys.

Nicholas liked Megan and he felt uneasy about the whole incident. A few days later, he called on her but was politely told again that everything was fine. And when he rang the house a week later, the woman who answered said Megan did not want to speak to him.

The accident became a topic of local gossip. The tone of the newspaper article was sympathetic. With it was a photo of Kalajzich being carried up the cliff on a stretcher. The article began:

CAR ONLY FEET FROM WATER

MANLY FAMILY ESCAPE CRASH WITH SHAKING

The proprietor of a South Steyne restaurant was taken to hospital after the car he was driving plunged over a cliff on to rocks near Commonwealth Parade, Manly, late on Sunday night.

The story detailed the half-hour rescue effort under emergency lights to lift Kalajzich from the rocks. Megan was quoted as saying her husband had been driving slowly because he was not feeling well. 'If he had been going any faster we might have ended up in the water,' she said. There was no mention in the article of the fact that Kalajzich was not even in the car when it plummeted over the edge.

The next month, Megan and Kalajzich went on a holiday to Fiji. As soon as they returned, they sold their house in Condamine Street and moved to Fairlight Crescent. Megan rarely mentioned the car accident to anyone, but shortly after they returned from Fiji, Megan's widowed mother, May, moved into their new house to live with them. Mrs Carmichael had sold her unit in Crown Road and invested $20 000 in the house at Fairlight Crescent. When she moved in with Megan's family she quit her job as a cook at K's, now content to look after Michele and Butch at home.

FOUR

THE PSYCHIATRIST AND THE WEDDING DRESS

The Snake was not the sort of man who readily displayed excitement, but this time he found it hard to contain his elation. This was the breakthrough he had been waiting for and it had come from a most unexpected source.

It was three days after the murder when he got a phone call from Kevin Woods, a detective-sergeant he had worked with in the bomb squad and an old CIB colleague. Only four detectives were told about the call.

Woods had been contacted by a 'crim' who said he wanted to talk urgently. He was rattled and nervous: 'I want you to check whether that murder I heard about on the news—that dame at Fairlight—was it Fairlight Crescent, Manly?' the crim asked. 'Because if it is, I was offered that job weeks ago.'

Woods did some quick checking. Yep, Fairlight Crescent, Manly. He rang him back.

'Fuck,' George Canellis had said. 'I knew it.'

'Canellis wouldn't tell me who the murderer was,' Woods told Inkster later 'but he said the guy who set it up was a bloke called Orrock.'

At the post-mortem examination of Megan Kalajzich's body, on 28 January 1986, the government pathologist, Dr Oettle, was surprised at first to find no visible signs of powder burns around the two bullet wounds on her face.

Such burns were common in most shooting casualties. In every other way, the death was typical of a shooting death. He found two deformed bullets in the right-hand side of the base of her skull. She would have died quickly from haemorrhaging.

Using surgical scissors, Dr Oettle cut a piece of skin from around one of the bullet wounds and placed it onto a glass slide and examined it under a microscope. Only then could he see traces of powder residue. Whoever shot Megan Kalajzich had done so at close range. Dr Oettle handed the slide to Detective John Barber, from scientific, who was assisting at the post mortem.

'You can freeze that and have a look under a stereo microscope, John,' Oettle said. 'And we should get some pictures of it.'

The murder re-enactment had been Detective-Sergeant Bob Richardson's idea and Inkster liked it. It would give them a good idea of the amount of light in the room at the time and they would be able to tell whether the killer had used a silencer.

'We can put some people in the upstairs bedrooms and next door and see if they hear the gun,' he told Inkster.

So, on the third night after the murder, eight detectives, including one each from ballistics and scientific, arrived at the Kalajzich home at 9 pm. They spent three hours making a detailed examination of the bedroom and setting it up as they believed it had been on the night of the murder.

Shortly after 1 am, they re-enacted the shooting. They tried every possible scenario—scaling the balcony, climbing the stairs, with and without silencers.

Richardson was pleased with the results: 'We're pretty sure a silencer was used, Bob,' he told Inkster when they'd finished. 'He must have been standing practically right alongside her, as we thought. We'll know a bit more when we get the test results back on those four cartridges, but he was pretty close— and he would have known who he was shooting.'

'You don't think she was mistaken for him?'

'No way. There was plenty of light. It took our men just twenty seconds to adjust to the light in the room and with the light from the bedside clock radio, you could almost see their faces. It was very easy to see who was who.'

'Hmm. Just as we thought. Are you going to have another word to Kalajzich?'

'Yeah. Maybe later today or tomorrow. But I might wait for the ballistics tests on his pillow to come back. Oh, and John Barber said the body's been released from the morgue. We ought to make some security arrangements for the funeral.'

Inkster went home exhausted, but unable to rest. The simple pleasure of a night of unbroken sleep was forgotten. It was the same every night. As hard as he tried to sleep and as much as he needed it, he could not shut off his mind. It was the challenge of the puzzle—the tragedy—which excited and ensnared him.

He turned on the light in the study at the back of his house and sat down at the desk. He had bought the desk for his children to do their homework, but these days he seemed to use it more. He sat there long after the family had gone to bed, reading over statements and analysing the day's events.

Inkster, like Richardson, had had his share of 'loonies'. A letter and pornographic photos had arrived at Manly police station claiming Megan was making blue movies. He had to admit the woman in the photos looked very much like Megan, but it wasn't her. And there was the 'eyecatcher model agency' story: Kalajzich supposedly running an escort agency from the Manly Pacific. Rubbish, too. There was also the phone call which led him to the accident in 1973. The tip-off came from a woman: 'Someone tampered with the brakes on her car. You should be looking to see if she's ever been in an accident.' She refused to say more and hung up.

It wasn't much to go on but Inkster checked through the

road accident reports and found that Megan had been involved in a minor car accident in 1973. But there was no suggestion of sabotage.

Inconclusive leads, maybe, but Inkster smiled to himself. He still had Canellis.

He yawned. He should go to bed. He wanted to be in the office by 7.30 am to go over the running sheets before the 8 am conference when they'd organise the day's jobs. It was important to keep generating interest, get feedback from the public. Maybe another press release . . . Inkster turned out the light.

It was little wonder that Inkster found nothing suspicious when he checked out the details of the accident at Commonwealth Parade. Police at the time had logged it as a routine traffic accident.

Nobody, apart from Kalajzich's doctor and his wife, knew the effect the accident had on him. Kalajzich was confused and could not understand his actions. To be capable of killing his wife and son was unthinkable.

As a professional habit, at the end of every psychiatric consultation Dr Donald Hill jotted down a few key points about the patient he had just seen. As the visits continued, the notes formed a helpful potted history and provided a reference for the next consultation. After Kalajzich's first visit on 15 September 1973, Dr Hill wrote:

> Left mother-in-law's or mother's house at 9.45 pm near the Manly pool on night of the accident. The car was doing about five miles an hour when he got out and the car went over the cliff. His head hurt and his head hurts when he tries to remember.

During that first session, Kalajzich gave his version of the crash. He also gave Dr Hill a brief outline of his family history and he talked about his relationship with his parents. Dr Hill concluded that Kalajzich was suffering from mental exhaustion. He prescribed a course of sedatives and made another appointment for four days later.

Kalajzich had been referred to Dr Hill by his family doctor, James Clarke. Dr Clarke had not been surprised when the Kalajzichs called and asked him to come and see them on 11 September at their home. He had read about their car accident and he was concerned about Megan, considering her history of migraine and hypertension. But, when he arrived, he soon realised it wasn't the accident that was troubling them. Or so it seemed. He was surprised. They seemed almost unconcerned about their brush with death.

'Yes,' said Kalajzich, almost matter-of-factly, 'I'm very lucky to be alive. If I hadn't been able to get out before the car went over the cliff, I would have been seriously injured because it fell on the driver's side. I was lucky to escape.'

Megan quietly agreed: 'Yes, we were very fortunate. It could have been much worse.'

To Dr Clarke, she seemed withdrawn and on edge. He was about to ask about her headaches when Kalajzich spoke up: 'There's something else we'd like to discuss with you, doctor. Megan and I are having some difficulties in our marriage, and we've decided that I should see a psychiatrist. We wondered if you could arrange an appointment.'

'I see,' said Dr Clarke. 'Well, yes, of course. And you've discussed this between you?'

'Yes,' Kalajzich continued. 'There is a third party involved. Megan and I think we would like to try some counselling.'

Megan started crying. Dr Clarke was shocked. He had never seen her shed a tear in all the years he had treated her. She was a true stoic, keeping a brave face no matter how severe her pain or discomfort. But here she sat before him, sobbing uncontrollably.

Dr Clarke was worried. He wondered how long the 'marriage difficulties' had been brewing and he saw at last a logical explanation for Megan's migraines and depression. He wanted to talk to her but realised she was too upset. The marital problem was probably best left to a psychiatrist, anyway.

'Well, I think that's a very good idea. I know someone suitable, a practitioner at Mosman. I've referred other patients to him. I'll make an appointment for you first thing tomorrow.'

Megan accompanied her husband on his second visit to Dr Donald Hill, yet it was not until the consultation was well under way that the subject of marital problems arose. After the couple had left, Dr Hill wrote:

> People say he is having an affair, believes people are talking about him and a third party. Says he is having a platonic affair with a woman from South America. Megan said she thought the affair was over 18 months ago.

When Lydia read *The Manly Daily* and saw the photo of Kalajzich—an unrecognisable bundle being carried up a cliff on a stretcher—she fell apart. She became anxious, weepy and deeply depressed. It was not the homecoming she had expected. Worst of all, she couldn't contact him, at least until he returned to work. Perhaps she could get a message to him through Irma.

But two days after the accident, Irma came home from work early. Tony had dismissed her.

'He said I was being sacked because I was giving Andrew your letters,' Irma told her sister. 'He also asked me whether Andrew had paid for your air ticket from Brazil. I told him that he hadn't.'

Lydia broke down. Andrew's family knew all about her. Far from being accepted, she was spurned. And now poor Irma had lost her job.

On 20 September, Kalajzich was admitted to Alanbrook, a private hospital near Dr Hill's rooms at Mosman. He stayed for a week. Dr Hill saw him about twice a month after that. Kalajzich still seemed preoccupied with the car accident. On 25 September, Dr Hill wrote:

> Little boy in the car, not sure how he helped, he kept asking them all the time if they were all right. His wife

thought they were going to stop. Goes home this way every day, knows the corner is very dangerous. Personally cautious, knows the risks involved, no major accidents before, no traffic offences. Good fortune rather than ability . . . Wife and brother think he wanted to kill them.

That same day, Megan visited Dr Clarke. 'It's those tension headaches again,' she told him. 'They're still bad. And I seem to have been having a lot lately.'

Dr Clarke was now sure that the headaches were directly related to the Kalajzichs' marriage problems. He prescribed Valium to ease her hypertension, checked her blood pressure and recommended some multi-vitamin tonic.

Dr Clarke had reviewed Megan's medical files after his first home visit following the accident. She had first seen him—for depression and mild hypertension—in 1966, four years after she was married, and had seen him regularly for treatment during the next three years. Then, in 1969, the symptoms developed into migraines. She had never volunteered any reason for her depression.

In September 1971, Dr Clarke had became so concerned by her failure to respond to various therapies that he suggested a neurological assessment. She had refused. Now he was sure her symptoms had been no more than a cry for help. He should have realised what had been wrong all those years ago. At least now she was getting some help. He was pleased that the Kalajzichs had started regular marriage counselling.

Lydia did not hear from Kalajzich for a month after his accident until he appeared unexpectedly one morning at Irma's house. Lydia cried when she saw him. He was pale, drawn and upset.

'I've been taking sedatives,' he explained. 'But I'm not sure how I feel about you or anything any more. I'm very confused.'

Lydia sat opposite, listening, tears in her eyes. 'Don't cry,' he whispered, 'please don't cry.'

They began to meet again, but not often. Kalajzich sometimes visited or telephoned but they talked about everyday matters. The relationship seemed to have changed drastically. Lydia still loved him despite the new constraints. Although his divorce was not directly discussed for several months, she trusted him and believed that some day, somehow, they would be married.

If Andrew Kalajzich's personal life was in a shambles, it didn't seem to affect business. By the mid-1970s, he had consolidated his position on the Manly Chamber of Commerce—now the most influential local body, its power exceeding even the council or the local state member. Kalajzich was outspoken on all issues concerning Manly's development and he had a strong ally in the newly elected Mayor, his friend Joan Thorburn. And the lucrative Kalajzich businesses continued to dominate the South Steyne corner of the Corso.

But to others, including some employees and small business people who had dealings with them, the Kalajzichs were hardheaded business people. Among his employees, and behind his back, Andrew Kalajzich senior was known as 'old pussycat', because of his habit of padding around in a pair of loafers, checking up on the workers. The Kalajzichs ran a lean business with few perks for the employees, although the labourers who renovated the flats above K's each got free fish and a scoop of chips for lunch.

Every Sunday night, Andrew senior and his sons would lock themselves in the office near the cool rooms to count the weekend takings. They would sit around a large table piled with notes—thousands of dollars—from their busy cash-only weekend trade.

Megan was often the one bright spot in the workers' day. Whenever she passed any of them who had slipped outside for a quick smoke, she would smile and say hello. If Kalajzich caught them it was a different story. 'Go on, get back to work,' he would hiss. 'We're not paying you to stand around and smoke.'

Kalajzich sometimes sent some of his employees up to his house to landscape the back garden and tend to the harbourside lawns. There, Megan would provide lunch: orange juice, fresh bread rolls and cups of tea, brought out on trays.

Although Kalajzich stuck at marriage counselling he had been unable to forget Lydia. His obsession lingered, and so he kept her like a jewel just outside his reach. He continued the fantasy he had created while she was in Brazil, deluding himself and her by promising they would marry.

In 1975, Kalajzich told Lydia he had resolved some sort of property trust problem which he blamed for delaying the divorce. 'I am a free man,' he told her excitedly. He began speaking of Megan as his ex-wife and told Lydia his 'ex-wife' wanted to move into a new house.

Lydia collected their wedding papers from the registrar's office and filled them in. She gave them to Kalajzich, along with her passport. They chose a wedding ring, a plain gold band for $75 from Proud's jewellers in the city.

'Have your name engraved on the inside,' she told Kalajzich. 'It is a custom from Brazil.' Kalajzich took the ring and promised to do as she wished. But for several months their plans went no further.

So despite his continual assurances, Lydia was still surprised when Kalajzich arrived unexpectedly at Irma's house one afternoon early in January 1976, and announced: 'We are getting married—tomorrow. At the Boulevarde Hotel. Nine o'clock. I'll pick you up.'

As soon as he left, Lydia went looking for a wedding dress. Her mother cried with happiness when she heard the news. Lydia called her office and told them she would not be at work the following day.

She barely slept all night. The next day began as a beautiful hot January morning but when nine o'clock ticked by, Lydia knew something was wrong. She turned from the window and glanced around the room at the small group of relatives who were now looking more like they were gathering for a wake.

The day grew warmer. Lydia picked up the phone and called the Boulevarde.

'No, I'm sorry, ma'am,' said the woman. 'We have no bookings for wedding ceremonies at all this morning . . .'

Lydia did not bother listening to the rest of the reply. She hung up and quickly dialled another number.

'Ocean Foods. Can I help you?'

She took a deep breath to steady her voice: 'Is Andrew Kalajzich there?'

'No, he's not. Haven't seen him all morning. Who's speaking?'

Again Lydia hung up. She fumbled in her handbag for a tiny brown notebook. All eyes were on her as she turned to one of her relatives.

'Could you ring this number please and ask for Andrew?'

Lydia stood at the window and stared outside. She could hear a voice speaking and then the sound of the receiver being replaced.

'A woman answered,' Lydia's relative said. 'She said that this is not his home phone number any more.'

The first tears rolled from Lydia's cheeks, staining her wedding suit.

Four days later, Lydia received a message from Kalajzich. He rang Irma's house and asked her to tell Lydia not to worry, that everything would be OK. But Lydia didn't know what to think any more. She was humiliated and crushed. He had violated her trust, the one thing that had sustained her through three years of waiting.

She took a few days off work to try to recover and to decide what to do. She felt helpless and nervous, unsure of her future. She found herself wishing she had never returned from Brazil. She decided she wanted nothing more to do with Kalajzich and his empty, bankrupt promises. She would be strong, and she vowed not to give in to him again. Kalajzich helped her to keep her promise. For the next year she heard nothing from him. He stopped ringing her and he no longer called in to Irma's. As for the wedding plans, he never even bothered to explain why he hadn't appeared on their intended wedding day.

Kalajzich still visited Dr Hill, but he rarely spoke about Lydia. Now his talk centred more on his plans to buy a new fishing boat, his business and his ambitions.

In the mid-1970s, Manly's commercial district was depressed. In less than a year, three big retail outlets—Waltons, Goodways and Adrian's Shoes—had left the Corso. When a fourth, David's World of Fashion, announced that it, too, intended leaving, Kalajzich began rallying. As head of the Chamber of Commerce he was determined to dispel the growing image of Manly as a commercial wasteland. On 9 January 1976, he announced a tourism promotion levy on all local businesses. 'There's no way Manly will become a ghost town,' he said.

Among the many commercial casualties was a thriving takeaway food shop, Seaside Snacks, two doors down from Ocean Foods. When the Kalajzichs bought the business, it capped off their monopoly on the southern beachfront corner of the Corso.

FIVE

THE MANLY PACIFIC HOTEL

The Manly Centennial Ball in January 1977 was advertised as the 'Ball of the Century', the glittering finale of a busy week of local celebrations.

Earlier that day Kalajzich had posed for the local media with a group of underprivileged children for the official cutting of a Centenary Cake outside the council chambers. He had walked the streets with the Tourism Promotion Committee, watched parades and attended exhibitions. He had listened to jazz concerts and cheered at the boat races. All in all it had been exhausting.

Marlene Watson caught Kalajzich's eye across the floor of the St Patrick's College ballroom and smiled. She was dressed in an elaborate period gown with an embroidered, off-the-shoulder neckline which exposed the smooth, milky skin of her shoulders and throat. Her shining dark hair was cut gently around her face to soften her features.

She was 30 years old. Kalajzich had known Marlene for two years. She was a secretary at the Manly Municipal Council and worked with his ally, Alderman Joan Thorburn, and often came in contact with Kalajzich in his role as President of the

Chamber of Commerce and Chairman of the Tourism Promotion Committee. She was competent and she had won his respect.

Leaving Megan chatting with friends, Kalajzich moved through the crowd towards her. As they stood talking, a local newspaper photographer, looking for celebrities, turned his camera in their direction. They looked such a handsome couple. The camera captured Marlene's confident smile, her arms outstretched, Kalajzich holding her hands up high as if they were about to dance.

MARLENE WATSON.

DOB 11.5.46.
Divorced.
Flat 3, 66–68 North Steyne, Manly.
November 1982: Employed as secretary to the General Manager and Sales and Marketing Manager Manly Pacific Hotel.
November 1983: Promoted to Executive Assistant of the Manly Pacific Hotel—position created by Andrew Kalajzich. Currently still employed as same . . .

She had certainly come along since her days on the Manly council, thought Inkster as he flicked over the report again. *Position created by Andrew Kalajzich.* Yes, she had done very well: promoted to personal executive secretary in a successful international hotel in the space of one year. Obviously good at her job, he mused. Without looking up from the cluttered mess on his desk, he took a mouthful of coffee. It was cold and left a bitter taste in his mouth.

He was sitting at his desk at the back of the house. He could hear the quiet ticking of the clock in the lounge room whenever he stopped tapping on the electric typewriter. He preferred to write most notes by hand. Late nights were routine for him now. His most pressing task was to compile a chronology. 'If you keep things in chronological order, the story usually leaps out and hits you in the face,' he often told his offsider, Kerry Flood. But so far, nothing jelled, only rumours, and what said they prove?

Inkster had heard the rumours about Marlene and Kalajzich. It was, it seemed, a favourite topic of gossip at the hotel and he had already started checking it out. He had put them both under surveillance but, so far, nothing unusual had surfaced. Sure, she spent a good deal of time in his company at the hotel, but she *was* his personal assistant.

He flicked through the surveillance reports. The house at Fairlight Crescent had been emptied. Inkster had expected that. He also expected it would be up for sale soon. None of the family had returned to the house since the murder. They were living with his parents in Queenscliff and he doubted they would ever go back to Fairlight Crescent. That was understandable. Inkster remembered seeing the remains of the bed in the downstairs rumpus room. John Barber had cut a huge chunk out of it for scientific tests, and the bloodstained remnants had been temporarily abandoned at the bottom of the stairs. Inkster presumed someone from the hotel had eventually removed it.

Inkster had checked and rechecked the house for any evidence of a forced entry, any clue that burglary was the motive. He had found a slight bend in a window frame near the meter box, but the window was still locked and intact. Now he was certain of at least one thing: the person who murdered Megan Kalajzich had not broken into her home. He would bet his life on that. So many things just didn't add up. Next Inkster turned to a surveillance report from Trevor Cheers and Kay Whitty—two of the five Bureau of Criminal Intelligence (BCI) 'dogs', or surveillance detectives, Inkster had seconded to the investigation. They had begun shadowing Kalajzich on 5 February following a briefing by Inkster and Detective-Sergeant Mike Hagan, one of his senior men.

Cheers and Whitty had spent most of the next day sitting outside the Manly Pacific. Finally about 3 pm, Kalajzich had emerged. 'Hey, here we go,' said Cheers. 'There's our man.' He nudged Whitty, who put down her newspaper. He wrote the time and date in his notebook: 1500 hours, 6 February 1986. The two detectives were sitting in an old Holden panel van parked near the intersection of North Steyne and Raglan streets, Manly. They watched Kalajzich, dressed in a pink business shirt and dark grey trousers, walk out of the front entrance of the hotel with another man.

'What did I tell you,' said Cheers, as the two men walked over to a black, late-model sports car with registration plate '3' parked in the driveway. 'I figured he'd have had something to do with those fancy wheels.'

1505: The car moved off, Kalajzich in the passenger seat.

The panel van followed it north to Dee Why, where it stopped outside Bill Buckle Toyota, a luxury caryard in Pittwater Road. Cheers and Whitty parked opposite. They watched Kalajzich and the driver go inside and up some stairs. For the next seventy minutes, Kalajzich remained upstairs, his tall frame sometimes passing by the window.

1630: The window closed, the blinds were pulled down.

Kalajzich came downstairs alone and strolled along the footpath looking through the showroom windows. He waited for five minutes before he was joined by the driver and another man, who led them into the showroom. Kalajzich was shown a brand-new red Toyota Supra sports car. The detectives watched as Kalajzich settled into the passenger seat.

'Probably just wants to buy himself a present to make him feel better,' said Cheers sarcastically.

'Yeah. The Snake'll be interested in this,' said Whitty. 'A week since his wife's been murdered and he's out looking at sports cars. So much for the devastated husband routine.'

Cheers and Whitty watched as the two salesmen removed advertising signs from the Supra's window. With the sports car driver behind the wheel and Kalajzich sitting comfortably beside him, the car eased out of the showroom.

1635: Kalajzich leaves in new sports car.

'Damn,' said Cheers, 'they'll be hard to tail in this traffic.' The panel van nosed into the peak-hour crawl. Up ahead, the Supra was weaving its way effortlessly in and out of the lanes.

Within fifteen minutes, the police had lost sight of it, heading for Manly.

As the detectives waited at another set of traffic lights, Cheers had noted on his pad: *Vehicle unable to be followed due to the manner of driving.* Still, this was not proof of murder. Inkster picked up another sheaf of typewritten pages and began reading over a summary he was compiling:

> Without evidence to the contrary . . . police were faced with the murder of Megan Kalajzich and an attempted murder of Andrew Kalajzich . . . It was difficult to accept that an assassin would commit a murder in the circumstances outlined and then fail to effect the murder of the second intended victim from such a short distance . . .

The Snake looked up from his notes, closed his eyes and went through the scenario in his mind yet again. There was something comforting about working in this room. He had grown up in this house. Then he had bought it from his parents and had lived there all of his married life. His father's family were from the Shetland Islands, migrating in 1915. 'Inkster is like Smith up there,' he told people, although he had never visited the country of his ancestors. He had no desire to travel. He could still remember the lilting Scottish brogue of his grandmother and he had inherited the Inksters' 'common sense' approach to life.

His father, a boiler maker, was born in the nearby suburb of Queenscliff, the same suburb where Andrew Kalajzich senior now lived. He had been Manly Boys High's first school captain and Inkster's son had carried on the tradition. His mother was a New Zealander.

Funny in some ways, him ending up a cop. The job of accident underwriter had been stable enough, but there was his next-door neighbour, Alan Fitzgerald. He was a cop and a good one too. The young Bob Inkster admired him and was already used to investigating fires and burglaries for the insurance company. It seemed a natural progression.

Kalajzich's pillow bothered him. It was obvious that it hadn't been moved after the shots were fired into it, and yet Kalajzich was adamant he had grabbed it after the shooting and held it over Megan to hide the blood from her mother when she looked into the bedroom. And then there were Kalajzich's claims that he hadn't heard or seen anything before or after the shooting. You'd have to be deaf—or lying, Inkster thought.

There were three ways the killer could have entered the bedroom. Inkster glanced at the summary. The most obvious way was to scale the balcony and come in through the sliding door, which had been left partly open. The flyscreen had been closed but not locked. But the flyscreen door squeaked loudly when it was moved because the runners had been corroded by salt air.

And even if the killer had not woken Megan or Kalajzich, he or she—or maybe they—would then have had to walk around Kalajzich to get to Megan to shoot her—with the gun about ten centimetres from her head, according to scientific—take a step back towards the foot of the bed and fire two more shots, missing Kalajzich from about one metre away; run past Kalajzich, without being seen or heard; and exit through the balcony door, closing the noisy flyscreen behind them. As Inkster had written in his summary: An unthinkable proposition.

Coming in through the balcony and leaving through the house was just as unthinkable. The killer would have had to find the way downstairs in a house he had never seen before, without being seen or heard, after having fired four gunshots.

Coming in through the downstairs door unaided also seemed impossible. There was a Yale lock on the back door, and it was such a tight fit that it would be too difficult to slip even a plastic card between the doorjamb and the edge of the door. May Carmichael said she had made sure it was locked before she went to bed and Butch hadn't come in that way when he got home. It would have to mean that either the door was later unlocked from the inside by one of the occupants or that the killer had a duplicate key. Inkster read on:

If this was the case then there was a strong suspicion of assistance by person or persons living therein, which, of course, was family only. Evidence showed that Andrew Kalajzich was the last person to go to bed that evening and was therefore the only person other than the deceased having the opportunity to unlock the door after it had been locked by Mrs Carmichael.

Inkster thought back to something that Constable Delores Lassen said to him at the scene. She'd told him Kalajzich had said something like: 'I forgot to lock the downstairs back door, did anybody check it?' Interesting comment, thought Inkster. Kalajzich was obviously worried about the back door. He went back to his summary . . .

However, there was no conclusive evidence at the time to connect Andrew Kalajzich with the murder of his wife or the events of 11/1/86 when she was assaulted in the grounds of her home.
 It was quite apparent from the murder that the two incidents must have been connected. There was no apparent motive as to why any person would have reason or cause to kill Megan Kalajzich, a lady well known in the Manly area and a person of excellent repute . . .

No conclusive evidence and *no apparent motive.* The words had a depressing finality but the Snake was determined to find a motive—and a killer.

The next day brought better news. George Canellis, the crim who had contacted Detective-Sergeant Kevin Woods, had agreed to talk.

'Yeah, well who am I going to talk to, Kevin?' Canellis had been suspicious when Woods rang him. 'It's got me worried. I don't give a fuck who killed her but if they've got my gun and if that fuckin' maggot comes after me, I'll fuckin' kill him I tell you.'

'It's OK, George.' Woods was used to Canellis' outbursts. 'There's a bloke called Inkster in charge, George. I know him well; he's a good man. He wants to talk to you as soon as possible. How about we meet somewhere near you?'

'All right. But I'm not talking to anyone unless you're there, Kev. I know what those bastards can do.'

'I'll be there, George. Where'll we meet?'

'At the Settlers Arms Hotel at Gosford—you know it?'

'No, but we'll find it. We'll see you there about noon tomorrow.'

'OK. I'll see you then.'

Inkster decided to keep the meeting a secret, except from Richardson, Rope and Mike Hagan. Inkster had already locked away all the Kalajzich files in a heavy-duty, free-standing safe borrowed from Chubb, the company he used to deal with in his days at the breaking squad. He kept one safe key, and gave the other to Mike Hagan.

As an extra precaution, he kept the brief of the investigation, including the top-secret information on Canellis, hidden in the superintendent's office at Dee Why station. Inkster wanted to make sure that information didn't fall into the wrong hands. It wasn't that he didn't trust his men, but Inkster was careful. If the information was wrong, it could throw them completely off the track. And he still didn't know a lot about Kalajzich. He wasn't sure how much or who Kalajzich knew—or who he could get to. One slip of the tongue could ruin the inquiry.

By the late 1970s, Kalajzich had recovered from what his family regarded as a minor nervous breakdown, probably brought on by the pressures of work.

Emotionally, he felt stronger than he had for many years. He no longer needed psychiatric consultations with Dr Hill and the marriage counselling sessions with Megan had long finished. She seemed happy enough. She had the children and her home, and she spent a lot more time with Jeanette Humphrey, her closest friend. They shopped and socialised together—and she still enjoyed working in the restaurant.

In 1977, he began phoning Lydia again, at her office. He acted as though nothing had happened but Lydia kept their conversations brief and he stopped ringing.

Then, in 1978, Lydia's mother died. Kalajzich decided to send his commiserations. Lydia was at work when a woman came in to see her. She introduced herself only as Shirley and explained that she had come on behalf of Andrew Kalajzich. Lydia felt that old familiar knot tightening in her stomach.

'He asked me to tell you that he was sorry to hear about your mother's death,' Shirley said awkwardly.

Lydia had not heard from Kalajzich for almost a year and now he was sending an emissary. Not a day went by when she didn't think of him, but now she felt angry. How dare he intrude once again into her life. And he didn't even have the guts to pay his respects personally.

'If he was a man, he would say that himself, not through somebody else,' Lydia snapped. She turned away, quickly, not giving Shirley a chance to see the tears in her eyes.

Early in 1980, Andrew Kalajzich was offered the chance of a lifetime: an opportunity which promised even greater wealth, achievement and power. It was an ambitious project, an international hotel on the Manly beachfront, the brainchild of fellow Yugoslav Larry Radovan and his partner, Noel Lobb, long-established builders and developers on the Manly peninsula.

Their plan was courageous. Many considered it crazy to even contemplate a world-class hotel 21 kilometres from the city and even further from the airport. But Radovan was nothing if not optimisitic: 'It will be the best outside the city limits,' he boasted proudly in *The Manly Daily* in February 1979, the eve of final council approval for development.

Despite Radovan's faith and vision, the planning had not been easy, and it would get tougher yet. Their original idea back in 1977, for a fourteen-storey hotel had to be modified to eight storeys after complaints from a local church and school. They objected that it would overshadow the playground, that it was too high and bulky, would generate traffic, detract from the coastline, block the sea breezes and 'attract the kind of people whose lives would lead to violence and disease'.

But finally, in April 1979, almost two years after they had lodged their original proposal, Manly council approved a $9 million eight-storey complex on the site of the old Manly Pacific Hotel. In its heyday the sixty-year-old hotel had been a popular honeymoon retreat and weekend hideaway. More recently, neglected and outdated, it had changed hands several times—once as a prize in an art union lottery—before Radovan and Lobb bought the site and planned the new hotel. In 1978, confident their plans would be accepted, they were already operating a new drive-in bottle shop on the site while they waited for the final decision on the hotel.

Just as soon as the council approved the plan, though, another problem arose. A statewide economic squeeze meant money was hard to raise. Banks were wary, and even slightly risky business ventures were shunned. To reduce their own personal risk, Radovan and Lobb were forced to invite a cashed-up partner into their plans.

Tony and Andrew Kalajzich were an obvious first choice. They were Yugoslavs, and Radovan knew and respected their parents. Also, they were good businessmen with the capacity to raise the necessary money, and Andrew was chairman of the Manly Tourism Promotions Committee. He was widely regarded as Manly's biggest force behind tourism and Radovan was sure he would be interested. More importantly, Radovan and Lobb had no choice. They needed financial help if they were to get the hotel up and running.

Kalajzich's parents were enjoying a quiet winter holiday in Omis when they received an excited telephone call from their sons.

'We're thinking of opening a hotel on the beachfront,' Andrew told them.

His father, who loved a challenge as much as his sons, was enthusiastic but felt bound to voice caution and concern. 'You have plenty to do without it,' he replied. 'You have the shop and the restaurant. It sounds like a big risk to me.' But he knew nothing he said would deter his sons.

Two weeks later the deal was on. A fifty–fifty partnership

was formed with Radovan and Lobb on one side, and Tony and Andrew Kalajzich on the other—for the time being, anyway. The Kalajzich brothers raised their money, and in April 1980 the first bulldozers rumbled onto the site. As local interest in the project grew, the sceptics came out in force. Kalajzich was ready and proved to be more than a match for them. He promoted the hotel at every opportunity, working hard to win support wherever and whenever he could.

On one occasion, despite heavy rain, he and Joan Thorburn led 200 delegates from a New South Wales government tourism conference on a tour of Manly. The delegates arrived by ferry from the city and traipsed around the suburb in the wet weather. A local pipe band entertained them as they walked up the Corso from the wharf. Their planned lunch at Shelley Beach went ahead—under tarpaulins—and after lunch they got even wetter as they followed Kalajzich to the hotel site where he enthused about its progress and potential.

Kalajzich also promoted the hotel in the local press, where it was no longer touted as an initiative of Radovan and Lobb. Under the company name Gumligen Pty Ltd, the developers were more often described as a consortium headed by Andrew Kalajzich.

In September 1980, after $2 million worth of work had been poured into the project, disaster struck. It seemed the sceptics had been right. With little warning, the bank which had backed the Kalajzich brothers pulled out of the deal. Costs soared as work stopped and the brothers desperately sought another backer. The weeks dragged by—painfully and agonisingly slowly.

Then, just as suddenly as the first bank had withdrawn, another—the State Bank, owned by the New South Wales government—came to the rescue. A new loan of $5 million was negotiated and the construction of the hotel went ahead despite the nationwide economic recession. For the State Bank, the move was a considerable coup, the Kalajzichs being one of the bank's biggest success stories. The cover of its 1983 annual report boasted the tale of the struggling migrant family made good: '. . . while they learnt the language, they let their cooking speak for them,' it said.

'Ambition and pride,' Kalajzich told *The Manly Daily*, were the two main reasons *he* had decided to build a hotel in Manly.

'I attended endless meetings with committee representatives and developers in attempts to influence someone to develop here. But no-one could be convinced that Manly was ready for the operation.' So, he had decided to go ahead himself, he said, making front-page local news, again, accompanied by a photograph of him in front of the hotel's shell in January 1982.

In 1982, Lydia read about Kalajzich's increasing success with a mixture of resentment and melancholy. There were so many places that still reminded her of him and whenever she read the local paper, it seemed he was featured. She tried counselling, which helped, and she was advised to confront the man who had caused her so many problems. That would enable her to start afresh in a healthier relationship with someone else. She had attempted to have a relationship with another man the previous year, but this had failed.

Full of trepidation, she picked up the telephone one day and dialled his number. 'I have to talk to you, Andrew,' she said, her voice unsteady with emotion. To her surprise, he agreed.

He picked her up that evening. They drove to a street near Manly beach and sat in his Mercedes looking at the view, saying nothing. After several minutes, Lydia turned on him: 'You are a big bastard.' Tears filled her eyes. 'You had no right to do what you did to me. Why did you hurt me so much? You had no right . . .'

She broke down, sobbing quietly into a handkerchief. Kalajzich said nothing. He did not know how to comfort her.

'Don't you know what you have done?' she said when she regained her composure. 'You caused me so much disappointment and hurt I cannot even have a relationship with another man because of you.'

She began to cry again. 'You should have told me honestly that you wanted to stay with your wife and children. I would have understood. You shouldn't have to feel sorry for that. And if I had known that, I would have felt a lot better, even if I would have been very sorry at the time. But you led me on. I never knew who I was or what you would do next and now I doubt myself as a woman.'

For several minutes they said nothing, then finally he spoke in a low whisper: 'Lydia, what can I say? I am sorry. I feel disgraced.' He said nothing more and soon after he drove her home.

He rang her the following week to see how she was. She felt better, she said. Their talk and her tears had been cathartic, but she was still not sure if her feelings for him would ever fully be resolved.

'I will be all right,' she said, 'but you had to know what you have done to me.'

Lydia resumed her life as best she could and Kalajzich revived their friendship slowly, ringing regularly for a chat and making sure she was well. Although guarded, Lydia enjoyed the renewed contact. Then one day he asked if he could see her again. She agreed.

They arranged to meet at a home unit her family owned at Dee Why. She was cleaning the flat before new tenants moved in when Kalajzich arrived at the door. Lydia closed the door behind him. As they spoke she was overcome with memories and emotions. She remembered how much they had loved each other and how strong their passion had been. Soon they were kissing. Later she would say that she couldn't remember how or why it happened. Her resolve, which she thought had been hardened during the past nine years, turned to water.

They said very little to each other afterwards, and then Kalajzich left. He returned three more times and each time they made love. Their affair went against everything Lydia believed in, but she felt no guilt. She had broken all the rules, slept with a married man. He had always made her feel as though her life was intrinsically linked to his and somehow out of her control. The last time, they lay in each other's arms and talked until the evening light disappeared and they were enveloped in darkness. He chatted happily about the hotel and his children.

Then Kalajzich walked out of her life once more. He rang her occasionally over the next few years but usually at work and usually on the pretext of business to enquire about the European money market, exchange rates, and the possibility of importing shares from overseas. Once, Lydia asked him if he could help a friend emigrate to Australia. But it would be three years before she saw him again.

Megan Kalajzich had softened with age. At 40, her figure had become matronly. She wore her thick dark hair shorter, but always perfectly styled. In middle age, she was attractive and her warm smile, her cheeks dimpling, was still her trademark.

The beginning of the 1980s were good years. She had her friends, her work, her family. Then, before she knew it, Michele was married. Her wedding to a successful real estate salesman, Jim Economides, had been wonderful. Megan had thrown herself into its organisation, helping to choose the wedding dress and formal gowns for the four bridesmaids.

She took photographs at the wedding to show her dressmaker. 'The dresses were fabulous, but the crowns of flowers kept falling down on their noses,' she laughed. She was so happy and proud.

Kalajzich was flying high. Too high for some. As he poured his time and energy into the hotel development, anger, envy and discontent fermented among some of his competitors around the Corso. That Kalajzich appeared to them to have cultivated an arrogance, almost contempt, for some of his former colleagues, did not help. Nor did his constant self-promotion as some sort of saviour of Manly sit well with some. They felt he was pushing too hard and he was not consulting enough.

In mid-1982, signs of this growing resentment surfaced publicly for the first time. During the annual Chamber of Commerce meeting, moves were made to depose Kalajzich as president. Kalajzich knew that he might lose his position if proxy votes were allowed from businessmen who did not attend the meeting but were eligible to vote. The proxy votes were tipped to go against him.

'A search of the Chamber's articles has revealed that proxy votes could not be accepted,' Kalajzich told the Chamber. But, it was mooted that proxy votes be accepted for the election of the president and the two vice-presidents. The meeting was adjourned.

The Manly Daily, represented on the Chamber, proved a key player in Kalajzich's fall from office. The paper sought legal advice and found that the proxies were valid. Their reporter was briefed before the next meeting that Kalajzich would fall.

When the Chamber next met, the election went ahead—with proxies. Of the 139 votes cast, Kalajzich received only 29. He was out. As he stood to leave, defeated, he looked around the Chamber incredulously. 'Is this all I get?' he said. Well, to hell with them. While they fretted over parking spaces and paving, he had his sights set much higher.

Not long afterwards, in October, Kalajzich drew plaudits from a source far more influential than the local Chamber of Commerce. The State Treasurer, Ken Booth, praised Kalajzich publicly for his efforts in developing tourism. During a visit to Manly to launch one of Kalajzich's latest ideas—a beachfront tourist information centre—Booth told the local press: 'I pay tribute in particular to Mr Andrew Kalajzich, who has regarded tourism development as essential to Manly's growth.'

Booth also praised the efforts of the local Chamber under Kalajzich's presidency. He also announced that the Manly Pacific Hotel would be opened by the Premier, Neville Wran, on 1 December 1982. Kalajzich could not have paid for a better advertisement.

On 1 November the hotel was ready for its first public inspection. It was a low-key affair, a 'soft opening', the fanfare and celebrations reserved for the grand opening. There were still signs of unfinished work—trucks laden with building materials out the front and workmen in shorts still on the site—but the glass doors of the grand entrance foyer opened early. Kalajzich stood watching for the reaction from the crowd which had begun queueing outside much earlier.

From the outside, the Manly Pacific Hotel was a rather ordinary eight-storey building. Although moderate in height, the sheer bulk looked cumbersome against the sleek lines of North Steyne. In later years, with more development at that end of the beach, it became less obtrusive.

Kalajzich had carefully packaged it as Sydney's first five-star beachside hotel, and it seemed there were many who wanted to experience luxury at the local beach. Within an hour of the hotel's opening, the ground floor restaurant, Nell's, was alive with the clinking of new china. The aroma of freshly brewed coffee wafted through to the foyer.

Neatly dressed staff smiled and welcomed visitors who went up the marble staircase, past the rosewood panelling, exploring the hotel and inspecting the guest rooms, the upstairs lounge and the promised sweeping ocean views. By early afternoon the Charlton Bar downstairs was doing a busy trade as customers soaked up the sea views through tinted glass windows. Kalajzich was pleased. Almost every comment had been favourable. So, too, was the publicity. He posed for another front-page picture in *The Manly Daily*, at a table in Nell's with his sister, Olga, and two of her friends.

Two weeks later, the hotel opened its grand ballroom for its first gala function, a fund-raising ball for the Manly Museum. The guest of honour was Joan Thorburn. The event received a full page in the social section of *The Manly Daily*.

The new hotel was the talk of the town. Dalleys, the nightclub had a 3 am licence and drew big crowds. Almost half the hotel's rooms were booked for the opening night. As a gesture of support, several of Kalajzich's business associates booked in.

By six o'clock on the opening night, 500 people had crowded into the hotel's grand ballroom. Megan, Andrew, Tony and Sue Kalajzich, wearing white name tags, greeted guests as they arrived. The VIPs included the Premier, Neville Wran; the Lord Mayor of Sydney, the portly Doug Sutherland; the Minister for Sport and Tourism, Mike Cleary;

the Mayor, David Hay; representatives from the Yugoslav consulate and notables from the Manly business set. Olga and Andrew Kalajzich senior had returned from Yugoslavia for the opening.

The hotel staff mingled, serving platters of prawn cutlets, chicken wings and savoury croissants. As guests sipped champagne or beer, Wran stepped up to the dais beside a huge, and by now slightly sweating, metre-high margarine replica of the hotel which had been made especially for the opening. Behind him stood the Kalajzich clan—brothers, parents, wives and children.

Wran described the opening as 'an important event in the development of one of the tourist meccas of the South Pacific'.

'The investment of more than $16 million in the project by the owners represents a bond of faith in Manly . . . The New South Wales government is delighted to see bold initiatives such as this which not only bolster the standard of tourist facilities but also demonstrate to the world our long-term prospects are boundless . . .'

To many, this night seemed a fitting reward for the Kalajzichs. They looked the picture of success and the crowd applauded them. Larry Radovan stood in the background. Wran had acknowledged the hotel as the dream of a 'group of far-sighted people' but that was it. It was as if Wran's speech was written by Kalajzich for Kalajzich, he thought.

Radovan knew that his and Lobb's ideas about running the hotel were too different from the Kalajzichs'. He and Lobb were builders. In November 1982, just after the hotel's 'soft opening', they had offered the Kalajzichs the option to buy them out. The brothers had leapt at the chance. But despite it all, Radovan felt a certain pride as he watched Megan and Wran cut the margarine sculpture.

Detective Bob Richardson studied the papers before him, a statement from John Thomas—Kalajzich's accountant.

When the final building was completed in December 1982, it cost $12.5 m and the extra was financed through Barclays Bank and Citicorp.

The hotel became known as the Manly Pacific International Hotel. The first years of trading were difficult ... but the hotel is in a sound financial position. Its value is estimated at around $32 million. . .

Inkster had assigned Richardson to look into Kalajzich's financial affairs. They needed to know whether money was a motive in the murder.

Thomas was one of the directors of the company which owned the hotel and he knew exactly how much Kalajzich was worth. It was Thomas who negotiated the loan from the State Bank.

There are no life insurance policies on the family, however there was a policy of $5 million on Andrew to cover the $5 million loan from the State Bank.

The deceased's estate has been simply established and Andrew does not benefit financially or personally from her death. Andrew Kalajzich is not under any financial pressure. He has $800 000 invested with the State Bank, he is a workaholic, his financial success is due to this, the responsibility of the family life was left to Megan ... Tony is the executor of Andrew's estate, however Tony and his family do not gain financially from Megan or Andrew's death. The people to benefit from both their deaths are the children.

SIX

FINDING A VILLAIN

Warren James Elkins was by no means a crook. His criminal record occupied no more than a few lines of a standard police computer printout. As he neared his thirties, his assets amounted to little more than his fantasies of power, wealth and women. And although Elkins never had much trouble attracting the ladies, the closest he ever got to big money and power was in his dreams.

He was thirteen and living in Newcastle when he committed his first offence in 1967. Three years later he was caught stealing his first car. Stealing was his stock in trade—petty pilfering, reflecting his desire for the better life. He was not prone to violence, and he didn't like getting his hands dirty or committing anything that would more than blemish his record. And, after his most serious lapse from virtue on 2 September 1970, he appeared to be cured.

But there remained a hankering for a better life. A desire to shortcut the path to wealth. Perhaps experience gained in the various institutions where he served his minor sentences had rubbed off. Whatever the reason, he preferred a life where you helped yourself to wealth. At the age of eighteen, he moved south from the steelworks city to Sydney, where there was more opportunity for money.

By 1980, Elkins was indulging in good clean living. He got married and had a daughter. He told people he was a JP and he worked for a while as a chef in Crystals Restaurant on the Corso at Manly.

In December 1980, he found a job tailored to his needs: an ordinance inspector with the Manly council. He liked the uniform and the power that went with it, small-time as it was. As a ranger, he was the prosecutor—fining dog owners who didn't use leads, chasing kids out of parks—and for a while he enjoyed the role. Using his gift of the gab, he cultivated contacts in the local police.

But within two years, he was bored again. He was on his way up the ladder of respectability and there was no excitement, or sign of the life of luxury he coveted on a salary of $19 000 a year. His duties now included being the official council driver. He relished the contact it gave him with local dignitaries and their milieu—important people, powerful and wealthy—but the job offered nothing more than a humdrum, predictable future. He was always on the lookout for something better.

In his private life, he was a snappy dresser, charming and personable. Despite his mediocre salary, he managed to drive a flashy green Mazda RX7 car. With his wavy black hair and lazy smile, he considered himself a ladies' man. Cars and clothes were the status symbols of the wealthy, and Elkins tried hard to emulate them. He had the knack of being able to talk his way into anything.

Elkins first met the man who was to change his destiny while he was driving the Mayor, Joan Thorburn, back to the council chambers after a function.

'I'd like you to pick up Andrew Kalajzich on the way back,' directed Thorburn, a woman with the buxom proportions of an opera singer.

'Fine, Madam.' Elkins was practised in the art of being obsequious, always agreeable, never overstepping the mark. He knew Kalajzich and the Mayor were old friends.

From that first meeting, Elkins had trouble pronouncing the name of the man who, later, he would call simply 'the boss'. An old speech impediment surfaced, causing him to pause and stutter when he tried to say Kalajzich. He compensated by calling him 'AK'.

The two men represented opposite ends of the spectrum. Kalajzich was a self-made millionaire who had worked his way up from gutting fish to owning an international standard hotel; Elkins was after the same trappings of wealth but was not interested in the hard work required to achieve them. To Elkins, AK represented opportunity. Here was a man of money, style and ambition, a man willing to take a chance, possibly the right man to help fulfil one of his dreams—to own his own security business.

He looked for an opportunity to meet Kalajzich again. Apart from his council job, Elkins was also involved in a local security company, the Seaboard Cardinal Security Group, where he moonlighted as a security guard. Elkins talked one of the guards he worked with into watching over Kalajzich's hotel while it was being built. The gamble paid off. One night they found seven youths having a party in one of the hotel's unfinished rooms. A small offence, but it suited Elkins' purpose. He marched them down to the Manly police station and later called Kalajzich.

'Well, sir, we just found them there enjoying themselves,' he told Kalajzich matter-of-factly. Then he made his pitch: 'If I may say so, our company would be able to do a much better job of security at the hotel.'

He followed up the phone call with a letter to Kalajzich, offering to patrol the Manly Pacific. He couched his ideas grandly: 'We will have uniformed guards in the doorways and foyers of the premises to show that we protect security and discourage vandals and villains alike.'

He said his company would offer a 24-hour guard service and the guards would also act as escorts for guests. He added that during a recent trip to Europe, he had attended seminars on security and visited several firms to check the latest over-seas techniques and equipment. Elkins wasn't unduly worried about 'extending the truth' a little—as long as it helped convince Kalajzich to take him seriously.

Elkins' plan worked and the company got the contract shortly after the hotel opened. Dressed in a uniform and carrying a pistol, Elkins began working at nights as a security guard at the hotel, while during the day he continued his job with the council. From there, Kalajzich also offered him the job of disc jockey at Dalleys.

Kalajzich initially liked the idea of his guests seeing armed guards in the foyer when they arrived. Two months after the hotel opened, though, he decided they'd look better in suits, more like personal bodyguards.

Within a year of opening, the Manly Pacific was doing a sound trade, as well as attracting a sprinkling of pop stars and politicians. In February 1984, the Australian Olympic Federation held a breakfast meeting there. A testimonial dinner to a former national rugby league hero, Ken Arthurson, was also held that month, attended by the Federal Minister for Sport, John Brown.

Kalajzich liked to be associated with success. He displayed a limited edition scale model of the *Australia II* yacht, the winner of the America's Cup in 1983, in the hotel foyer. Later that year, transport ministers from all around Australia met at the hotel for a national convention—Manly was a welcome change from the city. Celebrities who stayed at the hotel included the singer Olivia Newton-John and the rotund then Queensland Minister for Roads, Racing and Local Government, the late Russ Hinze, who posed obligingly for photographers on the balcony of his hotel suite.

Megan was now reaching a new phase of her life. Her children were adults and, for the first time in many years, she had free time on her hands. Kalajzich was working an average ninety-hour, six-day week away from home. She was the wife of a millionaire, although she rarely saw her husband. She was not involved in the running of the hotel but, as usual, she accepted her husband's long absences without complaint. Megan settled for hobbies and joined the local women's travel league. In February 1984, she flew to London with Joan Thorburn and Jeanette Humphrey for an annual international women's travel convention, where they tried to promote Manly to the British travel industry.

Megan was always available for business functions at the hotel, and every Tuesday night she cooked dinner for the family—Butch, Michele and Jim, and her husband. It was not until later in 1984 that rumours about Kalajzich having an affair began to make her doubt his fidelity.

In the past, Megan kept any concerns or suspicions she may have had to herself. Jeanette Humphrey could only remember one occasion when Megan had mentioned infidelity in her marriage. She had spoken of a Yugoslav woman who had worked in the fish shop. Kalajzich had helped her with her tax. She had never known Lydia's name. So, Jeanette was surprised when Megan raised the subject again years later, this time referring to Marlene Watson.

'Do you think there's any truth in it, Jeanette?' she asked during one of their shopping trips.

'Oh, Megan, no,' she said. 'I'm sure it's just gossip. You know how Manly loves to talk.'

'Well,' said Megan, 'I've talked to Andrew about it and he says it's simply not true.'

Megan preferred to believe this version of events. She knew Marlene quite well. She and Andrew had dined at her Manly flat once. And she knew Marlene and her husband played tennis together each week with a small group of friends, and that sometimes he would go back to Marlene's unit afterwards. Megan did not play well enough to join in.

So, whenever doubts surfaced in her mind, Megan tried to quash them. Once she mentioned the 'Corso gossip' to her mother. 'You have a happy, loving relationship, darling,' Mrs Carmichael had said. Again, it was what Megan wanted to hear. And in the end *she* was his wife. Megan never mentioned the rumours to Jeanette again. Instead, she grappled with the torment alone.

But she was also reminded how she suffered at the time of her husband's 'platonic' affair with Lydia. She tried hard to disguise it, but found it more difficult now that she was not occupied daily with the restaurant. It was a time of life when she was supposed to reap the benefits of all those years of hard work and become a lady of leisure. But it was a role she was uncomfortable playing.

In November 1983, Marlene Watson was promoted from executive secretary, shared by Tony and Andrew Kalajzich and the sales and marketing manager, Merrill Barker, to being Andrew Kalajzich's executive assistant.

She saw Kalajzich almost every day, often dining with him. As his second-in-charge, she also had the power to sign cheques. Hotel staff knew that Marlene had to be treated well. She was efficient and Kalajzich relied on her. She often worked until 8 pm. Marlene added personal touches to his desk and sometimes chose the material for his suits from a local tailor.

His modern office was sparsely furnished with matching desk and display cabinet. He chose a colour photo of the Manly ferry, the *South Steyne*, and a gilt-framed certificate of merit for his services to Yugoslav migrants to hang on his walls. On the wall opposite his desk he had a framed quotation from John Ruskin.

> It is unwise to pay too much but it is worse to pay too little
> When you pay too much, you lose a bit of money—that is
>   all.
> When you pay too little you sometimes lose everything
>   because the thing you bought was incapable of doing
>   what it was bought to do.
> The Common law of business bounds prohibits paying a
>   little and getting a lot.
> It cannot be done.
> If you deal with the lowest bidder,
> It is well to add something for the risk you run,

*And if you do that you will have enough to pay for
something better.*

In late 1984, the successful business relationship between
Andrew and Tony Kalajzich began to flounder. Megan confided
in a friend that family infighting was causing tension and she
was worried about her husband. Finally, in November, the
brothers dissolved their hotel partnership and severed all other
business associations. The family, which prided itself on keeping difficulties within, insisted the split was amicable. John
Thomas, Kalajzich's accountant, supervised the division of
assets.

In the end, Tony Kalajzich took over the running of K's and
the other family business interests, leaving Andrew to buy him
out of the hotel. Rather than weaken Kalajzich's position, the
split seemed to strengthen it. He was now the owner of one of
the biggest employers in Manly and he still nurtured his links
with the Yugoslav community, acting as interpreter at the
Manly court whenever he could spare the time.

Kalajzich gradually moved in different circles and spent less
time with old friends. He made an effort to fraternise with the
new breed of Manly businessmen, the FOMS—Friends of
Manly—a social club whose members considered themselves
the Manly 'movers and shakers', each with his own success
story. FOMS was formed when a group from the Manly Council met for drinks after a particularly successful Christmas
party. Women were not allowed to FOMS meetings after a
formal ballot on the proposal was held. The men had nick-
names and new members had to be invited to join. The FOMS
said they had one collective goal—to take Manly out of the
backblocks and turn it into an international destination for
tourists. But usually their meetings were social events. They
staged awards nights and presented prizes like the 'Dumb
Cunt Cup', for the most disreputable member who came
under notice of the other members. Kalajzich was pleased with
the invitation to become part of the 'in crowd'. He was welcomed as a man of foresight and a tough businessman.

Elkins had gradually ingratiated himself into a manservant whom Kalajzich trusted. In September 1984, Kalajzich gave him a reference for the ANZ Bank at Manly where he had applied for a loan to buy a unit in Fairlight. Kalajzich wrote that Elkins, still a disc jockey at Dalleys, held an 'executive position' at the hotel and earned $40 000 a year. 'We want to make it look good,' he told Elkins.

Elkins became Kalajzich's eyes and ears around the hotel, an arrangement that suited them both. Elkins relished spying on other staff, reporting on staff disloyalty and the minutiae of hotel life. When Elkins showed him a 'spy' briefcase he had bought, Kalajzich was impressed. 'I need a bug,' he told Elkins, 'and you being in the security industry, you should know someone.'

Elkins took Kalajzich's instructions to a man he knew only as Scotty, whom he had met at Dalleys. A week later Scotty returned with a black briefcase, listening devices and a phone bug the size of a fingernail. Kalajzich paid Elkins $2000 for the lot.

Elkins, although still involved in Seaboard, had decided he would form his own security company and was desperate for the hotel security contract, worth $140 000 a year. He never missed an opportunity to point out that Seaboard should be sacked. He used his position with Kalajzich to ensure he remained as a director of Seaboard Cardinal, telling the boss, Mark Hopcroft, that they would lose the hotel business unless he was involved. Elkins was retained by the company without making any financial contribution to it. He was paid contractor's fees of $380 a week and given a company car for promoting the company and securing new clients. He did no actual security work. He had also given up his daytime job as a council inspector.

He reported back to Kalajzich on even the slightest slip-up by Seaboard Cardinal. Once, when a silvery-blue Mercedes, similar to Kalajzich's own car, was scratched while parked in the hotel garage, he accused the security men of not doing their job. 'It could easily have been your car, boss,' he told Kalajzich.

In November 1984, Elkins came unstuck. He was sacked as a director of Seaboard. Kalajzich had asked Elkins to steal 150 paving bricks from the Manly council yard for the front of his hotel. Elkins was caught loading them into his company car. The other directors called it theft, gave Elkins a week's salary, confiscated his company car and sacked him.

Elkins was forced to swap his suit for a uniform and found various casual jobs as a security guard. In January, he convinced Kalajzich to give him the job of night manager at Dalleys, which was worth $500 a week, less payment for the disc jockey. The previous nightclub manager was sacked after Elkins told Kalajzich he had been stealing and one of the items stolen was Kalajzich's gold pen.

Despite his meagre salary, Elkins now travelled business-class. He always paid cash and rarely went anywhere with less than $2000 in his wallet. He bought suits of fine grey and black wool from the more expensive menswear shops in the Hilton Hotel arcade. He kept his hair neatly trimmed, his neck and hands were adorned with gold and he wore Cartier sunglasses. He flaunted the trappings of wealth but still could not quite shake his conman image.

Elkins was a keen gambler and he supplemented his wage with his winnings from the horses. But there were also rumours in Manly that part of Elkins' money came from selling soft drugs. Elkins felt he was made for his new job at Dalleys. He assigned his best waitresses to customers who were to be treated as 'VIPs' and he occasionally sent elaborate cocktails with seaside names to tables of attractive women, compliments of the house. His job was to police drugs coming into the disco and check on the staff and standards of dress. Elkins worked hard: six days a week, Monday to Thursday from 6 pm until 1 am, Fridays and Saturdays from 6 pm through to about 3 or 4 am.

Kalajzich seemed happy with his performance. He wrote a

second reference for Elkins for the ANZ Bank, this time stating he held 'a confidential position' at the hotel and that he was paid $800 a week. Kalajzich even went guarantor on the loan which Elkins took to trade in his old BMW for a new Nissan Gazelle.

They worked in close proximity. Kalajzich trusted him and knew Elkins would be discreet. It was Elkins who brought the drinks when Marlene and Kalajzich dined alone in his office. And it was Elkins who would play Frank Sinatra's 'New York, New York' when Kalajzich ordered him to 'Put on my favourite,' on the few occasions when he and Marlene danced alone in Dalleys before it opened for the evening.

Once 'the boss' told him to drive him to Marlene's unit, only a few hundred metres from the hotel, to drop off a mirror. She was waiting for them.

'Thanks. I think I'll hang it on the wall over there,' she said. Kalajzich dismissed Elkins. He stayed behind.

Another time, Kalajzich ordered a porter from the foyer to bring his Mercedes around to the front of the hotel. Marlene had been shopping and he told the driver to take her home.

Kalajzich did little to hide from Elkins his deteriorating relationship with Megan. He seemed to regard and treat her with contempt. On one occasion, Megan called in to see her husband. The three of them chatted amicably.

'I think we'll go out to Cottage Point tomorrow,' said Kalajzich.

'Oh,' said Megan, frowning, 'but what about my shopping, I—'

'Fuck your shopping,' Kalajzich cut in, in a tone Elkins had come to recognise. For a long and awkward moment there was silence. Megan's face was flushed. Elkins was embarrassed for her.

Elkins continued to talk about the new security company he was forming and got a pistol licence in June in preparation. 'We're going to call it International Prevention Security Services,' he told Kalajzich.

He tried to impress Kalajzich with his security expertise.

When Yugoslav business delegates stayed at the hotel for a Trade Fair, Elkins organised extra security. On another occasion, using his old contacts at the Manly police station, Elkins warned Kalajzich the hotel was 'going to be hit' (robbed).

Kalajzich and Elkins never mixed socially except one night mid-year when Kalajzich took Marlene, Merrill Barker and Elkins to dinner at the club lounge of the Sheraton hotel in the city. After dinner, they went on a nightclub spree to check their opposition.

Nothing was too much trouble for Elkins, who carried out his boss' instructions with unquestioning devotion. But he was not prepared for the request from Kalajzich which came late in June 1985. He was working late in Dalleys when he was summoned to Kalajzich's office.

'I'm being threatened, Waz, and I want to get a gun,' he told Elkins.

'What about you become a subby on my licence, boss?' Elkins said. It was legitimate and easily arranged.

'No, I don't want that,' said Kalajzich firmly. 'I want a gun without any paperwork. Here's some money.'

Elkins looked at Kalajzich. He could see the boss didn't want any questions asked. He shrugged his shoulders. 'I'll see what I can do,' he said. Kalajzich handed him $1000 in $100 bills.

'I have one, boss,' Elkins said the next morning, handing Kalajzich a bag containing a .38 five-shot short-barrelled hand gun and a dozen bullets.

Kalajzich emptied the bag and fingered the gun carefully, turning it over in his hands.

'Now, Waz, how do you use this thing?' he asked. Elkins showed him how to load it. 'Does it make a lot of noise?'

'I'd say so, boss.'

Kalajzich put the gun and bullets into a drawer in a small filing cabinet near his desk and said nothing more about it until a week later when he called Elkins back into his office.

'Warren, I need a gun that doesn't make as much noise.'

'Well, what about a small-calibre gun? That's probably what you need.'

This time Elkins went to a local gun supplier, the Ron Harding Sports Store, where he knew one of the salesmen. He called in on a Saturday afternoon, with his friend David Packer, whom he had chosen as a partner for the new security company. They had met a year or so previously, when they were both escorting entrants in a beauty contest. Elkins had told him that they would get the Manly Pacific security contract and Packer planned to quit his job.

Elkins looked at some guns and decided on a .22 automatic rifle. 'It's for the boss,' he explained to Packer. 'He's off on a weekend shooting trip.'

This time, Kalajzich said the gun was too long. Elkins sawed off the barrel and butt and took it back to Kalajzich, slipping it into his briefcase to show how easily it could be concealed.

'No,' Kalajzich said. 'It's too bulky.'

Elkins packed the rifle away. He walked dejectedly out of the office. What the hell was he going to do now, he wondered. Maybe if he just forgot about it.

During the next few weeks Packer quit his job and he and Elkins officially formed their security company. Elkins assured Packer they would have the hotel contract by December and that they could also get the security work for John Humphrey's newsagency on the Corso. On 5 November they each leased a Fairlane sedan from a Brookvale caryard for $620 a month and planned to run a limousine service for hotel guests. But as the weeks went by, there was no still sign of the contract. Packer, without an income, was becoming desperate. When was Elkins going to finalise the deal with Kalajzich?

'I have to find the right time to approach him,' Elkins said. 'You don't understand, he's a moody sort of a guy.' Elkins got Packer a job as a busboy at Dalleys to see him through while they waited.

Elkins decided to store the second gun Kalajzich had rejected in the boot of his new Fairlane. Just when he thought

Kalajzich had given up the idea of getting a gun, Elkins was called into his office again.

'I need a gun with a silencer,' Kalajzich said. 'I need to bump someone off.'

Elkins was dumbfounded. 'Why?' he asked.

'It's none of your business,' Kalajzich said calmly. 'I've been double-crossed. I can't tell you about it. Do you know anyone in that line of work?'

Elkins bowed his head. 'Um, no.'

Kalajzich said nothing for a few seconds. He smiled: 'How much do you like your job, Waz? You *do* want the security contract for the hotel, don't you?'

'Um . . .'

'Don't double-cross me, Waz,' Kalajzich cut in before he could answer. 'And I want to know how much it will cost to arrange it.'

'OK, boss, I'll see what I can do.'

Megan had decided she should try to win back her husband's attention. In August 1985, she decided to learn how to play tennis. If they could just spend more time together, share each other's interests more. Although she had big plans for the weekender they had bought at Cottage Point a few months earlier, she had only managed a few cosmetic changes. Megan hoped to turn it into a comfortable little hideaway but she never seemed to manage time for the work involved.

At least through tennis she could fit in with Kalajzich's social group which played on Wednesday nights at the Evergreen tennis courts at Dee Why. There was Marlene, deputy Town Clerk, Wayne Collins, the council's chief administrator Jim Hunter, and two friends, Vicki Laing and Sandra Hopkins.

Megan asked Jeanette if she would like to learn too. They started taking lessons from Ernie Cannon, the coach at Evergreen. He and his wife Joan had often eaten at K's and were fond of Megan. Megan and Jeanette began playing round robin with other beginners and practised, so they could make it to the Wednesday night games.

Elkins realised he was now scared of Kalajzich. There was something in his presence that could fill him with fear; something about the way he spoke, a menace that chilled him. He knew better than to question the boss, but he had to find a hitman. He decided to ask Ken Phillips, a former police officer who had just become a partner in Seaboard Cardinal. Elkins found him drinking alone in the downstairs bar. He bought a beer and joined him. After the usual small talk, Elkins said: 'Ken, how hard would it be to have someone bumped off? Do you know how much it would cost?'

Phillips was bemused by the turn in conversation. He wondered whether Elkins was serious. He knew Elkins' style—a flashy little big-man.

'How long is a piece of string?' Phillips teased, smiling.

'I'm serious, Ken,' Elkins said.

'Oh, between nine and thirteen grand, I suppose.' Phillips snatched the figures out of the air.

'Who is it?' Phillips asked.

'I don't know,' Elkins mumbled.

Towards the end of 1985, Megan's fears about her husband's infidelity resurfaced. The Corso gossip continued to bother her and now it was troubling the rest of the family. Michele, Megan and Mrs Carmichael had a brief private family conference but Kalajzich convinced them there was no truth in the stories.

Elkins still had to find a gun and a silencer. In September, he made an appointment to see Peter Rabbidge from Commercial Guns Enterprises, who sold guns to New South Wales police department. Rabbidge had recently sold Elkins a .357 Smith and Wesson revolver and Seaboard Cardinal Security also dealt with him.

'I need some leather equipment,' Elkins said, 'a pistol with a harness.'

Rabbidge could see Elkins was nervous. Glancing at Rabbidge's secretary, Elkins asked if he and Rabbidge could have a 'private conversation'. Rabbidge asked his secretary to close the door behind her.

'You see,' said Elkins as he sat down, putting his briefcase carefully beside him, 'I'm working on behalf of an Arab interest.'

Rabbidge made no reply.

'Some very wealthy Arab oil men who are staying at the Regent hotel. While they're here, I'm acting as their bodyguard. I was wondering whether you could supply .38 revolvers—pistols with silencers?' Elkins added the last words as nonchalantly as he could.

Rabbidge looked him straight in the eye. 'I can supply you with licensed pistols or revolvers,' he said, 'but certainly not with silencers. They're illegal in this state.'

Elkins picked up his briefcase and opened it. 'It's worth a lot of money to me,' he said, showing Rabbidge the wads of bank notes in the case. Rabbidge noticed the white and gold colours of $100 and $50 notes. He guessed there were a few thousand dollars there. Elkins closed it again. 'My clients are prepared to pay a lot of money.'

'Look,' Rabbidge said, 'that's not the way I conduct my business. And I'm very busy.'

'Well,' he said, 'could you tell me where I could get them?'

'Only in South Australia as far as I know, mate,' said Rabbidge.

A few weeks after his visit to Rabbidge, in October, Kalajzich called Elkins into his office again. 'I still need that person, Waz,' he said.

'But I don't know where I can find that person, boss.'

'Well, go to the Cross and find someone,' Kalajzich ordered. Elkins didn't argue. 'And don't you double-cross me, Waz. You know too much not to go through with this.'

Elkins remembered Trevor Hayden. He lived in a flat at Kings Cross, Sydney's main red-light district. Elkins was seventeen and hitching a ride outside Newcastle back in 1971 when he first met Hayden, who was nicknamed 'Garfield'.

Hayden had offered him a lift. He knew Hayden drank at the Rex hotel, so he went there first.

Elkins found him at the bar. Hayden, tall and balding, had once won awards for his salesmanship. Elkins used to think of him as a 'penpusher', always busy with his job. But that was a long time ago. Now, at 42, he had been out of work for six months, depressed and increasingly relying on alcohol to keep him going. Elkins began by offering him a job at the security company he was setting up. 'We'll make a lot of money, you know, Trev, and if you're after a job . . . I mean, you can't say no this time. You're 42, Trev, and you're on the dole. I could offer you about $400 a week . . .'

Hayden listened and nodded. Then Elkins got round to business. 'How do you get in touch with people like that? You know, those heavies you meet inside? I'm in the market for guns at the moment. I know an overseas customer who's keen to get one with a silencer,' Elkins said.

'OK, I'll ask around the Rex,' Hayden said.

'Give me a ring if you think you can come up with something.'

Before he left, Elkins gave Hayden his pager number. He carried his pager everywhere, so that Kalajzich could reach him whenever he was needed.

A few days later, Kalajzich cornered Elkins in the hotel foyer. 'Have you done anything more about that business we spoke about, Waz? The villain?' he asked.

'I'm still looking. I'm waiting for someone to get back to me.'

Kalajzich reminded him about the security contract. 'I should hear something this week,' Elkins stalled.

The following day Hayden rang. He'd come up with a gun. Elkins paid him $750 for it, and then found it was useless. He took it back.

'That's a toy gun,' Elkins said. 'I want the real thing and I want my money back.'

Instead, Hayden put him off, promising he'd call him soon with a real gun. He rang two days later. 'I've got what you want,' he said. 'It'll cost two thousand-five hundred.'

When Elkins went to Hayden's unit, there was another man present, sitting in the lounge room. There were no introductions. Hayden produced a sawn-off .22 Stirling rifle with a silencer attached. 'It's a survival rifle,' he said. It looked more like a small hand gun and Elkins liked the look of it. He asked to test it so Hayden brought out a bulky yellow-pages telephone book. The bullet made a dull thud as it hit the paper.

Elkins nodded with relief. 'I've got a market overseas for people who want guns,' he said for the benefit of the other man, while putting the gun in his briefcase. 'I'll send this one off.'

Later that day, Kalajzich unwrapped the gun from a piece of yellow towelling and held it in his hands. 'How much noise does it make?' he asked.

'I'll show you,' said Elkins. He left Kalajzich's office and got a phone book from the receptionist's desk. It was the first volume of the white-pages telephone listings, a bulky book about 8 cm thick.

Elkins assembled the weapon and loaded it carefully. He put the telephone book on the floor, took aim and fired.

Kalajzich looked at the hole the bullet had made. 'Give me a go,' he said.

Kalajzich held the gun carefully and aimed at the book in front of him. He fired a single shot. 'Oh, shit,' he said. 'It's gone right through.' There was panic in Kalajzich's voice as he saw the marks on the skirting board.

'Just say you hit the skirting board with your chair, boss,' Elkins suggested quickly.

Elkins lit up a cigarette and exhaled smoke around the room to cover the smell of the gunpowder. Kalajzich sat down behind his desk, the gun still in his hand. He turned it over several times, studying it, then pointed it straight at Elkins.

'Don't ever double-cross me, Waz,' he said quietly. His face was cold, expressionless.

Elkins stared straight at the gun. It was an automatic, and it still had another bullet in the breech. He also knew it was a light trigger. 'Of c-c-c-course not, boss. Of course not,' he stuttered.

Kalajzich gave him back the gun. Elkins relaxed a little. 'This is how you dismantle it,' he said in what he hoped was a businesslike tone. He took out the magazine, removed the bullet and wrapped it all up again in the yellow towelling. He handed the parcel back to Kalajzich.

'I still need that villain,' Kalajzich said.

Elkins nodded.

Elkins waited until much later that night to set out on his mission. He was driving a BMW. The drive to the Cross took about twenty minutes. He slowed the car to a crawl as he passed the nightclubs and strip joints in Darlinghurst Road. As he neared the top of the main drag, he reached one of the Cross's landmarks, the El Alamein fountain, then he turned down a narrow lane behind the Rex hotel. He watched a woman cross in front of him. 'Hey, love,' he said, 'you got a minute?'

The girl liked the look of the car. She approached Elkins' window, ready for business. She had dyed hair and a red heart tattooed on her thigh. She looked like a drug addict.

'Get in,' he said. 'I wondered if you knew of anyone who could hurt someone, physically.' He pulled out his wallet.

'Well,' she said slowly, 'there is someone, but I don't know where he is. I'll have a look and see if I can find him.'

She left and returned, a few minutes later, with a man in tow. Brian Stokes opened the passenger-side door of Elkins' car and sat down on the front seat. He pulled the girl, Trudy, onto his lap. As Stokes put his hands around the girl's waist, Elkins noticed a spider's web tattooed on his right hand.

'Do you want to make some money?' Elkins asked.

'Doing what?'

'Just to bash a bloke.'

'How much?'

'Five grand—just to bash him.'

'I'll do it.'

'Would you shoot someone for five grand?'

Stokes hesitated. 'I don't know . . . I'll have to think about it.'

Elkins opened his wallet. 'This is five thousand. It's yours if you'll do it.'

Elkins gave Stokes a $50 note and handed Trudy $20. 'Can I meet you here next Saturday night?' he asked. 'At the fountain?'

'OK,' said Stokes and he left, smiling. He spent his $50 that night on alcohol.

Back in Kalajzich's office, Elkins reported the latest.

'But, can we trust this guy?' Kalajzich asked. 'Is he for real?'

'Well, I don't know the answer to that, boss.'

'Tell him I'll give him ten thousand to do the job.'

Not surprisingly, Stokes didn't show the following week. Elkins rang Hayden, described Stokes, and asked him to track him down. One of Hayden's scouts, Black Ralph, the piano player at the Tennessee Inn, found Stokes two days later. Hayden paged Elkins. Stokes would be waiting that night, at midnight, on the council bench outside the Sebel Townhouse in the Cross.

'I need someone bumped off,' Elkins told Stokes later that night. 'Can you do it? It's worth ten grand if you can.'

'Yeah. OK,' said Stokes. 'You set it up for me and I'll make sure it's done.'

'All right,' said Elkins. 'Meet me at Manly wharf on Saturday, say eight o'clock, and I'll give you the details.'

Stokes said he'd be there.

Kalajzich wrote out a list of instructions for the hitman. He handed them to Elkins, saying: 'Get this letter back off him. And give him the gun and the money.' Kalajzich handed over the gun inside a large Tupperware lunchbox.

It rained that night. Elkins waited at Manly wharf in the drizzle, his eyes fixed on the phone booth nearby. More than an hour after Stokes was supposed to show, he drove slowly back to the hotel, dreading Kalajzich's reaction.

Kalajzich looked up as he walked in. 'Well?'

'H-h-here's the gun and the letter, boss,' Elkins said. 'He didn't show.'

Kalajzich's face hardened. He snatched the lunchbox and letter from Elkins.

'S-sorry, boss,' Elkins stammered as Kalajzich ripped up the letter.

'You're too involved in this to pull out now, Waz. Just remember that,' Kalajzich snarled. 'And don't think about double-crossing me. You know what happens to people who double-cross me. You can get back up the Cross and find him again.'

Elkins had turned to leave when Kalajzich spoke again. 'I might as well tell you who it is, because you'll find out sooner or later.' Kalajzich dropped his voice. 'This is how we're going to do it. I'll pick my wife up, take her to dinner, come home about ten o'clock, drop her off and return to the hotel . . .' Kalajzich paused.

'What?' Elkins said. 'What do you—'

'I've got everything to lose, Waz,' Kalajzich cut in, 'and I've been double-crossed.'

A few minutes later Elkins sat in Dalleys, more scared than he wanted to know. He poured himself a drink. And another. The victim was Megan.

Later that night, he went to Hayden's unit. 'You see, Trevor, I need someone who'll bump someone off—a business rival of these people I'm working for,' Elkins lied. 'Do you know anyone at all? It'll be worth your while.'

'Well,' Hayden hesitated, 'I know Bill.'

'Bill who?'

'Bill Vandenberg . . . my flatmate. He was just saying the other day, someone came in and ripped him off, and he said he knew someone that could break bones. I could ask him, I suppose.'

SEVEN

THE MAN WHO LOVED ANIMALS

Franciscus Wilhelmus Vandenberg had the angular features of the archetypal Dutch immigrant. Although he had lived in Australia for thirty years, his accent was still noticeable. In Australia he became known as Bill, a shortened version of his middle name. He spoke in a quiet, almost apologetic voice. At 44, he was thin and had gone bald prematurely. His baldness emphasised his large ears, and the dome shape of his head lent him a physical maturity beyond his years. He walked with an awkward shuffle, the result of an industrial accident.

Vandenberg migrated to Australia in 1955 at the age of fourteen with his mother, and the rest of her eight children. His father had joined the underground during World War II, so his children hardly knew him. Soon after the war was over, Vandenberg's parents divorced. During those war years, the family regularly stole food to stay alive. After curfew, Vandenberg's mother made ends meet by running a black market in what they had bought, begged, stolen or traded.

From a very early age, Bill was different from his brothers and sisters. As a baby he had been prone to fitting. He would suddenly stop breathing, hold his legs up and clench his fists tight, sending his eldest brother John, the family's de facto father from the age of seven, running to the neighbours screaming, 'Bill is dying.' The fits seemed to affect his personality. Then and later, he had the timidity of a frightened rabbit. Usually a loner, the only close friendships he formed were with children, and he had a protective instinct, especially towards small animals.

In Australia, the Vandenberg family first settled at the Bradfield Park Commonwealth Hostel on Sydney's North Shore. As a teenager, Bill spent all his pocket money on the latest Johnny O'Keefe records and the Vandenberg brothers started rock 'n' roll dances every Friday and Saturday nights in the hostel hall. Bill revelled in his role of dance-hall disc jockey, and became more confident for a time, despite his unprepossessing looks and his poor English. Now fifteen, he refused to go to school for his final six months even though the Dutch embassy badgered his mother about it, insisting that attendance was compulsory in Australia.

Bill drifted into odd jobs after he left the hostel, starting as a storeman at Woolworths. He remained introverted and occasionally lapsed into depression. Once, while rushing between jobs, he ran over a cat. After hitting it, he stopped his car and stood in the middle of the road looking at the dying animal. When it was dead, he carried the warm, furry body to the side of the road and then slowly drove away, full of remorse. The dull thud his wheels had made hitting the cat played havoc on his mind for days. The same sentiment emerged later when Vandenberg bought a dog. One day he found his nephew eating the dog's excrement in the backyard. He decided to take the dog to the RSPCA pound. He was torn by his decision, often wondering if the animal survived, slipping into bouts of depression when he realised it was probably dead.

A more severe depression that recurred throughout the rest of his life was caused by the death of his nephew and godson, Anthony, the first and only son of his brother, John. Ever since Anthony's christening, Bill had taken his role seriously, visiting regularly with presents and spending time with the boy.

Then, at the age of nine, Anthony was diagnosed as having muscular dystrophy, a condition in which his muscles slowly deteriorated.

Each year Anthony would grow gradually weaker as Bill and his family watched helplessly. Bill often slept in Anthony's room when he visited, and was with him, holding his hand, when he died three months after his 21st birthday in 1983. Anthony's death shattered Bill. He had loved him as a son and he never recovered from the death.

Bill tried to emulate John's popularity and respect within the Vandenberg family, but try as he might, he never quite achieved the same quiet command and authority. Apart from Anthony, Bill had established an odd de facto family of his own. With the money he saved from his various jobs, he rented a large house at Chatswood, sub-letting the rooms and presiding as landlord.

At 24, women were still an enigma to Bill. He was awkward in their company and preferred to be with men. His marriage surprised everyone. His bride was one of his tenants, a young woman who had fallen pregnant. Bill felt sorry for her. Both families were against the marriage. John Vandenberg seriously doubted that Bill was the father—in fact he doubted that the marriage was ever consummated. 'You can't expect me to love that man,' John claimed she told him privately. 'I couldn't live the rest of my life with an ugly bastard like him.'

Despite the family's misgivings, Bill seemed happy. He and his wife and her daughter moved north to Kurri Kurri, not far from Newcastle, where Bill set himself up as a painter. After four years he bought an empty shop in Newcastle which he turned into a small grocery store and milk bar. The couple made money from the shop. Bill delighted in showing off his new Chrysler car to John. It was much more expensive than John's old Holden.

As if the long hours weren't enough, Vandenberg also took on voluntary work, five nights a week. He became chairman of the Kurri Young Citizens' Association, and helped start a gymnasium for young people to keep them off the streets. He became chairman of the local Rotary Club and helped set up a committee to organise tree planting in the town. He also became chairman of the Kurri Development Association, and was a foundation member of the Kurri Civic Committee.

In 1972 his marriage ended. Although it had always seemed inevitable, Vandenberg later blamed himself. After they sold the shop, Bill went to work at Commonwealth Steel at Newcastle, New South Wales' biggest steelworks. One of his co-workers was Kerry Orrock, whose girlfriend, Gloria, had worked in Vandenberg's shop. After they married, they became Vandenberg's 'adopted family' and Vandenberg moved in with them and their two children. Kerry Orrock had just bought a service station in Kurri with some compensation money he was awarded from an industrial accident at the steelworks.

After a few months, Vandenberg left the steelworks. For the next few years he drifted, starting up businesses which ended up bankrupt. Then he started drinking—a vice he had so far avoided.

In 1980, back at Commonwealth Steel he had a bad accident, falling several metres onto a scrap-metal heap. He spent almost a week in the intensive care unit of Newcastle Hospital and was left with an awkward stoop. Unable to return to the steelworks, Vandenberg thought he was unemployable. Finally, after several months, he was offered a job as a senior assistant in a Sydney hotel.

Vandenberg had always suppressed his homosexuality. But now, he headed for the streets of Kings Cross where he could anonymously solicit young men in hotels. Andrew Tregurtha, then about fifteen, would later write about his first encounter with Vandenberg in 1980, when he was living on and off the streets of the Cross. Tregurtha, who was later convicted of the murder of the Sydney Greek consul, had just recovered from a drug overdose when a friend asked if he would be interested in working at Vandenberg's hotel one and a half hours from the Cross by train. Tregurtha and his friend had met Vandenberg at a nightclub in the Cross where Vandenberg often drank.

Vandenberg offered him the job without a formal interview, despite his being under age and lacking experience. At first Tregurtha could not understand his good luck. After a few weeks, one night when he finished work, Vandenberg suggested he stay at his nearby flat because Tregurtha was working a double shift. Vandenberg insisted they had sex. Now Tregurtha knew why he had been employed. The next day he quit his job.

Over the next few years, Vandenberg moved from one hotel to another, mainly in the suburbs. While managing the Sundowner hotel in Punchbowl he started informing for police. He was mixing on the fringes of stolen car rackets and some of his information was good. The local detectives were uncomfortable with his homosexuality, but his information was usually spot-on and they knew he could not sustain a lie for any length of time.

In 1985, Vandenberg moved to Kings Cross and got a job running the Sea Galleon restaurant at the Rex hotel in the heart of the Cross. It was a rundown, seedy pub that attracted all sorts. He found himself a flat behind the hotel in a bland fifteen-storey block with a carport underneath, named Ithaca Gardens. The small, two-bedroom unit had a good view of the Harbour. The furnishings were frugal: two coffee tables, a comfortable old blue chair with some of its stuffing missing, and an old sideboard by the window where he kept a game of Trivial Pursuit. On the walls hung some of his favourite drawings—naked women in tortured, Bosch-like poses.

In August, Vandenberg found himself a flatmate. He had known Trevor Hayden, a regular at the Rex, for about twelve months. As time passed, Vandenberg came to believe Hayden was one of the grubbiest men he had ever met. More than once Vandenberg, who was fastidiously clean, would come home from work in the early hours to find the sink full of dirty plates and cockroaches running about the kitchen. Hayden was unemployed and was at home most of the time.

In late September, Vandenberg was robbed of $500. It had been inside his jacket pocket in the flat. Vandenberg had been robbed before, but this time he was hurt and angry and was not going to be left looking like an idiot.

He was still smarting when his friend Orrock came down to Sydney a few weeks later. Orrock now had a private investigator's licence and was in Sydney to get a gun. He picked up Vandenberg on his way to the gunsmiths.

'Do you know any heavies?' Vandenberg asked as they drove out west.

'Yeah, mate,' said Orrock. 'There's Black George. He lives in Kurri, but he's a real heavy. He's been in jail for murder. He put a bloke in hospital for six months—and he's kicked someone's head in. You don't double-cross him.'

'How hard would it be to get in touch with him?'

Orrock looked at his mate. 'Well, he lives at Weston.'

'How well do you know him?' asked Vandenberg.

'Pretty well. When I had the garage, he did a couple of days work for me driving my tanker—remember? I was having union troubles.'

'Yeah. Well, someone's ripping me off and I'd like to get this young fellow and teach him a lesson that he can't mess around with me. Vandenberg was sure he knew the culprit. 'How much would your bloke charge?'

'Oh, about three hundred for breaking one leg, five hundred for two and a grand for doin' the whole job.' Orrock was hazarding a guess. Canellis had never really discussed prices.

Orrock assured Vandenberg he would see what he could do. The mere thought of revenge seemed enough for Vandenberg. He was practically gloating the next morning when he told Hayden his plans: 'They won't mess with me again,' he said triumphantly. 'A friend of mine knows someone who'll fix up whoever took my money.'

A few nights later one of the waitresses told Vandenberg someone wanted to see him outside. It was Hayden, waiting on the footpath. Vandenberg could smell alcohol. Hayden slurred his words and swayed slightly as he asked: 'That bloke you were talking about . . . the one who could do certain jobs. Do you think he would be interested in knocking someone off?'

'I don't know, Trevor,' Vandenberg said, surprised.

'Well, could you ask him? Elkins wants to know.'

Vandenberg remembered Elkins. He had met him at his flat about two months previously. Vandenberg had just had a shower and was getting ready to go to work when Elkins dropped in for a drink with Hayden. A big spender, Hayden had said, telling Vandenberg that Elkins had given him some work tracking down someone in the Cross. Hayden didn't get the money—or so he said. Vandenberg hadn't paid much attention at the time. Hayden was always cooking up schemes to make money. He had once asked Vandenberg if he wanted a trip to Singapore to follow a man from the plane to his hotel for $1000. But nothing came of it.

Now this Elkins wanted something from him. When he saw Hayden the next morning, Vandenberg was sure he'd forgotten his request. So he was surprised when, during the quiet part of the morning, just before the hectic lunchtime crowd arrived, Vandenberg looked up and saw Elkins standing in front of him.

'G'day, Bill. How's things?'

'Fine,' said Vandenberg. He offered him a coffee. Elkins was someone who would bring clients to the restaurant—a man who came to spend money, thought Vandenberg. They chatted for several minutes until Vandenberg said he had to get back to work.

'So,' Elkins said, 'did Trevor speak to you last night?'

'Yes, he spoke to me about a few things.' Vandenberg paused, hovering like a bee above a flower, unsure whether to land or fly away. He noticed Elkins had lowered his voice.

'Did he ask anything special?'

'Well, you know, he spoke to me about a few things, something about this job he wanted done.'

'Yeah,' said Elkins. 'Do you know anyone who could do away with someone? Rub someone out?'

The words sounded to Vandenberg like the script for a detective thriller. 'Yeah, he mentioned that,' he said slowly.

'And what did you tell Trevor?'

'I told Trevor I'd ask around. I may know someone.'

'And have you inquired about it yet?'

'No, I haven't.'

'Why not?'

'Well, I didn't think he was fair dinkum.'

'It's worth ten thousand.'

'OK, I'll make some inquiries.'

Vandenberg finished his coffee. Surely not. This was a joke. This couldn't be serious. These things didn't happen—not to him, anyway. And yet he felt a surge of excitement. It was like reading a good book, he thought. He wanted to find out what happened next.

EIGHT

BLACK GEORGE

George Canellis was proud of his hands. His long, slender fingers were more like those of a pianist than a hitman. They had escaped the usual hazards of his profession.

At 43, Canellis, also known as Noel Sherry and Black George, was taut and muscular. His slim build belied his strength but there was menace implicit in his canny, tomcat eyes. He moved with a rare animal grace, like a leopard, sailing along on the balls of his feet. He was handsome in a rugged, weatherbeaten way. At times he looked Aboriginal with his smooth, dark skin; at other times his almost black eyes and thick dark hair seemed Mediterranean. Whatever his origins, with Greek adoptive parents and a name like Canellis, most people assumed he was Greek. Canellis didn't know or care. He had accepted many years ago he would never know his real mother. She had left him for adoption at Newtown Hospital, behind the Hub Theatre in the inner city, when he was six weeks old in March 1942.

It was a tough start to life, but Canellis proved tougher. His adoptive parents were poor. They lived in a one-bedroom flat in Surry Hills. Canellis' step-father, a burly man who worked at the fish markets at Pyrmont, usually reeked of stale sweat and fish. He often argued loudly in Greek with his wife. When Canellis was a few years old, the family was evicted for not paying the rent. Canellis' father came home to find George and his mother sitting in the gutter, their meagre possessions strewn around them. Canellis had never seen his father so angry. He marched up and down the footpath screaming and ranting, while Canellis cowered behind his weeping mother.

The Canellis family moved to a derelict, rat-infested two-bedroom cottage off Cleveland Street, Redfern, which they eventually bought and restored. During one of their first nights there, George was bitten on the face by a rat as he slept. He woke screaming, blood trickling down his cheek. The rat left a half-inch scar under his left eye, a reminder of his past.

Canellis would tell tales of those early days—how the first police officer he remembered was one who had visited their house and wound up in an argument with his father. On his way out, the policeman had squashed Canellis' favourite toy, a red train.

Inner-city Redfern was a tough neighbourhood but Canellis was a fast learner. He managed to hold his own, even among some of the older kids. By the age of eight he was smoking cigarettes and into petty theft. At ten, he 'torched' his first car. It belonged to a teacher who was in the process of getting Canellis expelled from the local public school. Canellis was barely into his teens when he gave up school. Although he was too young to have a licence, he drove an old 1937 Ford for several months until he crashed into a tram outside the Cauliflower hotel in Waterloo. Despite 'banging the arse out of the tram', he climbed through the car window and took off before the police arrived.

By the time he was fifteen, Canellis had left the streets of Redfern for Kings Cross. He was young, strong and fit. He soon got a job as a nightclub bouncer and proved himself a fair match for the troublemakers and drunks, especially the visiting American sailors in Sydney on R & R during the Vietnam War. Canellis was lightning-quick and merciless with his hands. He usually gave better than he received. He decorated his arms with tattoos—blue hearts and anchors.

Quick to learn the pecking order, he slipped easily into the nocturnal sleaze of the Cross. He soon knew who controlled the strip joints, the gambling dens, the nightclubs and the girls. He also found out which police were on the take and how much they got.

In his cheap suits and high-heeled boots, Canellis got a job as a 'sitter', looking after prostitutes working for some of the nightclubs. Part of his job was paying protection money to police. He would brag of his conquests: how he thrashed a Yugoslav twice his size who had demanded his money back and threatened one of the women with a knife.

If the women were 'pinched', Canellis would bail them out. The boss always paid. Sometimes the magistrates would let them off with a warning, sometimes a fine. Canellis would be there to collect them from court.

For a while Canellis lived with one of the prostitutes who was a few years older than him. They moved into a a a flat at Double Bay. As far as he was concerned, when she came home from work and had a shower, he was the only man in the world for her. When she left him eighteen months later for another man, he shrugged his shoulders. Such was life.

Gradually, Canellis moved from protecting prostitutes to collecting debts. He also set himself up buying and selling stolen goods. For a brief time he even tried his hand at a legitimate daytime job, carving leather belts, bridles and saddles at a shop in Newtown.

In time, Canellis became a self-taught expert with a gun—not only the technical aspects, but how to use one. By the early 1970s, he had already notched up several convictions for stealing, larceny, street fighting and assault and robbery. His love of guns had earned him charges for illegal possession of firearms and he had also been found guilty of living off the earnings of a prostitute.

He spent several short stints in jail but he managed to survive inside just as well as he did up at the Cross. If he beat the jail heavy at chess, he slept with his eyes open that night.

And it was to the Cross that he always returned when he got out. His notoriety brought him plenty of business. He was good at it: debt collection, threats. There were standard rates for everything from scaring people to breaking legs.

He carried a gun most of the time but he boasted that he could kill, if necessary, with his hands alone. He developed a street awareness that was always with him and he never sat with his back exposed. He would research his victims with the tenacity of a palaeontologist studying a fossil, knowing their movements in detail before he struck. His language was coarse and colourful.

Canellis eventually married and it was after he had five children, he found himself in the most serious trouble so far. In 1978, he was charged with murder, having killed a man who had assaulted his son. He agreed to plead guilty to a lesser charge of assault occasioning actual bodily harm. It got him five years although he was released two years and eight months later.

On his release in 1980, Canellis was penniless and the cops had made it clear he was finished in Sydney. He would be back inside to serve the rest of his five years if he breached his strict parole conditions. So Canellis took his wife and five children and moved to the Newcastle district. They lived with a friend in a caravan park until a housing commission home became available.

Canellis still did the odd job when the opportunity and the money arose, although most of his money came from truck driving.

He bought a second-hand cut-down Stirling .22 rifle from the local poundkeeper at Kurri. It was an old gun, with cobwebs in the barrel, but Canellis fixed it up. For practice he took pot-shots at the mongrel dogs that rummaged through his garbage early on Friday mornings. He used a silencer, which he'd bought in South Australia years ago, so he wouldn't wake the neighbours. He also trained a couple of

Rottweiler pups as attack dogs, but instead of the usual commands of 'go fetch' or 'sit', Canellis' rotties—as he called them—were taught to respond to commands of 'bastard' and 'kill'.

Canellis made few friends, but Kerry Orrock was one of them. Orrock ran the local BP petrol station where one of Canellis' sons did work experience. Canellis started calling in for a chat with Orrock whenever he stopped for petrol.

Orrock was eleven years younger than Canellis. He had a thin face and short, thick, dark hair. His pale grey eyes were often dark-ringed from pain, a legacy of an accident at the steelworks where he used to work. He still suffered from headaches and backaches and he was disfigured by a 3 cm wide scar which stretched across his lower back between his hip joints.

Canellis liked talking and Orrock liked listening, especially to Canellis' colourful tales of the Cross. Orrock had lived in Kurri all his life. He left school at the age of eleven, and his life had been ordinary. Some of Orrock's police friends at Kurri had warned him not to get involved with Canellis. He was bad news, they said, and he had a long criminal record. But Orrock liked him, and he'd done nothing to worry him or his family.

Apart from his petrol station, Orrock owned a petrol tanker and drove wholesale Queensland petrol betweeen Raymond Terrace, near Newcastle, and the Hunter Valley. In July 1982, hundreds of angry Newcastle truck drivers set up blockades on the main highways to protest about a new government fuel tax. Orrock was one of the rebel tanker drivers who continued to deliver blackmarket petrol. But he was threatened with a flogging and he didn't have the stomach to keep delivering, even though the money was good. He asked Canellis if he wanted to give it a go. Canellis agreed, for a quarter of the price Orrock would get for the load. Armed with an iron bar, chain and a double-barrelled shotgun, Canellis drove from Raymond Terrace to Muswellbrook and back to Kurri with little resistance. After the strikes were over, Canellis worked for Orrock for a few months. Each time he brought the truck back, he'd stop for a coffee and a chat.

By 1985, though, the work had dried up. The two men didn't see each other for several months. Then, about three days before Christmas, Orrock called.

'G'day, George. How's things? You busy?'

'No, not really, mate,' said Canellis, a little surprised.

'What's doin'?'

'I might have a job for you.'

'Yeah? Well, don't talk on the phone. Come over and see me this afternoon. About five?'

Orrock arrived in his white former police highway patrol car. Canellis went outside to meet him and the two men sat on the bonnet of the car. Both lit cigarettes.

'Are you interested in doing a job, George?'

'What sort of a job?'

'A knock job.'

Canellis paused for a few seconds. 'Who is it?'

'I don't know yet. I'm just asking if you're interested and how much it's going to cost them. They want to know your price.'

Canellis thought again. 'My price is thirty grand—that's if I use my own gun. If they supply the piece, it's twenty-five.'

'They'll even supply the car —'

'Fuck that,' Canellis cut in. 'I'll use my own fucking car.'

'OK. Well, how about we take a run down to Sydney and see them?'

'Tonight? Get fucked. You get in touch with them, and let me know if they want to go on with it under my conditions. Then I'll think about going to Sydney.'

'Why don't you jump in the car and we'll go and ring them from my place,' Orrock said. He had not expected the figure to be so high, but Canellis knew all about that sort of thing.

Orrock's house, a white aluminium-clad bungalow in Edward Street, Kurri, was three kilometres away. Canellis greeted Orrock's wife and children, then went through to the bedroom with Orrock. He sat on the bed and watched Orrock dial a Sydney telephone number and heard the voice at the other end say: 'Sea Galleon Restaurant.'

'Is Bill there?' Orrock asked.

'Hang on, I'll get him.'

Canellis walked out into the kitchen, satisfied that he had an address for Orrock's contact. A few minutes later Orrock followed him: 'I've got that bloke on the phone. Do you want to talk to him?'

'Yeah, OK.' Canellis picked up the phone and said hello.

'G'day, my name's Bill.' There was a trace of a European accent. Canellis guessed the man was about the same age as himself—early forties.

'This friend,' the man went on, 'he wants someone rubbed out, and he's willing to pay ten thousand and —'

'No fucking way,' Canellis cut in. 'You tell your friend if he wants me to do the job it'll cost him twenty-five grand and I want the piece supplied as well.'

'OK. I'll tell them.'

'Yeah, and when you're ready, you ring Kerry and let me know whether it's on.'

'OK. Put Kerry back on.'

Canellis gave the phone back to Orrock and walked into the kitchen.

The two said little during the short trip home, but as Canellis closed the car door, he leaned inside: 'Do you trust your mate?'

'Yeah,' Orrock said, 'I trust him.'

Elkins became more determined in his pursuit of the hotel security contract. Late on the night of 30 November, the hotel master keys mysteriously disappeared. David Lyle, a security guard with Seaboard Cardinal, had left them on the counter at reception. When he returned a few minutes later, the keys were gone. Elkins was nearby. He said he had not seen them. Lyle felt sick.

Elkins went to Kalajzich who was furious and insisted that Seaboard Cardinal pay to have the locks changed for the entire hotel. The way was now clear for Elkins to take over.

Vandenberg was relieved that Canellis had refused the job for $10 000. Vandenberg was sure Elkins would be just as adamant about not paying $25 000. He hoped, in one way, that that would be the end of the whole affair.

He contacted Elkins and arranged to meet him at the Sea Galleon. Vandenberg was glad when Elkins shook his head. 'Twenty-five thousand dollars?' he repeated. 'My client will never agree to that, he'll never go for that . . .'

That was the end of that, the game was over. But Elkins was surprised at Kalajzich's reaction: 'Is this guy for real?' he had asked. 'Go back, just go back to meet with him again to make sure he'll do it.'

A few nights later, on the Boxing Day holiday, Vandenberg looked up and saw Warren Elkins sitting at one of the tables in the Sea Galleon. He took a coffee over to him. Elkins stuttered slightly: 'My c-c-client is willing to pay twenty-five thousand.' Vandenberg was shocked.

'He also wants you to ask if it makes any difference if it's a woman,' Elkins said. 'And ask him if he wants a gun.'

Within an hour, George Canellis' phone rang. It was Orrock: 'Everything's sweet,' he said. 'The job's on and they'll supply the piece. You can take it up with Bill.' He gave him Vandenberg's phone number.

Canellis called him ten minutes later. 'Is that you, Bill?'

'Yeah, mate. I've checked with them and everything seems OK. When can you come down and discuss the matter?'

But Canellis was in business mode: 'You listen to me,' he said. 'You can fuckin' tell them I'm not going down there for nothing. I want five grand up front before I even start, and the balance within two hours of them hearing it on the news. And if they're supplying the gun, I want to see it before I do the job.'

Vandenberg said he'd call him back. Within an hour, Vandenberg rang him from the post office at Potts Point. The money and the gun would be waiting for him, he said. 'And they wanted to know if it made any difference if it was a female.'

'No difference at all to me,' said Canellis. 'It's just a job. But it better be a good piece if I'm going to lose five grand for it.'

'Well, they said it cost ten thousand, so it must be good. It's got a silencer.'

Kalajzich closed the door of his office. Elkins stood at the side of his desk with his briefcase open. Kalajzich passed him bundles of notes—$25 000—and the sawn-off .22 Stirling survival rifle and silencer. Elkins packed them in the briefcase, then ran through his instructions again: 'I've booked the room at the Travelodge. I'll leave twenty thousand in the briefcase there. After the job's done, I'll put the room key in Vandenberg's letterbox.'

Kalajzich nodded. Elkins was relieved that it was finally arranged. Now, maybe, the boss would get off his back.

He and Vandenberg met on the roof of Ithaca Gardens. When Elkins opened the briefcase to show him the weapon, Vandenberg said: 'There's no point in me even looking at that. I know nothing about guns.'

They met at the Tennessee Inn, a smoky little bar in an arcade, back from the bustle of the main drag at the Cross. 'How will I know you?' Canellis had asked.

'I'll be easy to spot, you can't mistake me,' Vandenberg replied. 'I look like Billy McMahon. I've got big ears, a bald head and glasses.' Canellis had laughed.

When Canellis walked into the bar, Vandenberg recognised him straight away. Orrock's description—dark, but not Aboriginal—was perfect.

Canellis was late. His car had broken down at Peats Ridge on the way to Sydney. He just made it into a petrol station and looked under the bonnet. It was the transmission. He had rung Vandenberg to tell him he'd be late: 'The bloody clutch has slipped. I can't get any revs out of the bastard, but I'm still coming. I should be there in about an hour. Just wait for me.'

Vandenberg waited in the near-empty bar for more than an hour. It was just on two o'clock when Canellis walked through the door. The first thing he noticed was Vandenberg's ears. They seemed to stretch from the top of his jaw to his eyebrows.

'Hello Billy McMahon,' he said, grinning. Vandenberg laughed and offered his hand.

As Canellis sat down he noticed the briefcase next to Vandenberg's chair. The money and the gun, he assumed.

'OK, Billy,' he said. 'I want some details. Who is it and where?'

Vandenberg handed Canellis the scrap of paper Elkins had given him to pass on to the hitman. It was torn from a Sydney phone directory and had the words '31 Fairlight Cresc rust Jap' written on it.

'There's two Fairlight addresses,' Vandenberg said. 'One's a street and one's a crescent—so don't get them mixed up.'

'How will I fuckin' know which one's the right one?'

'Well, I've been told the garage doors of the house where she lives are white with brown trim and that the house is at the back, dropped below street level. There's a block of flats opposite.

'The best position to get the woman is after she parks her car in the garage and walks down the back pathway to the house. The tilt-a-door opens automatically. She'll press the remote button before she arrives and then the door'll open. You'll know it's her when the car goes in the garage. You can wait at the back of the garage and get her there.'

'What does she look like?'

'She's in her late forties, well-groomed. She'll be on her own, the only one at the house.'

'And what's this "rust Jap" mean?' Canellis asked, pointing at the scrap of paper.

'She drives a red Japanese sports car—I don't know what make . . .'

Canellis looked up and noticed a man standing outside. He had a camera, and was looking inside.

'Is that bloke with you?' Canellis asked, nodding to the door.

'What bloke?' said Vandenberg, turning slightly. 'No, I've never seen him before.'

'Are you sure?' said Canellis.

'No, I don't know . . . I've never seen him.'

'Well, he's fuckin' trying to photograph us,' said Canellis. Vandenberg was scared. Canellis saw he was as jittery as all hell.

'This is the first time I've done this sort of thing,' Vandenberg said. 'I just hope everything goes all right.'

'Have you got the gun and the money?'

'Yes, I picked them up this morning.'

'Is it a pistol or what?'

'A pistol. They said they paid ten grand for it.'

'You're fuckin' kidding, aren't you? What is it—gold? Have you seen it?'

'No. They said it's a .22. It's in the briefcase with a silencer and the money.'

'OK, then,' said Canellis, 'you tell them I'll have the job done within 48 hours. As soon as you hear on the news that such-and-such has happened, I get paid. Otherwise, I'll come after you. Understand?'

'OK, I'll tell them.'

'Good. Come with me. We'll walk out the back, and I'll take the briefcase when we're outside.'

'There's one more thing,' said Vandenberg. 'The briefcase combination lock is 519 on the first lock and 915 on the second. And it's my briefcase. I wondered if I could have it back, later, if possible?'

'Sure.' Canellis smiled. 'You go through the front and keep an eye on that bloke with the camera while I walk to me car.'

As soon as Canellis got back in his car, he opened the case. He counted the wads of $20, $50 and $100 notes. The $5000 was all there. Next, he checked the gun. 'What the fuck . . .' he said out loud. It was a cut-down survival rifle, with a hand-made modified pistol grip. A bodgie screw through the centre held it all together. The barrel had been cut off to about 20 cm long with a thread for a silencer. The silencer was a factory-made model, painted black. Canellis was disgusted. Piece of churned-out shit, he thought to himself as he closed the case.

He drove to a friend's house nearby for a better look. Inside the magazine he found three hollow-nose bullets. 'Who the fuck do they think I am? Three fuckin' bullets? Fuckin' worthless piece of shit,' Canellis said as he shoved the gun back inside the case. So much for the pistol they promised. He put the money in his pocket and drove home to Kurri.

'What's their fuckin' go?' Orrock cringed as Canellis shouted down the phone. 'They tried to charge me five grand for a piece I could buy in Brisbane for about $180. You can tell them to get fucked.'

'Hang on, mate,' said Orrock. 'I don't know nothing about it.'

'Well, you fuckin' tell Bill if they think I'm going to use this heap of shit—I'll use me own and five grand goes on the bill.'

Ten minutes later, Vandenberg rang Canellis. 'What's the matter, mate?'

'There's no way I'll pay five grand for this fuckin' cut-down rifle—it's not worth a pinch of shit.'

'They told me they paid ten grand for it.'

'Well, they must be a bunch of fuckin' dills. I won't use it, I'll use me own.' Canellis still had the old Stirling .22 semi-automatic he'd bought to take care of the dogs.

'I'll tell them what you've said,' said Vandenberg.

'Yeah,' said Canellis, 'and you just tell them to make sure there's twenty-five grand instead of twenty when I come to collect.'

'I will,' said Vandenberg. 'Oh, and they also said to tell you the best time for the job was to wait for her to get out of the car and walk down the path, but be sure to get her before she gets to the house.'

'How will they know if it's done?' Canellis said.

'They'll know straight away. Within thirty minutes they'll ring a man in North Sydney, I'll pick up the money for you and I will make the payment at a prearranged place.'

'OK,' said Canellis. 'I always do my jobs within 48 hours.'

Early the next morning, Canellis decided to test the cut-down anyway. Standing near his back verandah, he fired two shots. The explosions sent his wife running out the back door:

'What the hell do you think you're doing?' she asked. 'What's going on, George?'

'Nothing, love. Just testing a gun. I got it for the dogs.'

'Well, you scared the living daylights out of me, and you'll have the police down here next.'

'Yeah, yeah, all right.'

He had to agree with her about the noise—and that was with the silencer. He tried some of his own ammunition, standard lower velocity bullets, but it was still way too noisy. Useless bloody silencer, Canellis thought. Damn it. He'd have to use his own gun.

Two days later, the first day of 1986, George Canellis drove to Manly.

NINE

SMILE FOR A STRANGER

On any fine summer's day, Manly is a carnival of colour. The surf sparkles, and the blue of the ocean is peppered with myriad sails of windsurfers and sailboards. The babble of playing children drifts above the breeze and crowds of daytrippers wearing the iridescent colours of summer wander along the Corso to the beach. The smells of summer—fish and chips, and salt from the sea—infuse the air. Lifesavers bump over the waves in rubber-duckies herding straying swimmers back between the flags, and families picnic on the grass under the shade of towering Norfolk pines.

On New Year's Day 1986, Manly was a spectacle of summer at its best. Canellis joined the crawl of lunchtime traffic hoping for parking spaces along North Steyne. He could have been one of the hundreds of daytrippers out to make the most of a sunny public holiday at the beach. But Canellis was on reconnaissance. After checking out the beachfront, he drove back up Commonwealth Parade to Fairlight, parked his car, and walked along The Esplanade which ran along the front of the Kalajzich house.

It was now afternoon, hot and humid. A few low clouds had

appeared on the horizon and the water of Forty Baskets Beach had turned dark grey-blue. Canellis smoked as he ambled along, taking in the view and listening to the sounds: the tinkling of the yacht masts, and the waves slapping against the rocks. He noted the position of every street and pathway exit off The Esplanade.

He had already viewed the back of the house from the street. He had seen the garage door Vandenberg had described. But nothing else Vandenberg had told him seemed to match. The flats he had been told were opposite had turned out to be next door, and not only was there no sign of a red Japanese sports car, there was a blue four-wheel-drive Suzuki in the driveway. So, who owned that car? Canellis wasn't pleased. He didn't want any witnesses.

As he approached number 31 from the front, he slowed down, stopping on a rocky ledge opposite the sandstone fence at the front of the house. It had an uninterrupted view of the bay. Wild brambles grew over the ledge below and each side was framed by manicured rockeries bursting with blooms that rustled in the afternoon breeze. Canellis sat on a bench and, pretending to read the inscription—to Harold Hilbold Bowan (1913–1985)—he examined the house through his dark sunglasses.

It was a three-level place, brick and timber, with two back exits: a sliding glass door on the ground level and a small balcony on the second. He noted all sorts of details: the windows opened outwards and there was access to The Esplanade on either side of the house. A lawn ran across the front of the block and ended at a small sandstone wall. Anyone entering from The Esplanade could do so through a small wooden gate. The wall and the gate were no more than a metre high. Leaving would be easy. He could not see anybody inside, so he walked through the unlocked gate for a closer look.

As he stood inside the gate, he noticed a youth coming around the side of the house. Canellis tried to appear confident.

'What are you doing? This is private property,' the boy said.

'I was just comin' in from the bay . . .'

'Well you can use the pathway for the units next door.' The boy indicated the steps beside him.

'I don't like it, Billy. Not one bit, I can tell you now . . .' Canellis was ringing Vandenberg from a public phone box. 'You tell them I want some more details. There's no fuckin' red Japanese car and the garage door isn't at the back at all. There was another car there, a blue Suzuki. I want to know if it's hers. I've got the rego. What's more, the fucking son or someone—a young bloke—came out and caught me in the act.'

Vandenberg promised to get more information. When Canellis rang back, he was ready: 'I've got the rego number of the car. It's not red. It's rust-coloured. The number plate is MK 203.'

'Who owns the blue Suzuki, then?'

'I don't know.'

'Well find out. They're not going to fuck me around. You tell them I want to know what's going on.'

That night Canellis booked into a room at the Manly Hotel, opposite the Manly ferry wharf. He decided to see it out for another day and at least have a look for his target.

Early the next morning he wandered across to a cafe for breakfast. From his table by the window he saw the early beach-goers arrive by ferry and meander down the Corso. He had a clear view of Commonwealth Parade and he watched the cars and buses as they rounded the bend down into Manly. He was on to his second cup of coffee when he saw the car. It was a reddish-brown Toyota Celica with black-and-white personalised plates: MK 203. As the car came closer, he saw that the driver was a woman. It must be her.

Canellis threw a $10 note on the table and ran out to his car. The woman had stopped at traffic lights outside. Soon Canellis was in the traffic behind her. Two left turns and she pulled into a car space at the Manly fruit market. Canellis drove into a carpark opposite, then followed her inside.

He walked behind her as she wandered along the aisles to

the rows containing lettuce and tomatoes. The first thing he noticed was her hair: not a strand out of place. She was wearing a loose, floral dress and casual shoes. Despite her informal clothes she had class written all over her, Canellis thought. He wondered why someone wanted her dead. She picked up a lettuce, some shallots and tomatoes and took them to the checkout.

Canellis grabbed some bananas and grapes and followed her. He stood beside her in an adjacent queue. He was still looking at her when she turned and smiled at him, almost as if she knew he was there. Canellis smiled back. She had a soft, round face and warm eyes, he thought.

Canellis followed her out, double-checked her number plate and then followed her car up Commonwealth Parade and into Fairlight Crescent. She pulled into 31. It was her all right. Then Canellis noticed the other car in the garage—a silver-blue Mercedes. And that blue Suzuki was now parked opposite. 'Shit,' Canellis said. He drove straight back down the hill.

'What the fuck is going on?' He was on the phone again to Vandenberg. 'You'd better get over here, Billy.'

'Why, what's up?' asked Vandenberg.

'You tell me there's nobody here except her, and now there's two other fuckin' cars in the driveway. Something stinks. You find out who owns them—I'm not having people watching me.'

'Um, yeah, well,' said Vandenberg apologetically, 'they told me there's a husband, and a son as well.'

'Well fuck you,' Canellis shouted. 'I'm not walking in there in front of the husband and son and blowing her head off. I'd have to take them out, too, and they're not paying me for that.'

'OK,' said Vandenberg, 'I'll get back to them.

These idiots were unbelievable, thought Canellis. But still, he'd stick around. He had other business to see to in Sydney that week anyway.

He had decided the best way to approach the job was to make it look like a robbery gone wrong. That way he didn't necessarily even need to use a gun. He could break her neck as she walked down those steep stairs from the carport to the house, smash her head against a rock, and steal her handbag.

The days passed but the job had not been done.

'He's fucking with us.' Kalajzich's anger had returned. 'I want the job done now or I want the money back,' he told Elkins. 'Is this guy for real? I want you to go back, Waz. Go back and meet him again and make sure he'll do it.'

Elkins called Vandenberg. They had to talk. This time, Vandenberg visited Elkins. He had not been to Manly for years. He caught the ferry over from the Quay the next afternoon, Saturday 4 January. They met at Marineland, just around the bay from the wharf, at 4.30 pm.

'My client is losing millions of dollars a day,' Elkins said. 'She's ripping him off—selling his shares. It's important the job's done tonight.'

'Is it a political murder?' Vandenberg asked.

'No, it's a domestic murder, mate,' Elkins said. 'It's nothing like as big as that Chinese murder—you know, Stanley Wong. It'll only hit the papers for a day or two and that'll be the end of it.'

'Well,' said Vandenberg. 'I am meeting him later on, so I'll tell him. That's all I can do. He says he will do it when the time is right.'

'It's got to be done tonight,' Elkins stressed. 'Make sure you tell him. It's very important. He can't wait any longer.'

Vandenberg walked back to the wharf, where he had arranged to meet Canellis. He was worried. He knew that no matter what he told Canellis, it wouldn't make any difference. If only the whole thing was over. He wondered who Elkins' client was. Someone from Manly was all he'd been told.

'G'day, Billy.' Canellis startled him from behind.

'Oh, hello, George,' Vandenberg said. 'We have to talk. They're not happy about things.'

'Well fuck them,' Canellis cut in, 'because neither am I. Let's have a talk and some dinner at that Greek joint down the road.'

As they ate, Canellis told Vandenberg he had seen the woman and followed her inside the fruit market. 'She's a good-looking woman,' he said. 'Classy, all right. I could have done the job there and then; knocked her off her feet.'

'They say the job has to be done within 24 hours,' Vandenberg said. 'It's important. She's costing him millions. You've got to do it.'

'Don't rush me, Billy.'

'I'm just passing on the message.'

'I'll do the best I can tonight. But if I can't tonight, I'll do it as soon as possible.'

'They won't be happy if it's not done tonight. When you've done it, contact me.'

'OK, Billy,' said Canellis, picking up the bill.

Vandenberg walked back to the wharf to catch a ferry. Canellis drove out to Liverpool, in Sydney's south-west, to finish some business out there. Then he drove home to Kurri.

Fuck that lot, he thought. He had made up his mind he wasn't going to do their hit that night or any night. Bunch of amateurs. He'd keep their five grand, too. For his trouble. They'd screwed him around enough.

The 24 hours came and went. Then 36. Come Monday morning, Kalajzich summoned Elkins to his office at the hotel. After they'd spoken, Elkins rang Vandenberg: 'Tell your man he's sacked and my client wants the gun back.'

Vandenberg waited a few minutes to compose himself before he dialled Canellis' number.

'Oh yeah?' George shouted. 'Well I'm really fuckin' pissed off, too. They didn't supply me what I needed, and the first person I have to protect is myself.'

'They want the gun back,' Vandenberg said.

'Yeah, well they can have that useless piece of shit. But you can fuckin' tell them they're not getting the five grand back.

And if they have any beefs about it they can come and see me and we'll sort it out one way or the other.'

'They haven't said anything about the five thousand dollars yet, so don't worry about it,' Vandenberg said.

'Too right I won't.'

But Kalajzich wanted his money back. Nothing infuriated him more than being cheated, and he suspected this Vandenberg character had ripped him off. Maybe there had never even been a hitman and now he had been robbed of $5000.

Carey Harvey had never seen so much money. She and Elkins sat on the bed in the room at the Travelodge in North Sydney and counted out the notes. $20 000 all up. Carey knew not to ask too many questions. She was Elkins' latest lover, a New Zealander whom he had employed at Dalley's as a waitress. Elkins' first marriage had finished long ago and he was practised at being single.

Satisfied the money was all there, he returned it to Kalajzich that day.

The following afternoon Elkins arrived at Vandenberg's flat in Elizabeth Bay. 'My client wants the gun and he wants the money back,' he said. 'You'd better ring your man and tell him.'

Vandenberg sighed. He knew what Canellis would say but, for Elkins' benefit, he rang him anyway.

'No fuckin' way in the world,' Canellis bellowed down the phone. 'I spent four-and-a-half fuckin' days working for them, and I reckon I'm entitled to it.'

Vandenberg hung up, shaking his head.

'I'd better ring my client,' said Elkins.

Vandenberg listened as he passed on the news. There was a string of monosyllabic sounds from Elkins before he turned to Vandenberg: 'He wants to speak to you.'

Vandenberg hesitated, then took the phone. The voice he heard on the other end was deep and controlled. Its coldness chilled him.

'What happened to the money and the gun?' the voice asked. 'I don't believe anybody has been up there.'

'There has. I've been honest all the way through. I have,' Vandenberg pleaded.

'Well, tell me the name of the bloke who's got it,' said the voice.

'I can't tell you that because he's pretty heavy.' Vandenberg was equally terrified of Canellis. He spoke of human life in terms of payment for a job, nothing more.

The voice continued: 'I have people who can take care of people like him.'

'I may be able to get the gun back, but he won't give the money back.'

'I don't believe you,' said the voice. 'I don't believe you hired anyone in the first place. You've got the money and the gun, and I want them back.'

'But I'm telling you the truth,' Vandenberg pleaded again. 'I've done nothing wrong. I can't give you the name—'

The voice cut him off mid-sentence: 'Put Warren back on.'

When Elkins hung up, he said: 'My client is pretty upset. If you don't give me this man's name, he'll be after you.'

But Vandenberg was adamant. Better the devil you know, he thought.

'If I told him the bloke's name he would come and blow my brains out. I'd be better off doing the job myself than taking the risk of him coming after me,' he said to Elkins.

Elkins, now a desperate man, seized on Vandenberg's words. 'If you'll do the job yourself, I'll give you an extra ten thousand.'

'Hang on,' said Vandenberg, alarmed. 'I was only saying that it was too risky for me to give you his name. I don't intend to get involved in it that way.'

Elkins beckoned to him. The gesture seemed almost sinister. He walked to the fourth-floor window and pointed towards Elizabeth Bay with a sweep of his arm. 'He's a very powerful man, my client,' Elkins said. 'He has friends in the state government like Neville Wran and Gerry Gleeson.'

He pointed to Elizabeth Bay again. 'He has friends down there, friends in the Philippine embassy, and he could get anything done, anything at all ... Do you understand?' He paused. 'He's very, very heavy.'

'If he's got so many heavies, why aren't they doing the job?' Vandenberg asked.

'It's just that they can't do this particular job.'

Vandenberg had to speak to someone. He couldn't work it out on his own. The next night he rang Orrock. 'I need to talk to you, Kerry, but not over the phone. Can you come down here to Sydney?'

'What for, Bill? What's going on?'

'I'm in trouble again over George. This time it's serious and I need to see you. My life is in danger. I'm worried, Kerry. I just don't know what to do.'

Orrock had visitors staying at the house. When he told his wife he was going to make the three-hour trip to Sydney, she wasn't pleased. But he went anyway, arriving shortly before midnight. 'Don't come to the flat,' Vandenberg had said. 'I'll book a room at the Crest hotel. I'll see you there tonight.'

Orrock filled in the registration book and went up to his room. When he walked into the foyer again, he saw Vandenberg waiting for him. They sat down and had a coffee.

'Let's go up to your room,' Vandenberg said. Orrock had never seen Vandenberg so nervous and scared.

As they sat in room 705, Vandenberg explained what had happened. He kept reproaching himself, saying, 'I have to speak to Elkins.' He called Elkins' pager number repeatedly, but got no reply.

'So, who's this Elkins?' Orrock asked.

'He's a go-between—between me and a guy who owns a big hotel and his wife is selling millions of dollars of shares a day. The guy wants to get rid of her. There are politicians involved. It's very heavy.'

Orrock listened. He had agreed to help his old friend; he felt responsible. After all, he had introduced him to Canellis.

Vandenberg left the hotel for a while and the phone rang thirty minutes later. Orrock picked it up.

'Is Bill there?' a man asked.

'No, he's gone.' The line went dead.

Orrock pulled on his boots and went into the streets of the Cross. He knew where to find Vandenberg—at The Taboo, a gay bar. They went back to the hotel room, where Vandenberg tried to call Elkins again that night without luck. The following morning, Orrock went across the road to Woolworths and bought himself a razor and some toothpaste. When he came back, Vandenberg looked distressed.

'I'm in real trouble now; big trouble.' He took a piece of paper from the hotel's folder on the desk. He wrote the name 'Warren', a phone and pager number and then 'Manly Pacific Hotel'. On another line he wrote; '$30 000'. Handing the paper to Orrock, Vandenberg said: 'If anything happens to me, get in touch with this bloke and get the money and hold it for me.' Orrock folded the note and put it in the back of his bank deposit book.

Later that day they drove to Fairlight Crescent so Vandenberg could see the house. It was the first time he had driven to Manly for years and after they crossed the Spit Bridge, he missed the sign to Manly and almost ended up in Dee Why. Finally, they backtracked and found the Manly ferry terminal. Vandenberg left the engine running and went into a newsagent to buy a map. He traced Commonwealth Parade with his finger until he found Fairlight Crescent.

'That's where the woman lives that George was supposed to do. He was right,' he said, as they drove slowly past. 'George was right. The units are next door, not opposite, and the door's on the other side.'

Back at the Cross, Orrock went to his hotel room and left Vandenberg at The Taboo. When he went back later, he saw that Vandenberg had made up his mind to get drunk. He was sitting at the bar, drinking steadily, a half-empty bottle of red wine in front of him. Orrock had a coffee and left when Vandenberg ordered another bottle. He stopped at a street stall and filled in an hour having his portrait drawn. Then he rang his wife.

He went looking for Vandenberg again and bumped into him on the street. 'I'm going back to Kurri. Gloria's not happy at all, so I'm leaving straight away,' he said.

'I'll come up tomorrow,' Vandenberg said, patting him on the shoulder, his speech slurred. 'I need a few days to think.' But the next day, when Vandenberg rang Orrock, he had changed his mind. 'Kerry, I need you to go to George's place,' he said, 'and pick up the gun from him. I've told him he can keep the money but he's agreed to give the gun back.'

When Orrock turned up, Canellis had the gun ready for him. 'You're welcome to it,' he said. 'I wouldn't give you the steam off my piss for that piece of shit.'

Canellis wiped the gun with a piece of towelling to get rid of any of his fingerprints, then he put it in Vandenberg's briefcase and handed it over to Orrock. 'Do you know the combination?'

'No, and I don't want to know,' Orrock answered.

Orrock rang Vandenberg. 'I've got the gun.' He could almost hear Vandenberg's relief at the other end of the line.

'I've got to get it to Sydney,' Vandenberg said.

'I can't come to Sydney. I'm in enough trouble with Gloria already,' Orrock replied.

'What about putting it in a taxi for me and sending it down with my briefcase? Put it in a suitcase with some clothes.'

'No, it'll cost you too much money. It'll be at least $150,' Orrock said. 'Also, taxis aren't that safe. I'll go and see my nephew and see if he'll do it.'

At first his nephew, David Orrock, refused. He was sick and not up to it, he said. But when Orrock offered $100, he agreed.

As soon as David stepped onto the platform at Hornsby station, he saw Bill Vandenberg's bald head through the crowd. Vandenberg had been sitting on a wooden seat on the platform, lost in thought. Vandenberg took the suitcase and handed David a $100 note.

At least he had the gun, he thought, as he drove back to the city. Elkins would be happy.

TEN

VANDENBERG STRIKES

Vandenberg parked the car, pulled on the handbrake, turned off the ignition and sat adjusting to the silence after the noise of the engine. In the rear-view mirror he could see the house and the garage door, illuminated by a streetlight. All was quiet. The street was deserted. He was hours early. It was 10 January 1986.

The house looked different at night. Vandenberg looked at the gun, lying on the passenger seat floor next to him. He stared at the brass numbers, 31, on the garage wall. Elkins had told him to be in position at 10 pm. The woman would arrive between 10.30 and 11.30 pm. Vandenberg felt sick as he sat dwelling on his instructions.

He had returned to Manly several times after that quick reconnaissance with Orrock two days ago. He had spent these visits driving around the backstreets and small cul-de-sacs near Fairlight Crescent, trying to memorise the best get-away route. Canellis had told him the house could be approached from the water or by road, and he had marked Fairlight Crescent in biro on his street directory.

Vandenberg had not been sure how to dress for the murder.

He'd started with a camouflage-green army hat that someone had given him. That would disguise his baldness. Then he had bought himself a black tracksuit, as there was nothing dark enough in his own wardrobe. He had hired a car, a white Falcon sedan, from Avis Rent-a-Car at Kings Cross, naively giving the woman behind the desk his real name and licence number.

He reached over and picked up the gun and the magazine. He had loaded the magazine before reaching the house. Orrock had shown him what to do—not too many bullets in the magazine, he had warned. He still had no real idea of how the gun worked, but he knew how to pull the lever back. Just aim and fire. It was that simple.

Shortly after midnight the woman finally arrived. She was on her own. Vandenberg saw her briefly, a shadowy figure behind the wheel, when the streetlight flash-lit her windscreen as she drove around the bend. The automatic garage door rolled open smoothly as her Toyota Celica approached.

She turned the car into the garage. As the door started to close, Vandenberg cocked the gun, as he had been shown, and got out of the car. He crept around to the back of the garage. The woman would be coming out of the rear door, he had been told.

As he crept alongside the carport, he caught his breath sharply. There she was, standing almost in front of him, fumbling with her keys. The door wasn't at the back, it was at the side. He dropped behind a beach buggy at the side of the garage.

He was sure she had seen him. He held his breath, his heart thumping. After what seemed like a minute had passed, he heard the keys jangling again. It seemed as if she was having trouble with the lock on the garage door. He would have to go ahead with it now. He was so close. He watched as she turned on a light above the steep concrete steps leading down to the house. She put her handbag on a ledge near the garage and began examining the bunch of keys. At last, she picked up her bag and turned towards the steps.

She had her back towards him, inviting the attack. Vandenberg stood up and crept towards her, cradling the sawn-off rifle against his shoulder, until he was so close that the tip of the barrel almost touched the back of her head.

His finger trembled as he curled it around the cold metal trigger. He pulled.

At the sound of the click, the woman turned, a puzzled look on her face. They looked at each other for a moment, the victim and her would-be killer, transfixed, neither knowing what to do. Vandenberg felt exposed, vulnerable. She had seen him now. He had to kill her.

He held the butt of the rifle in both hands and swung it like a club. He felt the dull thud as it hit the side of her head. Then he felt the rifle lighten suddenly. It wasn't until he was running past the carport and onto the street that he realised she had screamed.

He flung the rifle onto the back seat and turned the ignition key, his fingers shaking, coaxing the machine to life. Thank God, he thought. He fought the incredible urge to flatten the accelerator. He drove away carefully, a pledge he had made to himself.

A few minutes and a few kilometres later, Vandenberg checked the gun. It was then he realised that the silencer had fallen off. He had to get rid of the gun. He reached into the glove box and still shaking flicked through the street directory. Lane Cove National Park. Yes. He remembered going fishing there as a child.

On the way there, Vandenberg stopped every now and then, dropping some of his clothes in various garbage bins along the road.

At last he started the decline towards the national park. His last stop was Fullers Bridge. He stood there looking down into the swirling waters, then flung the rifle out as far as he could. He watched it spin away from him into the blackness of the Lane Cove River.

May Carmichael had long ago settled into her nightly routine:

bed by 9.45 pm, the radio playing softly as she drifted off to sleep. That night, something startled her. She sat up in bed, her eyes wide open, listening. She heard it again. A woman screaming. She fumbled for the light switch and headed for the window that looked out onto the front of the house. The front door bell rang.

She heard voices as she approached the front door. She unlocked and cautiously opened it. Her daughter stood there, pale and shaking under the hall light, blood dripping from a gash to her head. Mrs Carmichael recognised the young man supporting her—Anthony Vieceli, who lived in the units next door.

'What happened . . . what happened?'

'I was bashed,' Megan said, gulping for breath, her eyes wide and scared.

Mrs Carmichael helped her inside. Megan looked as if she would stumble and fall at any moment.

'Oh, my God. You poor thing. You'd better lie down on the couch,' said Mrs Carmichael. 'I'll ring the police.'

'Anthony heard me screaming,' Megan said, indicating the young man. 'Thank you, Anthony,' she said. 'Thanks very much.' He nodded and left.

Mrs Carmichael began ringing Manly police, then stopped and said: 'No. I'll ring Andrew and let him handle it, darling.' Afterwards, she brought Megan a sponge and cold water.

'Now tell me what happened,' she said, sitting next to her daughter. 'I've left a message for Andrew at the hotel, and asked them to ring the police. What a dreadful thing . . .'

Elkins' pager started beeping just before he was due to end his shift. But it wasn't the message he had been waiting for. Standing at the door of Kalajzich's office, he saw at once from his expression that something had gone wrong.

'This guy's fucked up,' Kalajzich said between clenched teeth. 'He's fucked up.'

'Why? What happened?' Elkins asked.

'He's only hit her over the head. That's all.'

Elkins said nothing.

'I don't think he even used a gun,' Kalajzich spat. 'Why would he have to hit her over the head? He must have used a nightstick or a club. I want you to find out what happened, Wazza, and fast.'

Constable Karen Ure scribbled in her police notebook. It was 12.40 am, less than half an hour after the attack, when the two constables arrived. 'Injuries: limp and cut on left side of head,' she wrote.

'What exactly happened?' she asked.

'Well,' said Megan, still lying on the couch, her husband now standing beside her, 'I drove into the garage and pressed the button to close the garage door. I got out of the car and came out of the side door. I put on the light at the top of the stairs and realised I had the wrong set of keys. So, I put my bag down and found the right keys to get into the house and walked down the step and I felt something on the right side of my neck. As I turned around I could see someone standing there . . .'

'I see. And what happened then?'

'He had a black balaclava and dark clothes on and it looked like a baton—about eighteen inches long. I screamed and he hit me on the left side of my head and took off. I heard a car door and a car take off. I came down the stairs and the boy next door came in . . . All I could see of the man was two eyes and a mouth.'

Megan signed her name. Underneath she printed: 'Megan Kalajzich, wife of Andrew Kalajzich.'

Constable Ure looked over the statement then turned to Kalajzich. 'Can you show me where it happened?' she asked.

As Kalajzich led her up the steps to the garage, he said: 'Maybe the person—whoever did it—thought it was me because Megan drove my car to the hotel this evening. Hers was being serviced.'

Ure made a few more notes in her notebook.

'I don't want this to get into the papers,' Kalajzich said suddenly.

Constable Ure looked at him: 'There's no reason why it should.'

'Well,' Kalajzich said, 'I'm the owner of the Manly Pacific hotel. I don't want it to get in the papers, that's all.'

As soon as it was light, Kalajzich went back to the area near the carport. He checked the garden carefully. There was no sign of the silencer.

Later that morning there were more police, detectives this time—O'Donnell and Hill. Detective Hill was the senior detective on duty that morning.

Megan tried again to remember the man's face. 'The only thing I really saw was what looked like one of your police batons—about eighteen inches long and about one inch in diameter. It was black, and he was wearing a black balaclava with holes for the eyes and mouth. That's all I can tell you.'

'Did this person say anything to you?' Detective Hill asked.

'No.'

'Did he try and take your handbag?'

'No. That's the funny thing. He had plenty of time to take it when I put it on the toilet roof.'

'Have you or your husband received any threats lately?'

'No, I haven't but you should speak to my husband about this because he told me that some former employee threatened to steal the hotel payroll.'

'Where could I contact him?'

'He's in a meeting in town at the moment. He's not due back at the hotel until some time after lunch.'

'I'll leave my name and the telephone number and he can contact me at his convenience. I'll be working until five today.'

'I'll get him to call when he gets back.'

Outside, Hill conducted a routine search of the garage and around the steps, but found nothing.

A telex was circulated to all police: 'Victim—Megan Kalajzich, 31 Fairlight Crescent . . . Police Action: P4D submitted. Manly detectives informed . . . offender wanted for injury and assault, assault with an offensive weapon.'

Back at the police station Hill also filled out a standard Crime Information Report. He circled the words 'not robbery' in biro next to a rough sketch of what happened. The following notations were added: 'Andrew Kalajzich, owner of Manly Pacific Hotel. Doesn't like police. Have to enter hotel from rear.' Another pen had added and underlined the words: 'Bullshit, not me . . . Friends high up.'

That afternoon, Kalajzich invited two of the hotel's security company directors, Mark Hopcroft and Michael Commerford, up to the house.

'What about an in-house guard, or installing an alarm system?' asked Hopcroft.

Megan wasn't keen. 'I don't know about a guard,' she said. 'I don't really like the idea.'

'Another option,' said Hopcroft, 'is to have security patrol men make unscheduled security checks of the house. Such patrols would be very random . . . We'd provide this service ex-gratia, of course.'

'Yes,' said Kalajzich. 'Let's start this evening, Megan. Can you also put a sign out the front and out the back mentioning the service?'

Hopcroft left after agreeing that his security men would patrol around the premises and inside the garage, but they would not patrol the grounds down by the water.

Megan's family flocked around her. She seemed to be recovering from the attack.

'When I heard the noise behind me, I thought it was Butch, playing games . . . I was expecting to feel his hands over my eyes at any moment,' she told them.

'I can't think of any logical conclusion as to why,' Tony Kalajzich said after they had all pondered the motive. 'Robbery seems unlikely—maybe attempted sexual assault, or even an indirect attempt to frighten you. It's very odd.'

However, her mother knew how fraught Megan had been

straight after it happened—not so much because of the bashing, but because of Andrew's apparent disinterest. Once Kalajzich knew Megan was all right, he seemed unconcerned about spending time with her while she recuperated. She responded by rarely referring to her injuries.

Both Vandenberg and Elkins thought they would be able to forget about it too. When Vandenberg rang Elkins shortly afterwards, Elkins seemed resigned that that would be the end of it. 'I mean, the cops will be involved for sure, now, and I'd say it'll be too risky for you to go back there,' Elkins said.

'Yeah, mate. I'm sorry, but that's what happened,' Vandenberg said.

ELEVEN

HUSH PUPPIES

Despite his part in the crime being over, Vandenberg was astounded at how much the events of the past 24 hours had affected him. He had assaulted a woman. He, who had never even been involved in a bar-room brawl before, he who was known as the mediator, the man who stopped fights in pubs.

This was his first act of violence. Every time Vandenberg closed his eyes he saw her face and its split-second metamorphosis, surprise to terror, as her features distorted. He felt nothing for his victim; the woman was a stranger, a leech on her husband's business affairs, selling her husband's shares under his nose—typical behaviour for a female. He was more amazed that he was capable of such a thing. What worried him was that she had looked at him. Could she recognise him again? What if she had given his description to the police? Vandenberg knew from his own experience that women were fickle. They could betray and deceive.

It was dawn again. Already. Although exhausted and fraught with anxiety and fatigue, Vandenberg welcomed the morning light. Things never seemed so bad in the daytime. He looked across his bedroom as the familiar shapes emerged under the weak, new light. It was in disarray—clothes strewn on the floor, even dirty coffee cups on the table—all proof that Vandenberg, normally fastidiously tidy, had lost all interest in life. He had no pride left and he spent every waking hour worrying.

He sat up, wishing his mind would stop. He went to the bathroom and peered at his reflection in the grubby cabinet mirror above the basin. Even without his glasses on, he looked terrible. He rubbed his face as if to wipe away the dark rings and bloodshot eyes. He had to talk to someone. He went into the lounge room, picked up the phone and dialled Orrock's number.

'How are you, Bill?' said Orrock, who was used to early morning calls from Vandenberg. He sometimes rang when he got home after working through the night.

'Mate, I've really done it now,' said Vandenberg. 'I've gone out last night and tried to shoot someone.'

'Oh yeah,' said Orrock. He often didn't know whether Vandenberg was serious. 'What happened?'

'I put the magazine in the gun but I never pulled the lever at the side of it and it didn't go off.'

'In other words, you didn't load the gun.'

'I'm not joking, Kerry. I hit the lady with the gun and it broke. There'll be something on the wireless later today . . .'

As soon as Vandenberg hung up, Orrock rang Canellis.

'You know that dame at Fairlight . . . yeah, well they gave her a serve last night. She got done at home,' Orrock said.

'What do you mean? Got knocked?' said Canellis, instantly curious.

'No. They would have sewn her up but the gun didn't fire. The bloke stood in front of her, pulled the trigger and the gun didn't work.'

'Yeah? Was it that fuckin' thing they gave me to use?'

'Yeah.'

'Well no fuckin' wonder,' said Canellis.

'He belted her over the head with the gun and the silencer fell off.'

'Did he pick it up?'

'No, he bolted.'

'That's fucked that, then. She'll get police protection, or security in the house. That leaves me right out of it. There's no way I'd go near that woman after they fucked up like that. But tell 'em if they put fuckin' thirty grand in my hand, I could knock her from a hundred yards away.'

'Yeah, OK, George. I'll get back to you.'

That'll sort them out, thought Canellis. At least now he'd find out just how serious they were.

Elkins had arranged to have dinner, midweek, with David Packer. It was time to concentrate on the security contract. Elkins also invited one of the hotel barman, Christopher Stear, and they met at Williams Restaurant at the Boulevarde hotel in Kings Cross. Elkins parked his Fairlane behind Packer's car in a laneway at the back of the hotel.

Over dinner Stear, one-time ambulance officer, bodyguard, journalist and diamond salesman, tried to sell Elkins a solitaire diamond, emerald and gold engagement ring. The previous day, Elkins had bought a gent's gold and diamond ring for $1150 from a jewellery shop in the city's Centrepoint complex. He was getting used to spending money. Kalajzich had recently bought him a gold wrist chain to replace one he had lost.

After dinner they returned to where they had parked the cars. As they entered the laneway, Elkins frowned. 'Shit. My car's gone,' he said. 'Oh, Christ . . .' he said, remembering the gun he still kept in the boot. It was the cut-down .22 automatic rifle Kalajzich had said was too bulky.

'It's all right, mate,' said Packer. 'It's insured. We'll go up to the police station and report it stolen.'

'But you don't understand,' said Elkins. 'There were some very, very private and important business papers in the back of the car. They were the boss' . . . and I think my service pistol was in the boot.' He looked at the empty space behind Packer's car. 'I just don't believe it.'

'Let's go and report it anyway. You never know, it might turn up, although I don't think you'll get your pistol back,' Packer said.

At 11 am on 15 January, Detective David Hill rang the Kalajzich home. He was fast losing patience with Andrew Kalajzich. Four days had passed since his wife had been assaulted and he still hadn't contacted him.

'Hello, Mrs Kalajzich. This is Detective Hill from Manly police,' he said. 'Is your husband there at the moment?'

'No, he's not,' said Megan.

'Where can I contact him? It's in relation to the assault on you.'

'He's at the hotel, I think. Why? Hasn't he rung you yet? I gave him your name and telephone number . . .' Megan was perplexed. Andrew had told her he would ring Detective Hill on Sunday, straight after she had given them a statement.

'No, not as yet,' said Hill. 'I'll ring him at the hotel now.'

'OK, then. 'Bye.'

Megan wondered what was going on. He must have rung by now, she thought. She was tempted to ring him then, but she decided to wait until he got home.

A few days after the assault, Megan had eventually agreed to visit the family doctor, Dr Wing Hong Chan. Her mother had been quietly reminding her to have her injuries checked, in case of infection.

'Yes, there is some swelling there I can see,' Dr Chan said after examining her head injuries. 'And the cut on your left leg, below your knee—it looks like it might be infected and there's some swelling.'

'I think that was when I fell over,' Megan said.

On 17 January, Megan rang him. 'I'm much better thanks, Doctor. I don't think I'll need to come and see you again. There's just a bit of bruising left, that's all.'

Also on 17 January, Hill decided to give Andrew Kalajzich one more chance. It was now six days after the assault. He rang the Manly Pacific hotel again. Kalajzich was busy. He left a message. Hill had a feeling he was wasting his time.

On Sunday, the day after the assault, Vandenberg found $2000 in his letterbox. After three days he started to feel better—he was able to sleep at night. But late on the third night, the phone rang unexpectedly.

'Andrew still wants the job done.' It was Elkins.

Vandenberg swallowed. 'What about the police? The place will be watched. Now there's been an assault and the police are involved, the job will have to be cancelled.'

'Don't worry about that. He's told the police she was attacked by Croatians. He's not happy with the whole situation. He can't find the silencer and he still doesn't even believe a gun was used—'

'That's bullshit,' Vandenberg cut in. 'I told you, I lost the silencer. It fell off.'

'Yeah, well he can't find it and he's not pleased. He wants the job finished.'

'I can't now . . . I'll need to find another gun. It's too risky to try again.'

'No, he's spoken to the cops. He's straightened it out with them. He told them that he had had threats from Croatians and he's blaming them. The cops told him to step up security around the house and the family, so the job can still go ahead.'

'Well, I still think its too risky, Warren . . .'

'Maybe, but it's got to be done. It's very, very important that it's done. He's insisting on it and you know what he's like. Can you try again?'

Vandenberg felt as though he was being sucked into a vortex. The harder he tried to free himself, the more entangled he became. He had thought of going to the police and confessing the whole story. He knew there were some who would listen. But this time, he was too involved and the man behind the plot could have high-level connections in the police force.

'Andrew thinks now you should go into the house and do the job while they're asleep,' said Elkins.

'No way,' replied Vandenberg. 'If I went in there while he was asleep, he could have a gun under his pillow and I would probably shoot her and then he would shoot me and say to the police that he was ready with a gun because his wife was attacked last week.'

'Maybe he wouldn't have to be there. I'll get back to him and ring you back.'

Meanwhile, Vandenberg had to find another gun. Later that night, he rang Orrock again. 'G'day, mate, what are you doing?'

'I'm in bed, strangely enough,' said Orrock sleepily. 'It's one o'clock in the morning.'

Time now meant nothing to Vandenberg. There was no normal routine to his life. 'Sorry, mate, but I need a gun. A quiet gun. I'm in all sorts of trouble again and I don't know who to talk to. I'm being threatened and there's trouble over that money George kept. These people want it and they are getting real heavy about it—'

'OK, Bill, calm down, just calm down.'

'I have to get another gun, Kerry, and they want the money back from George and they are threatening me and I'm scared. Can you get another gun and can you teach me how to use it this time?'

'I'll see what I can do. I don't have a gun but I'll ring George.'

'OK, but don't tell him who it's for.'

Later that day Orrock rang Canellis. 'Someone else has been found to do the job you knocked back,' Orrock said, coming straight to the point.

'Well fuck 'em, then. Is it the same cunt who bashed her?'

'I dunno. But I have to talk to you. I need a gun for Bill, for protection.'

'For what?' asked Canellis.

'Protection. He's being threatened by some heavies. I'll explain later. I'll come over to see you tonight.'

'If he's in trouble, we're all in trouble,' Canellis said. 'Yeah, all right, I'll be here.'

When Orrock knocked on Canellis' front door, Canellis was waiting for him in the lounge room. He gave Orrock the gun and a silencer. It was an old Stirling cut-down .22 rifle. 'It's the only gun I've got, but it's old and I don't even know if it still works. The only reason I've got it is to take care of those fuckin' mongrel dogs that keep rippin' me garbage to shreds.'

Orrock inspected the weapon.

'If you tell me who they are,' Canellis said, 'I'll fuckin' look after Bill, but I have to know who I'm supposed to be protecting him from.'

Orrock hedged. 'They still want that $5000 back and they're really heavying him.'

'If they want to sort it out, these cunts can come and see me.'

Canellis screwed the silencer on to the thread on the end of the barrel and the two men walked out onto his verandah. Canellis fired two rounds into the dirt, re-cocking after each shot.

'Yeah, it works. You can have this one. It'll cost you $100, but listen, if Bill's having trouble, you just tell me who they are and let me fuckin' sort them out.'

Orrock pulled a $100 note from his wallet and handed it to Canellis.

'I don't know about the silencer. It's fairly old. You can't have my other silencer, it's custom-made. I bought it in South Australia years ago. If this one doesn't work, you'll have to get one yourself and they're not easy to come by.'

Orrock took the gun home, tried it out with the silencer in the backyard, and rang Vandenberg.

'I've got a gun, but you'll have to get a silencer. And I don't want to get caught with it. I want to get it out of the house as soon as possible.'

'OK. I'll see what I can do,' said Vandenberg and he hung up. Vandenberg looked at the clock by his bed. 3.30 am. Although it was early, he decided to ring Elkins.

Elkins and his girlfriend, Carey Harvey, had not long been home from work at Dalleys. Elkins took the phone into the kitchen and Carey went into the bedroom. She was used to making herself scarce and complying with Elkins' odd requests.

'. . . Then South Australia's the go,' Elkins spoke into the phone. 'That's what I've been told by people in the know. You can buy them legally down there.'

'I've got another job to do,' Elkins told Carey as he came out of the kitchen.

'But I thought you weren't doing any more investigations,' she said. She knew how often Kalajzich called him into his office. She assumed it was all connected with the hotel security contract.

'Oh, it's only a little job. I'm not even involved. But I have to organise a quick trip for today to South Australia to pick up some equipment for snooping—it's the latest thing out.'

'Well, why don't you just send it up on air courier?'

'I think the guy needs to go down and sort out exactly what he's looking for. I need the return tickets for today.'

'Would you like me to ring up and ask?'

'Will someone be there at this time in the morning?'

'Yeah, I'll ring now if you want.'

'Would you do that, hon?'

'Sure.'

Carey booked Vandenberg on an 11.35 am plane with a return flight at 5.25 pm. That would give him plenty of time to buy a silencer, Elkins thought. Kalajzich wouldn't even need to pay for a night's accommodation.

It was now 16 January. Before he left for work that morning, Elkins gave Carey $500 to pay for the plane tickets. He went straight into Kalajzich's office when he arrived at the hotel.

'I'm going to need some more money for costs, boss,' he said. Kalajzich wrote a cheque for $1300 and Elkins left.

Vandenberg rang Orrock just before he left for the airport. 'I'll be up in a couple of days to pick up the gun. But I have to go to Adelaide to get some hush puppies.'

'What's a hush puppy?' said Orrock.

'A silencer—that's what they call them. I'm going there now.'

Above: 'Kalajzich Corner' — it was here at the southern side of the Corso, opposite Manly Beach, that the Kalajzich family first made their name in the early 1960s. Within a decade, the Yugoslav family owned two shops and a restaurant, K's Snapper Inn. (Photo by Mark Baker, courtesy John Fairfax Group) *Below:* From left, Andrew Kalajzich, Megan, and then Premier Neville Wran, Sue and Tony Kalajzich behind the margarine replica designed for the opening of the Manly Pacific International Hotel in November 1982. (Photo courtesy *The Manly Daily*)

Above: An aerial view of Commonwealth Parade, Manly, where the Kalajzich car plummetted over the edge in September 1973. Andrew Kalajzich, driving, jumped out moments before his wife and son hurtled over the embankment. Police now believe it was Kalajzich's first attempt on Megan's life. *Top right:* The murder weapon: a cutdown .22 calibre rifle was fired in court so that the jury could hear the sound it made when being fired. *Bottom right:* Minute paper fragments from a telephone directory found in the skirting board in Kalajzich's hotel office. Warren Elkins claimed he and Kalajzich had test-fired a gun in the office using a 1985 phone book to lessen the sound. Detective Sergeant Trevor Alt, of scientific, proved the fragments were from a 1985 A–K phone directory.

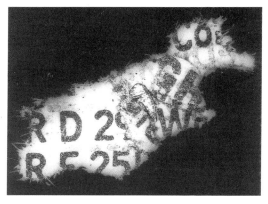

Above: A view of the Kalajzich home at 31 Fairlight Crescent taken from The Esplanade on the waterfront side of the property. The balcony door of Megan's bedroom is on the right-hand side of the second floor. (Photo by David Porter, courtesy John Fairfax Group)

Left: The Kalajzichs' bedroom where Megan was murdered showing the bloodstained mattress and Andrew Kalajzich's bloody fingerprints on the phone. He rang the Manly Pacific Hotel before ringing the ambulance.

Above: Detective-Sergeant Bob Inkster (left) and Detective-Sergeant Bob Richardson, the two police officers who, backed by a team of detectives, led the Megan Kalajzich murder inquiry. Inkster's motto to young constables, was 'Don't tell me. Show me.' (Photo courtesy *The Manly Daily*)
Below: Members of the Police Rescue Squad searched the grounds of 31 Fairlight Crescent on the morning of Megan's murder but no clues were found in the early days of the investigation. (Photo courtesy *The Manly Daily*)

Above: Andrew Kalajzich accepts condolences from John Webb, his solicitor, at Megan's funeral on 1 February 1986. (Photo courtesy *The Manly Daily*) *Left:* Andrew Kalajzich (centre) flanked by his pregnant daughter, Michele, and son, Andrew Junior (Butch), is comforted by a Catholic priest after the funeral service for Megan at the Mary Immaculate Church at Manly where Megan and Kalajzich had married in 1962. (Photo by Peter Rae, courtesy John Fairfax Group)

Above: The hearse carrying the body of Megan Kalajzich stops for one minute outside the Manly Pacific International Hotel on its way from the church to the Northern Suburbs Crematorium. Hotel flags were flown at half mast and hotel staff lined the main entrance as the funeral procession drove slowly past. (Photo by Peter Rae, courtesy John Fairfax Group)
Below: Bill Vandenberg (also shown in inset) shortly after his arrest, directed police to bushland off Millwood Avenue, Lane Cove, where he said he had thrown the murder weapon. Detectives recovered a silencer from the bushes and later discovered the gun in the Lane Cove River.

Left: Warren James Elkins being taken into custody after his arrest. Elkins was used by Kalajzich as a go-between to set up the murder. After giving evidence as a Crown witness at the trial, he was given a new identity on his release from jail. *Below:* Kerry Orrock enters the Supreme Court in Taylor Square, Darlinghurst, during the trial. Orrock was sentenced to life imprisonment for supplying the murder weapon to Vandenberg. (Photos courtesy *The Manly Daily*)

Above: Andrew Kalajzich and Marlene Watson pose for a photograph at the Manly Centennial Ball in 1977. Marlene always denied rumours that she and Kalajzich were having an affair before Megan's death. Kalajzich later admitted they had been 'intimate' but said their relationship started after 1986. (Photo courtesy *The Manly Daily*) *Below:* A police officer watches as Kalajzich, in handcuffs for the first time, is led from Manly Local Court to a police van after his first appearance on the charge of murdering his wife. (Photo by Tony Lewis, courtesy John Fairfax Group)

Carey Harvey picked up the tickets from a travel agent in Crows Nest. Elkins was waiting outside in his car.

'You'd better hurry,' she said, handing Elkins the envelope. 'You've only got an hour before the plane leaves.'

Elkins handed Vandenberg the tickets at a pub in the neighbouring suburb of Willoughby. 'Give me a call when you get back and let me know how you go. I'll meet you tomorrow in Manly,' Elkins said, 'at Marineland, where we met before.'

Elkins' stolen car turned up in the inner-western suburb of Leichhardt. It had been completely stripped. Only the engine block, one registration plate and a chassis was left. Not even the boot lid remained and Elkins knew he would never see the .22 rifle again.

Vandenberg drove to Kurri the day after he returned from South Australia. He had two silencers in his briefcase. When he arrived at Orrock's house, Orrock's wife Gloria was home. They all sat down and had coffee. As soon as Gloria went out, Vandenberg asked anxiously: 'You got the gun?'

'Yeah, I'll get it,' said Orrock.

Vandenberg opened his briefcase and took out the silencers. Orrock picked up one and screwed it onto the end of the rifle, then showed Vandenberg how to load it. They walked outside to the fernery. Orrock put a target on the ground and picked up the rifle. He fired eight rounds from the verandah in quick succession. 'Here, you have a go.' Orrock passed the gun and the empty magazine to Vandenberg.

Vandenberg had no idea how to put bullets in the magazine, let alone fire it. 'But, how do you load it again?'

'Here, watch me,' Orrock said.

Vandenberg's hands shook as he held the gun and aimed at the target. Orrock watched carefully. He could see Vandenberg was petrified. As he started firing, the bullets sprayed across the fernery. Orrock ran for cover, cowering in the laundry. Three of the bullets struck Orrock's son's bird-cage, which was seven or eight metres further down the back-yard. Vandenberg fired six shots into the backyard. They went nowhere near the target.

'God, you're dangerous with a gun, Bill,' Orrock said when the firing stopped. 'I wouldn't want to be anywhere near a room when you're using that.'

Vandenberg reloaded the gun, moved the target further away and fired another five shots, just as badly as his first attempt. Orrock decided it was safest inside the house so he didn't hang around outside to watch. Vandenberg had one last attempt, without success. When Gloria came home, Orrock quickly unscrewed the silencer and put it and the gun in Vandenberg's briefcase. He also gave him two boxes of bullets.

Vandenberg drove Orrock to collect his car, which he had left up the street. He leant across and opened the glove box. 'Here, mate, take this,' he said, handing Orrock a wad of notes.

'What's that for?' said Orrock. He guessed there was at least $2000.

'It's for the gun,' said Vandenberg.

'But the gun only cost me $100—you know that.'

'Yeah, well, I want you to have this. You haven't been work-ing since Christmas, you came down to Sydney to see me when I asked, and you put the Crest hotel all on your Bankcard; and all those phone calls and that—and you know I don't need the money. You take it.'

In the following days, Orrock paid $1000 off his bank over-draft, $300 off his Bankcard, paid the electricity bill and gave Gloria $400, which she spent on school clothes for the kids. He even had some money left over to pay some instalments off the council rates.

Vandenberg now had all the accoutrements of a professional hitman: a gun, a silencer. And Elkins had explained the layout of the house. All he needed were instructions. His prime concern was to keep everybody happy and, in a strange way, he was enjoying himself. Elkins would be pleased when he showed him the gun and the silencers and he in turn could pacify Kalajzich. Vandenberg had not allowed himself to think about his final deed—committing an act of murder.

That afternoon, about 4.30 pm, Vandenberg returned the Falcon to Avis in the Cross and replaced it with a beige Commodore sedan. Later that evening he drove to White Street, near Marineland, and waited for Elkins. When he arrived, Elkins sat in the front passenger seat.

'How'd you go? Did you have any worries buying a silencer?' Elkins asked.

'No, no trouble,' said Vandenberg, opening his briefcase and displaying his purchases. Elkins picked one up and pulled it apart to see how it worked.

'I fired a whole lot of rounds in the ground at Kurri,' said Vandenberg. 'We tested the gun. It works OK.'

'I know where we can try it out—at the old Manly Gasworks. The building's been demolished, no-one goes down there and I know the way in,' said Elkins.

'OK, you tell me where to go.'

The smell of coal and gas hung heavily in the still night air. 'Stop the car about ten metres from that wall,' Elkins said.

Straight ahead, lights blinked behind the top of the woolly black mass that was Middle Head. Vandenberg could just make out the white outline of the sandy beaches on the left. Elkins' voice startled him. 'Give me the gun and I'll try and thread the silencer,' he said.

Vandenberg opened the briefcase and pulled out the rifle. Elkins had to struggle to thread the silencer onto the end of it.

'We'll fire a few shots out of the car window. No-one around?' Elkins asked. He fired six shots. 'Here, you have a go,' he said, handing Vandenberg the weapon. Remembering how Orrock had shown him to load the magazine, Vandenberg reloaded and, not aiming at anything in particular, fired three shots out of the car window. It was enough to convince Elkins. 'Right, mate, I'll have a word to the boss and give you a ring.'

'Everything's in order,' Elkins told Kalajzich when he arrived back at the hotel. 'He has all the gear he needs.'

'OK, then,' Kalajzich replied. 'We'll set it up for Saturday night. I'll have dinner with Megan and drive her home about 10 pm. I'll go down the back stairs, unlock the rear door and the signal for him to come in will be when I drive my car away again.'

'Right, boss, I'll let him know.'

TWELVE

THE BUNGLES

It was well after midnight on 17 January when Vandenberg and Elkins arrived in Fairlight Crescent. They parked a block away and walked down to the waterfront along the public walkway until they came to the house. All the lights were out. Elkins opened the small wooden gate and motioned Vandenberg to follow.

It was the first time Vandenberg had been on the property since the abortive attempt near the carport. They walked up the pathway which ran along the right-hand side of the house up to the back garden. Elkins pointed to the balcony as they passed underneath: the master bedroom.

They stopped at a window just past the meter box at the other end of the house. There was a small crack in the bottom corner of the window and a slight bend in the aluminium siding. The white paint on the window frame was old and peeling.

'These marks under here will make it look as though it's a forced entry,' Elkins whispered. He motioned Vandenberg to follow him back down the pathway. They crossed the front garden and Elkins pointed to a wooden door on the left side of the house. 'That'll be unlocked for you to get into the house.'

They left as quietly as they'd come. Back in Vandenberg's car, Elkins asked: 'So, is everything clear?'

'Yes,' said Vandenberg, 'but you're sure no-one else will be there?'

'Yep. The plan is that the boss will have dinner with her, then drive her home about 10 pm. He'll unlock the back door and then he'll go back to the hotel to do some work. When his car drives off, you go inside. She doesn't usually watch television. She'll go straight to bed and she should be asleep within fifteen minutes.'

'And no-one else'll be there?' Vandenberg repeated.

'There's the mother-in-law—but she's old and deaf. Don't worry about her. She sleeps on the top floor, so she won't hear a thing.'

Vandenberg drove home, his mind replaying his instructions. He envisaged the inside of the house: right at the top of the stairs, bathroom ahead, bedroom on the right.

Megan liked the Friday and Saturday night dinners at the hotel with her husband, even if he was his usual preoccupied self— distracted and aloof. The dinners had become a regular feature over the past few weeks. So had invitations to other social functions, such as the dinner at the Southern Cross for the national tourism awards. And now, every weekend, instead of Megan eating alone at home or with her mother, Kalajzich had insisted she dine with him. Sometimes he would invite other guests, such as the interior decorator for the hotel.

Once, as she walked into the foyer, she met Elkins.

'Hello, Megan, how are you? You here for dinner again?'

'Yes. It seems like Christmas to me, with of all these dinners I've been getting,' she smiled.

Elkins walked away quickly. Inside Dalleys he poured himself a drink and lit a cigarette. There was no-one at the bar yet. He stood alone at the end of the room. Megan Kalajzich had no inkling of her fate. He was sure of that. Elkins swallowed.

The liquor warmed the back of his throat. He lit another cigarette.

It was not too late to stop it. But there were the death threats. One to Dalleys and another one late one night after work. Each time, it was a male voice, Australian. 'You know what you've got to do. If you don't do it, we'll do it to you.' Carey Harvey was with him both times. Now he slept with a gun under his pillow.

Elkins had noticed the change in Kalajzich's behaviour ever since he had begun plotting his wife's death. It was all part of the charade—making a point of seeing more of Megan at the hotel. But, Elkins had seen them fighting, eating in silence and sometimes arguing in Kalajzich's office. Then there was the time when she had been forced to sit in his office waiting for him while rock music blasted out from Dalleys. He knew she suffered from migraines and he had seen her rubbing her temples.

On Saturday, 18 January, dinner at the hotel went ahead as planned.

At 10 pm, Vandenberg watched as Kalajzich's blue Mercedes pulled up outside Fairlight Crescent. Kalajzich escorted his wife inside the house and then drove away towards the hotel. That was the signal to act.

Vandenberg walked quietly towards the block of units next door to the house, opened the gateway and headed down to the water. He crouched in the bushes on the other side of the footpath. About fifteen minutes later, the upstairs bedroom light went out. Almost twenty minutes after that, he walked across the lawn to the back door, the .22 Stirling cut-down rifle held tightly in his hand.

He turned the handle and it opened. Unlocked as planned. He walked inside. There was a small bathroom straight ahead, and he could see an exercise bike when his eyes adjusted to the dark.

He turned right and walked through a large rumpus room. There was a billiard table and he saw a fridge. As he walked, his shoes clattered on the polished wooden floor. Too noisy. He tiptoed outside again, and placed his shoes neatly together by the back door.

Vandenberg walked over to the wooden staircase on the other side of the rumpus room. It was a narrow stairwell, made darker by deep rosewood-stained panelled walls. As he looked up, he felt water oozing between his toes through his socks. The rumpus room had a seepage problem. He was standing in a puddle of water which had gathered at the bottom of the stairs. He stood on the first stair for a couple of seconds before he began his ascent.

As he neared the top of the stairs, he heard sounds—faint voices and music, possibly a television. He stopped. He saw light spilling from the room on the left, flickering on the walls as images from a television screen flashed in the darkness. With the gun held upright against his chest, he looked inside. Sprawled across an orange rug on the floor was a teenage boy. Vandenberg guessed he was about eighteen years old. He was wearing shorts and no shoes, and was perched on his elbows, engrossed in the screen before him.

Vandenberg fought against the rising panic in his chest and the urge he felt to run—as fast as he could—back down the stairs. He noticed the bedroom opposite was in darkness. The boy had his back to the door and was oblivious to Vandenberg's presence. Carefully, he turned and sneaked down the stairs, leaving just as quietly as he had entered. He grabbed his shoes and stopped himself from running to his car. He drove to a public phone booth near the wharf and rang Elkins.

'The son was home,' he spluttered, 'watching television in the lounge room. He was there when I got up the stairs. You said there'd be nobody there.'

'What?' said Elkins. 'He was supposed to be at a party. The boss said he wouldn't be home until twelve-thirty.'

'Yeah, well, he was there, in the lounge room. I did everything I was supposed to.'

'OK. I'd better tell him what's happened. Go down to the

churchyard at the back of the hotel. I'll meet you there.'

Elkins met him there twenty minutes later. 'It's all right,' he said. 'He's glad you didn't do anything because he loves his son and he doesn't want to lose him. We'll have to do something else.'

The next morning, Kalajzich called Elkins into his office. 'This guy's fucking with us,' he said evenly. 'Tell him no matter who gets in the way, he must carry out the task.'

Elkins stared. 'Are you serious?' he said.

'You heard me. No matter who gets in the way.'

Elkins rang Vandenberg. 'He's thought about it and he's decided it's a very important job and if you go in next time and his son happens to be in the way, or his mother-in-law, then you'll just have to take them as well.'

Vandenberg was as shocked as Elkins had been. 'No way. There's no way in the world I would take anyone young with me, Warren, no way.'

Vandenberg thought of Anthony, his nephew who had died aged twenty-one. Vandenberg was not made of the stuff it took to kill a child. 'That's just out of the question, Warren. I'm not taking him or anyone else with me.'

'Yeah, well, he wants you to try again,' said Elkins. 'I'll get back to you later.'

A few nights later, acting under instructions from Elkins, Vandenberg returned to the house. Again he left his shoes outside, this time sidestepping the puddle at the bottom of the staircase. He climbed the stairs and crept down the hallway to the bedroom. The door was open. He walked into the room. The bed was empty. The covers were neatly in place. No-one had been sleeping there that night. Vandenberg went straight back to the same phone and rang Elkins.

'What's going on? You told me she would be there, so I get all the way inside and the bed is empty. I don't know how many times I can do this, Warren.'

The following night Vandenberg crept into Megan's bedroom for a second time and again the bed was empty.

Elkins was just as confused as Vandenberg but he was more worried about confronting Kalajzich.

'I don't believe he's even going around to the house,' Kalajzich said when Elkins told him what had happened. 'Tell him he's being watched from one of the flats next door and see if that'll speed him up. And you can tell him I don't want any more fuck-ups. It has to be done and I want it done now. He can try again on Friday night.'

Elkins himself was beginning to doubt Vandenberg. Maybe Kalajzich was right. Vandenberg could be lying because he was scared. Elkins would have to talk to him again.

January 23, Fairlight

... If you have any spare bodyguards, I could do with one ...

Megan was sitting at a desk in the lounge room, watching the summer drizzle fall on the yachts outside. She gazed out at the bay. The familiar view and the boats swaying gently in the afternoon rain were soothing.

... The other night I came out of the garage to find some 'jerk' waiting for me with a black balaclava and a baton in his hand. He managed to hit me on the head but my scream scared him off. He knocked me off balance so I came down the stairs like the flying nun. So I'm covered in bruises and the nerves are shot to pieces. The most upsetting thing is no tennis for a while. I can't wait to see you. August seems such a long time away.

Two weeks had passed since Megan was attacked, but even recalling the incident in a letter to Vicki Laing, her friend who was working as a nanny in Switzerland, still sent a shiver up Megan's spine.

... Michele is feeling and looking a lot better. She is starting to get quite a tummy. Jim is going to buy her some 'fat' clothes for her birthday on Saturday. Butch is still

*having fun at Cottage Point. We all are ... He is still
planning to go OS in June. We will see. It's a miserable
day here today so Mum is knitting booties and bonnets.*

The thought of Michele's baby, her first grandchild, made
Megan smile. It was so exciting, although Michele had a few
months to go yet. A baby in their midst; it would be just the
lift she needed.

*... It's going to be the spoiltest baby ... Well Vic. Take
care and look after yourself. See you soon.*

Kalajzich had decided the job would have to be done after
midnight. This time he would have to be in bed with his wife.
That way he could be sure his instructions were carried out. 'I
want him to come into the house the same way when the
lights are turned off,' he told Elkins. 'He has to fire two shots
into her—she's on the left-hand side of the bed. Then he can
fire two shots into my legs.'

Elkins relayed the instructions. 'That would be stupid,'
Vandenberg said. 'You know what I'm like with a rifle. I could
aim for the legs and hit the head instead. That would be too
risky. The best thing would be for him to roll off the bed and
then I could put two bullet holes in his pillow.'

'No, he wants it to look like he's the target. You have to
shoot him in the legs,' said Elkins.

'Well, if he wants it that way, I'll try,' said Vandenberg.

It was now 25 January. That night, Vandenberg again hid in
the bushes and waited for the lights to go out. He knew the
garden well by now and crept over to the door in the dead of
the night without making a sound. He reached the door and
turned the handle. It was locked. He tried again but the
handle refused to yield.

'Apologise to the guy,' Kalajzich said to Elkins the following
morning. 'My mother-in-law put the lock on the downstairs
door. Will he go again?'

'Yeah, probably.'

'OK, then. We'll set it up for tonight, but tell him I've changed my mind. I don't want him to shoot me in the legs. I've decided to roll off the bed. Tell him to fire two shots into my pillow after he does the job.'

'Right, boss, I'll tell him.'

THIRTEEN

THE GAME OF SCRABBLE

The morning sky was heavy with full, grey clouds. Light drops of rain spattered across the bay and the yachts, masts leaning into the wind, looked forlorn. Damn, thought Megan, looking out from the balcony.

It was 26 January 1986: Australia Day and a long weekend. She had wanted the afternoon and evening to be fine. The morning didn't matter—there was the Australia Day naturalisation ceremony and lunch at Manly Town Hall—but she had plans for the afternoon. Today was Michele's birthday and they were all heading down to Cottage Point for dinner. Michele and Jim were already down there.

By 11 am, the day had become hot and steamy. Rain had forced the ceremony indoors. When the Kalajzichs arrived at the Town Hall, a large crowd was sheltering under the porticoes on either side of the shiny green front doors. Wet umbrellas clogged the foyer.

The Kalajzichs were among the official party of forty guests of the Mayor, Judy Mellowes, which crowded into the hall's main chamber. Megan signed the official guest book and

Kalajzich scrawled his signature beneath hers before they went through.

Afterwards, they went upstairs for a smorgasbord lunch. The Kalajzichs sat with Joan Thorburn and chatted with the Humphreys. It was Jeanette who had suggested visiting Cottage Point that afternoon.

'So, are you going to be able to come?' Megan asked her.

'Yes, everything's worked out well. My two younger ones are away, so we'd love to come,' Jeanette said.

'How are you feeling now, Megan?' asked Thorburn.

'Much better now thanks, Joan,' said Megan.

'I've got some security guards patrolling the house,' Kalajzich said.

'It worries me, things like that,' said Thorburn. 'In your own home, too. You just have to be so careful these days.' She went on, 'How about you come up to my place for dinner tonight to meet some friends from Japan?'

'Thanks, but it's Michele's birthday,' Kalajzich said. 'They're all down at Cottage Point and we're going to join them.'

After lunch the Humphreys dropped Megan home. Kalajzich said he had some quick business to do at the hotel. They decided to go to Cottage Point in the Humphreys' car.

The Humphreys picked them up just before 4.30 pm. Kalajzich and Megan were waiting, dressed in shorts, T-shirts and sandshoes. They drove along the main road—now busy with cars heading for Manly beach and the last of the late afternoon sun—through Seaforth, then onto the four-lane highway through the bush of Manly Dam Reserve to Belrose. Huge barn-like fruit and vegetable markets, nurseries, landscape supplies and saddleries replaced the houses along the roadside. Fresh flowers were selling for $1 a bunch.

'Let's stop for an ice-cream,' Kalajzich said when they reached Terrey Hills, just before the Cottage Point turn-off.

A few minutes later they were heading down the four-kilometre drive to Cottage Point, the road curling through the bush of the Ku-ring-gai Chase National Park, past waterfalls, tree ferns and banksias, and signs warning: 'Koalas Ahead'.

In the 1980s, Cottage Point had become an enclave for the rich. It was isolated, yet only an hour's drive from Sydney, and when an opportunity had come to buy a small weekender there the previous year, Kalajzich jumped at the chance. There were only 58 houses, crowded along the headland at the edge of the protected bushland by the Hawkesbury River.

The Kalajzich weekender, which Kalajzich named 'Maluska', was modest enough, nestling among the towering blue gums. It was a small, cream-fibro, two-bedroom house with a small lounge room, faded red holland blinds, thin white curtains, flyscreen doors and an outside toilet. Megan had so far only managed a few changes to the garden. The house's best feature was its position on the waterfront, the waves lapping gently under the red timber decking whenever a cruiser passed close by.

Cowan Drive, the Kalajzichs' address, was one of only three streets in Cottage Point, although it was more like a dirt track than a street. Its condition wasn't helped by the frequent passage of trucks during the week, carrying building materials to transform the neighbouring fibro bungalows into comfortable weekend retreats.

John Humphrey gingerly edged his Holden sedan down the steep driveway which took them halfway to Maluska. From there they went by foot, a tricky descent by steep steps that zigzagged down the slope. Megan made her way slowly. Her legs were still tender.

Butch, Michele and Jim, and two of their friends were waiting there to meet them. As the hot January sun began its descent towards the green river, they sat on the verandah under a large umbrella, sipping beer and chatting.

About 5.30 pm, Kalajzich's cousin John and his wife arrived in their cruiser. They joined the party for half an hour. The rain earlier in the day had rejuvenated the bush and the rays of the sun had released the rich, woody perfumes of the native shrubs and flowers.

As night came on, Megan and Jeanette began making dinner while Michele had a nap. Kalajzich took John Humphrey for a quick ride up the river in the runabout they used for fishing. After dinner, Butch and Jim took the boat out to do some night fishing. The others decided on a game of Scrabble. As soon as the game was over, Kalajzich seemed keen to go.

At 10.30 pm, the Kalajzichs kissed Michele goodbye and left. Although the way out was familiar to John Humphrey, he took the unlit road slowly. It was 11.10 pm when the Humphreys' car pulled up outside 31 Fairlight Crescent.

'I'll go and check out the place first,' said Kalajzich. 'You wait here, Megan.'

'I'll come with you, Andrew,' said John.

Ever since the assault, Kalajzich checked the house each time they arrived home, before they went inside. Megan had refused to have two signs staked in the front lawn stating that the grounds were patrolled by security guards. Instead, she agreed to a sign in the downstairs rumpus room window which read: 'WARNING! PATROLLED BY SEABOARD CARDINAL SECURITY GROUP'.

Soon the two women saw the house lights turn on and a few minutes later their husbands reappeared at the top of the stairs.

'Everything's OK,' Kalajzich said.

'Great,' said Megan.

They said goodbye. Humphrey glanced in his rear-view mirror as he drove off. He caught a glimpse of the tall silhouette of his friend standing at the top of the stairs as Megan slowly descended.

Vandenberg didn't hear the Humphreys' car pulling up. Although he had been there for forty-five minutes he was moving his car into a dead-end street nearby when they pulled up. Now, he was back in the bushes along The Esplanade.

He had occupied his time walking along the concrete pathway next to the units, past the row of letterboxes, up to Fairlight Crescent to see if anything was happening.

There were two plans. Vandenberg had been told Kalajzich would be leaving for the hotel shortly after they arrived home.

If the lights in the house went out then, Vandenberg was to go in and kill her, before Kalajzich came back. But if she didn't go straight to bed, or if the son came home, he was to wait for Kalajzich to return. Then, when everyone was asleep, he would enter the house.

Inside the house, as Megan unpacked in the kitchen, Kalajzich called Elkins at the hotel. 'Is everything ready to go?' he asked.

'As far as I know, yes,' Elkins replied.

'Good. I'll be down at the hotel shortly.'

Megan was watching television in the family room as he drove off.

Kalajzich parked his car in the hotel's delivery area out the back. Elkins met him in the foyer.

'Are you sure it's all organised?' Kalajzich asked again.

'As far as I know, he's already there waiting.'

Kalajzich went into his office and went through the motions of looking over the day's business. He kept looking at his watch. Just after midnight, he came out of his office. Neil Southerby, the hotel's night manager, was at the front desk as Kalajzich walked past. Southerby looked up from his computer screen.

'How's business tonight?' Kalajzich asked.

'Good,' he said. 'We've had a big crowd in Dalleys and the restaurant was almost full.' He walked with Kalajzich to the back office.

'Let me walk you to your car,' Southerby offered. He knew about the assault on Megan and Kalajzich's extra concern for security and had even driven him home on a couple of nights during the previous week. 'How's your wife?' he continued.

'Oh, much better now, but my mother-in-law had a funny phone call on Saturday morning.'

'Yeah?'

'Yes, someone who didn't talk when she answered the phone. And after a short time, a voice said "Wrong number" and hung up. It's worrying after the assault,' said Kalajzich.

'Really? I wouldn't worry too much about that. I doubt if it was related,' Southerby said, reassuringly.

Back at the house the lights were still on. Vandenberg had been waiting for two hours. It was almost 12.30. He walked up the path again, sticking close to the brown paling fence that separated the flats from the Kalajzich home. When he reached Fairlight Crescent, he saw the blue Suzuki in the carport. The son was home.

Plan A had failed. It was time for plan B. He met Elkins at the churchyard at the back of the hotel.

'The boss's gone home. He just left. He should be there now,' Elkins said, after Vandenberg told him about the Suzuki.

'So, we put plan B into action?' Elkins nodded. 'OK, Warren. I'll talk to you later.'

Vandenberg returned to his hiding place in the bushes. He was to wait for the lights to go out, the final signal. Every ten minutes, he walked over to the edge of the garden fence for a closer look.

Megan was still in the family room watching TV when Kalajzich came in. 'You still up?' he said as he walked inside.

'Yes, I got caught up with this movie . . . What's the time?' Megan yawned. She hadn't meant to stay up so late. She was already in her nightie.

'12.30.'

'Oh, I didn't realise it was so late. It's nearly finished anyway.'

Kalajzich walked into the bedroom. He kicked off his shoes, pulled down his tracksuit pants and shorts, and took off his T-shirt. As he put on his blue-striped pyjamas, he looked out the balcony door, down towards the water.

He picked up his clothes, took them through to the laundry and put them on top of the washing machine. Then he went into the kitchen and got himself a bowl of ice-cream. He walked into the family room and sat on the lounge next to Megan while he ate.

The movie finished at 12.50 am. Megan stood up. Kalajzich

yawned. 'Goodnight,' he said. He stared blankly at the television screen after she'd left the room and picked up a newspaper but the words blurred before him.

From the bedroom, he heard the clock signal 1 am: beep, beep, beep. He stood up, turned off the TV and switched off the lights.

FOURTEEN

TILL DEATH DO US PART

Vandenberg was sweating. The cushion cover had seemed like a good idea back at the flat. He had cut holes in it and turned it into a balaclava, but now his glasses fogged up from his perspiration. He pushed the cushion cover up off his face. At least it would disguise his baldness. He hadn't counted on the balmy night air and his body heat. For the last time, he crept across to the small sandstone fence and looked up at the house in front of him. It seemed to swim before his eyes.

The lights were off. He looked at his watch and waited while the second hand ticked steadily around the watch face. Fifteen minutes I'll give them, he thought. They'd be asleep by then. He had taken the gun out of the nylon bag. It lay beside him, alien and confronting. Even after so many abortive attempts, he was still not accustomed to its presence. He had stripped it down, taking off the trigger guard so he could conceal it down his trouser leg.

Kalajzich walked into the bedroom. Megan had left his bedside light on as usual. The clock radio played faintly. He looked at her as she slept, the blanket pulled up to her waist. He slipped into bed carefully, afraid his presence might wake her.

He turned out the bedside light. The radio would turn off automatically. Everything must be routine. A slight sea breeze stirred the curtain on the sliding door. Kalajzich held his breath and listened. Dead quiet. Then, a yacht mast clinking; Megan breathing; his heart beating.

Vandenberg glanced furtively behind him before he turned the handle. He eased the wooden door backwards, taking care not to scrape the tiles. His hands shook, but he forced himself to take it slowly. He left the door ajar and made his way across the rumpus room to the stairwell. Every sound he made seemed magnified. He climbed the stairs slowly, his socks silent on the wood. Clutching the gun to make sure the silencer didn't fall off, he had to concentrate on his balance. There was no banister to steady him.

At the top he cupped his free hand around a wooden knob on the railing at the top of the stairs and paused. He turned right and saw the bedroom door was open. He stood trans-fixed, looking at the gap which yawned before him. There was no sound. This was it.

Fear constricted his breathing. For a second, he thought of leaving, turning back down the stairs and out into the com-fortable darkness of the night. But he was drawn, inexorably, to the open door and moved towards it.

Once inside, the room seemed smaller than he remembered: the wardrobe, the bed and the sliding doors to the balcony were all within a few feet of each other. He moved along the narrow passage between the bed and the wardrobe. In the shadowy light he made out the two prone forms, sculpted mounds, before him. They were lying back to back, not touch-ing. The woman faced the wardrobe.

Vandenberg trembled. He raised the gun in front of him, the wardrobe limiting his manoeuvrability. He took aim, the muzzle inches from her head.

He pulled the trigger. A hollow thud. He pulled again. Almost simultaneously, the figure on the other side of the bed rolled off. Vandenberg swivelled the gun, aiming at the mattress where the man had been lying. He fired again, twice. Again he heard the thuds as the bullets hit the pillow. It was then he heard a low, gurgling animal sound.

Vandenberg almost fell going down the stairs. The rifle swung against the wooden panelling as he went, clattering loudly. But he didn't stop or look back. Outside, he rammed his feet into his shoes, unscrewed the silencer and pushed the gun back inside the nylon bag. He scurried across the garden, jumped the fence and ran up the pathway next door.

Kalajzich lay on the floor next to the bed. The acrid smoke from the gun seared his nostrils.

'Megan?' he called softly in the darkness. Nothing. He pulled himself up onto the bed. He thought the gunman had missed his target. She was lying exactly as she had been when he last saw her. He leant over her. 'Megan?' he whispered again. He turned on the light.

There was blood all over her face. He saw her gasping and heard a low gurgle. Blood flowed down the side of her head, staining the sheets. Her eyes were wide open, like a deer startled by the hunter. Kalajzich stumbled off the bed and ran into the corridor.

'Are you all right?' he called up the stairs to the bedrooms above.

He looked at his watch. It was 1.13 am. He went back into the bedroom. There was much more blood now, forming a wide arc around her body. Kalajzich had one more job to do. He hurried down the wooden steps through the rumpus room and locked the laundry door.

Vandenberg had been told by Elkins that he had seven minutes to get out of the area. He scrambled into the car and threw the rifle onto the back seat. As he approached the dark bushland, away from the traffic lights and buildings, he felt safer, heading for familiar territory. He rounded the last bend and saw the humpback bridge in front of him.

He drove past Fullers Bridge and did a U-turn outside the gates of the Northern Suburbs Crematorium nearby. As he neared the bridge again, he stopped the car for the first time, parking on the wrong side of the road.

He leant over to pick up the rifle which was inside the nylon bag. In his haste, his hands still clumsy with fright, he grabbed the trigger, forgetting that he had removed the trigger guard. The rifle recoiled from his grasp, the bullet exploding into the side of the car door. Vandenberg panicked. He grabbed the weapon again, but again it discharged. He jumped in fright, cursing his own stupidity, peering around him, tense, waiting for someone to come out of the dark. But there was no-one.

For a moment, in the silence as he looked at the water, he remembered standing on the banks of the river as a child, dangling a rod into the green-brown water as the sun forked through the eucalypts. It was as if the park, in its unchanged state, had accepted him in its midst, a lonely man as once he had been a lonely boy. Vandenberg thought about what he had done. He was an executioner. He had killed her.

He threw the gun into the water where he knew it would not be discovered by fishermen. Then he drove 200 metres down the road and flung the silencer into the bushes.

She was dead. Kalajzich stood at the bedroom doorway. Her eyes had closed. He had delayed long enough. He rang the hotel and left a message to ask Elkins and some security guards to come to the house.

James Taylor, the security guard, answered the page.

'Kalajzich called,' the message read. 'Send security around to his premises ASAP.' He'd better find Elkins, Taylor decided. This sounded serious.

At 1.17 am, twelve minutes after Megan had been shot, Kalajzich rang triple-0. 'Hello? Manly police? Look, we've been attacked. My wife has been shot. Quick, quick.'

'Just a minute, sir.' The telephonist transferred the call to police emergency.

'We've had a break-in to my house and I think my wife's been shot,' Kalajzich continued.

'Where's this?'

'At Fairlight.'

'Fairlight? What's the street number?'

'31 Fairlight Crescent ... Quick, get an emergency ... get an ambulance here quickly,' he stumbled over his words.

'What's your name, sir?'

'Kalajzich.'

At 1.20 am, Manly police cars were put on alert: 'To all Manly cars or cars in the area, proceed to 31 Fairlight Crescent.'

At 1.25 am Kalajzich rang again. 'Look ... look ... we've had a break-in in my house, only my wife's been shot.'

'The police and ambulance have already been informed, sir.'

This time Orrock knew Vandenberg was not joking. It was 6.30 am.

'Have you heard the news?' Vandenberg said.

'No, I haven't. I'm still in bed.'

'The job's been done.'

'When?'

'Last night, but I can't talk. Any questions you want to ask will be answered on the news tonight.' Vandenberg was strangely excited.

Orrock sat up in bed, the receiver still in his hand after the line had gone dead.

At 10.30 that morning Orrock was out in his backyard working on a granny flat he was building. Two friends, local police officers, were helping him. Orrock stopped hammering when he saw Canellis striding down the driveway. He could tell he was angry.

'What the fuck's going on, Kerry?' Canellis demanded.

'G'day, George. I don't know. What d'you mean? How's things?' Orrock tried to signal to Canellis to shut up. He steered him down the driveway to the front of the house.

'Have you heard the news?' Canellis asked, more calmly.

'No.' Orrock was playing dumb.

'Turn on the wireless and you'll hear it. I want to know what's going on. Where's the gun I gave you?'

'As far as I know, Bill's got it.'

'Well the job I was supposed to do—some bastard did it last night.'

'I don't know anything about it, George.'

'Well you get in touch with Bill and you tell him I want to see him.'

'He'll be up in a couple of days.'

Orrock waited until he had a quiet moment later that night and then picked up the phone and rang Vandenberg. 'George is looking for you and he's giving me one helluva hard time.'

'Tell him I'll see him soon. I'll look after George. Don't you worry about George.'

'Sure . . .'

'Did you see that her husband is Andrew Kalajzich?' Vandenberg asked.

'Yeah, I know. I saw it on the news on the TV.'

'You see, mate, there's four shareholders, and he and his missus are the major shareholders. If she'd kept on selling her shares at the rate she was selling them, he'd no longer have the controlling shares.'

'Oh yeah?' said Orrock.

'Well that was the reason she had to go. She was going to do something the next day. We had two plans—the first one failed and the second plan worked . . . but, by Jesus, I've never seen anyone move as quick as her husband . . .

'Anyway, mate, I'll have to lie low and I'll be up at your place in a couple of days. I'll give you a hand painting that flat and we can talk about it.'

'OK. Look after yourself then.'

'Oh, don't worry about me.' Vandenberg hung up.

He rang back several times over the next few days from the Cronulla Beach Resort hotel where he was lying low.

'Have you heard from George?'

'Yes and he's still ropable and he told me to tell—'

'Just tell him I'll be up very soon,' Vandenberg cut him short. 'Anyway, mate, they think I left the scene by boat—the cops do.'

The third time he called, he was more anxious. 'Look, mate, can you get a new moulding for the door of a car, a headlight and a blinker?'

'Why? What's happened to the door and the headlight?'

'I shot some holes in the door . . . I . . . I dropped the gun.'

'The way you use a gun I believe it. I'll see what I can do.'

'I've got to get them urgent. I've got to get the rental car back . . . And I'll need a new headlight . . . I'll be up soon. I'm getting paid tomorrow.'

Orrock went to a friend who owned the Holden dealership in Kurri.

'Bill had a bit of an accident,' Orrock explained.

'Oh yeah? I'd believe it,' the man laughed.

'Do you know who this is?' said the voice on the phone.

Elkins recognised the voice immediately. He was at home. Two police officers were in his lounge room asking routine questions about Mrs Kalajzich.

'Yes,' he replied, trying to sound non-committal.

'I'd like you to come and see me at my father's house in Queenscliff,' Kalajzich said. 'I want you to guard my daughter's house tonight. Is the security ready to go?'

'Yes.' Elkins cupped the cordless phone and walked into the kitchen. 'I'll be the only one armed.'

Packer and Stear reported for duty that night. 'Kalajzich is worried about his daughter. Whoever did that to his wife might also have a go at her,' Elkins told them.

'Is Kalajzich on the list of suspects?' Stear asked innocently.

'No, no. He wouldn't be a suspect,' Elkins said.

Elkins had bought a dozen brown uniforms for his new company with the insignia 'International Prevention Services'. He had already started inquiring about guns.

That morning, he drove to Kalajzich's parents' house. 'Your

son asked me to come down,' Elkins said when Andrew Kalajzich senior answered the door.

'It's Warren from the hotel,' Kalajzich told his son.

Elkins was invited into the dining room.

'Is everything OK?' Kalajzich was almost whispering.

'As far as I know, yes.'

Kalajzich lowered his voice: 'It'll look good if you protect Michele's place tonight. It's 9 Roberts Avenue, North Manly. I'll get in contact with you later on.'

Jim Economides, Michele's husband, briefed Stear and Packer when they arrived: 'My wife is pregnant and very upset. She won't be coming outside,' Economides told them.

By 9.30 pm, they were bored. 'I'll go and get a pizza from that place in Brookvale,' Stear told Packer.

An hour later, Elkins arrived with two pump-action shotguns he had picked up that day from the city. As he pulled up outside the house, the headlights from a car coming towards him dazzled him. It was Kalajzich, in a small red car driven by his sister, Olga. Kalajzich got out of the back seat. Packer and Stear watched from the roadside. Kalajzich got into the back seat of Elkins' Fairlane carrying a briefcase.

'I've got the money here to pay him,' Kalajzich said, indicating the briefcase. 'And also the bugging device and transmitter that's built into the briefcase—the one you got me. I want you to get rid of it.' He got out of the car, saying, in a louder voice which Stear and Packer could easily hear, 'You better take this in case they come around. Put this beside Marlene's desk. They're documents for the hotel.'

Kalajzich turned to Stear and Packer. 'Any problems?'

'No, everything's fine,' Stear said.

Kalajzich nodded a farewell.

'Well, I'm going to go and get a jacket. It's a bit cold,' Elkins said.

'Could you grab me something—a jumper?' Stear asked.

'Me too,' Packer added.

'Yeah. Won't be long.'

Elkins arrived at Carey Harvey's house at 11 pm. He had

already called in to his unit to count out the $20 000. Carey Harvey looked at him as he came in the door. She made him coffee.

'What's the matter?' she asked.

'I've been speaking with Dave and I've been thinking. It's not such a good idea to take on the hotel security contract.'

'Why? You were so keen on the idea before.'

'Well, I suppose because I think AK's a very dangerous man. And I don't know what he's into, but he scares me.'

'What do you mean?'

'I mean I don't want to be involved with a man whose business is bad. I don't want any hassles. I just want a security business.'

'I see,' Carey said although she didn't understand.

'And I don't want to be involved with anything around AK.'

It was the first time she had seen him so stressed. Elkins was more affected by Megan's death than he cared to realise.

'Where's the jumpers?' Stear asked when Elkins drove back to Roberts Avenue about 5 am. Daylight was already creeping through the suburban streets.

'Oh . . .' Elkins looked tired and drawn. 'I went home and fell asleep.'

The three men stood around in despondent silence. 'Look, why don't we sit in the Fairlane?' Elkins finally said. 'At least it'll be warm.'

In a few minutes they were all asleep. The idea for guarding Michele's house was short-lived. Later that week, in Elkins' flat, Stear put a few fresh marketing ideas to Elkins.

'Do you think Kalajzich will need personal protection now?' Packer asked.

'No, I don't think so. Anyway, if he did, we wouldn't be getting involved in it.'

Packer raised an eyebrow. 'Why not?'

'I don't want to get involved in that sort of security,' Elkins said. 'I just want to get into hotel security. That's all. Nothing else.'

Nobody said anything.

FIFTEEN

THE PAY-OFF

On either side of the Spit Bridge, the yachts bob enticingly, offering a fleeting glimpse to motorists whose eyes are fixed on the traffic as they descend towards the steel construction over Middle Harbour.

Elkins had chosen Parriwi Road, just past the southern side of the bridge, for the pay-off. It was a scenic winding drive, carved into the cliffs above the water, hidden from the bustle of Spit Road. It was 29 January, three days after the murder. As Vandenberg turned right into Parriwi Road, he saw Elkins' Fairlane parked further up on the left. He pulled up and Elkins came over carrying a briefcase.

'I've been down guarding the daughter's house,' said Elkins. 'What a joke! Working there just in case something happens to her—that's what he's told everyone. Anyway,' he went on, handing the briefcase to Vandenberg, 'it's all there, I checked.' Vandenberg had agreed to do the job for $20 000. Although Elkins had initially offered Vandenberg a further $10 000 to do the job, this was never mentioned again. The pay-off that morning was $15 000, calculated after Elkins deducted any expenses he had already paid to Vandenberg.

Vandenberg drove back to the Cronulla Beach Resort motel where he had been staying with a friend, Paul Blake. He counted the money in the briefcase, then checked out of the motel. He then deposited $4000 in his bank account at Sylvania, locked the rest of the cash in his briefcase and drove north to Kurri. When he arrived at the Orrocks's house, Gloria was home. There was no opportunity to discuss anything.

'So what did happen?' Orrock asked later when they stood together, paintbrushes in hand outside Orrock's granny flat. Orrock still doubted that Vandenberg had managed to kill someone.

'I walked around to the other side of the bed, fired two shots and the husband immediately rolled onto the floor. Then I fired two shots into the bed. It all happened in about ten seconds.'

'And how did you know she was dead?'

'I heard the death gargle.' The two men were silent. There seemed nothing more to say.

'Was it all worth it?' Orrock asked.

'I went into the house five other times, in and around the house, I mean—to do the job. I asked Warren what I should do if the kid was there, and the mother-in-law, and Warren told me at first that he loved the kid, and not to do anything to him. But he said later, if they got in the way, to take them both out.'

'Yeah?'

'I was only getting paid for one and I didn't want to take the whole family out,' Vandenberg said. 'The original plan was that I was to shoot him in the arm or leg, but maybe they heard about what sort of shot I was and they changed it to him rolling off the bed.'

'So how did you get in?'

'The husband ... he left the door open and I was to go in ten minutes after the upstairs lights went out ... it was well planned, mate. They sent people to New Zealand and Singapore to send letters back saying they were Croatians and sending threatening letters.'

'To make it look like they did it?'

'Yep. The bloke—the husband—left the door unlocked two nights before the murder, but on the night before the murder, he made a mistake and locked it instead of unlocking it.'

'What did you do with the gun? Have you still got it?'

'No, mate, no. I drove to this bridge. I had to turn the car around because I couldn't get rid of it on that side because that's where people fish. I threw it out of the window of the car. And I'll tell you something, Kerry, I thought this was a bit ironic. I was readin' the paper the other day—you know, about where her funeral is going to be and that, and I thought, "Well, that's where I got rid of the silencer" . . . I mean in the very cemetery where she was buried.'

The Settlers' Arms is a modern hotel just past the racecourse on the highway into Gosford. In the summer, patrons sit under umbrellas on the spacious verandah overlooking the tennis courts and order steaks from the chargrill.

Canellis was waiting in the public bar. As Kevin Woods introduced him to Inkster, on Thursday morning, 30 January, the two men sized each other up. They bought beers, ordered steaks and sat at a table away from the other lunchtime patrons.

The Snake knew instinctively that Canellis would be a good witness if he was telling the truth. And, although he had no plans yet to put Canellis in the box, he liked what he saw. Canellis came across as streetwise and credible. His motive was simple: he believed they had used his gun and he didn't want the blame. He was confident and had a quick, reliable memory. All in all, not bad.

'How do you feel about coming down to Sydney and giving us a formal statement?' Inkster asked after he had listened to Canellis' story.

'Well, I can tell you now, I'm not sticking my neck out for nobody,' Canellis said. 'Whoever done this is more than likely fuckin' capable of doin' it again and I don't want to be victim number two. And I didn't kill that lady and I'm not going to be loaded for a job I didn't do.' Canellis was clearly worried about Kalajzich's supposed heavy connections, the ones Vandenberg had mentioned.

'We're just as concerned about your safety as you are, George, but we can protect you. And you don't need to worry about being accused of the crime if you didn't do it. We can see about getting you indemnity—'

'What for?' Canellis cut in. 'I just told you I didn't kill her.'

'For any offence you might have committed in relation to the crime, like . . . if they did use your gun.'

'Well I'd want it guaranteed and I want protection for my family, I'm telling you now. If I have to move, I'd need money to do that. I can't watch my family 24 hours a day and I want them protected.'

Inkster paused for a moment. 'If you come down to Sydney tomorrow and make a statement, we can make some arrangements—apply for immunity from the Solicitor-General. We'll pay your expenses, of course.'

'How much?'

'Would five hundred cover it?'

'All right. But I'll come on one condition—if I give a statement, I want Kevin there when it's made.'

Inkster looked at Woods, who nodded. 'OK, I'll arrange it this afternoon.'

'You can ring me later, George,' Woods said. 'I'll let you know what's happening'

The following day, Friday, Inkster had arranged to meet the chief of the CIB, Bob Bradbury, and the Assistant Commissioner for Crime, Ross Nixon, at police headquarters. Woods was bringing Canellis. They were to meet in the media room on the fifth floor at 1 pm.

The Snake now had more evidence in his possession even though he still did not know who the killer was. Canellis had handed him a Christmas card he had found in the briefcase Vandenberg had given him with the money and the gun. On the front was a red-nosed dog sitting on a sleigh and wearing a purple hat. Inside, the card was addressed 'To Bill'. Inkster was already organising to have it fingerprinted. After making enquiries about immunity for Canellis, he had also applied for a warrant from the Supreme Court to tape conversations between Canellis and anyone else involved in the murder plot.

Nixon leaned back in his chair and studied Canellis. He had several papers spread out before him, including Canellis' criminal record. He threw a pen on the desk and folded his arms. 'You've got a lot of form,' he said.

Canellis leaned forward and looked him straight in the eye. 'Yeah, but I'll tell you one thing,' he snarled, 'I didn't kill the fuckin' woman.'

Eight hours later, Inkster and Canellis neared the end of a marathon record of interview they had started at Ermington police station at 4 pm. It was almost midnight. The room was heavy with smoke. An ashtray overflowed with butts, and empty coffee cups and the remains of takeaway chicken littered the desk.

Woods typed as Inkster continued: 'If it's considered necessary, would you be prepared to have further conversations with Bill or Kerry Orrock in relation to the murder of Mrs Kalajzich, should permission be granted by the Supreme Court to have that conversation taped?'

Canellis hesitated. 'Yeah, but I want you to understand this fully.' He spoke slowly so Woods could type his answers. 'If you feel that this is necessary, I am prepared to go to that length if you can guarantee my safety and that you can guarantee that any comment I have made in the past or the present cannot be used against me . . .'

Inkster stayed behind and read over the statement after Canellis and Woods had left. He was pleased. We're on our way at last, he thought, and permitted himself to smile. Canellis had given them the names of three of the people involved: Vandenberg, Orrock and a bloke named Warren— probably Warren Elkins, the security manager from the Manly Pacific, one step away from Kalajzich. Inkster wasted no time. By 2 pm the next day, Saturday, 1 February, the Snake, Mike

Hagan, and a technician from the electronic services unit arrived at Kurri. They met Canellis at the Spire Motel. The technician strapped a tape recorder, microphone and battery pack to Canellis' body. Then Canellis changed into a pair of heavy denim overalls that helped conceal the bulge.

'We want names more than anything, George,' Inkster told him. 'See if you can draw him out on this Warren character, maybe get a surname. And ask him if he knows the bloke who did the job, or whether Kalajzich was mentioned at all.'

'Don't you worry,' said Canellis. 'I intend putting the bounce right on Bill. I'd like to know who the bastard is, too. I've got my own arse to think about.'

They turned on the tape recorder and Canellis drove off to Orrock's house. Inkster and the technician parked two blocks away and listened through a transmitter. The reception wasn't good, but they could make out snatches of the conversation. Vandenberg and Orrock were inside when Canellis arrived.

'Come out the back and we'll talk,' said Orrock.

'Bring the smokes, Billy,' Canellis called. It was hot. Canellis was sweating heavily under his overalls. He concentrated the conversation on Vandenberg. Orrock drifted in and out.

'How you been, Bill?' Inkster picked up Canellis' voice.

'Good, good, good. I came here for a holiday but I've been bloody painting, mate.' So, that was Vandenberg. The Snake listened.

'You've got me fuckin' worried, Bill. Whoever these cunts are . . . I'm tellin' ya.'

'I don't worry, George, because as far as I'm concerned, we're out of it now.'

'Yeah, but are we out because of the five fuckin' grand involved? Whoever this cunt is, mate, he's no fuckin' idiot. What's to stop them from fuckin' puttin' him on my trail? To get their five fuckin' grand or get my blood?'

'Yeah, but they don't know who you are. They can only really find that out from me.'

'But if you know who the cunt is, I'd like to have the jump on him because if he comes near my fuckin' door, mate, anybody can walk up to my car or my fuckin' front door and start blastin' the fuck out of me and I don't know what I'm lookin' at.'

'Yeah, well, there's no worries. They're too happy with it as it is I think because it's too um, ah . . . I mean, they've gotta be fuckin' happy,' Vandenberg lapsed into talking tough. 'God, it's looking good for them, isn't it?'

'From what I read, I've got the feelin' that the old man's wanted her out of the fuckin' road himself, mate. There's a lot of money involved and maybe she didn't wanta play fuckin' ball from what you said—you know, like shares or somethin'— when they put that fuckin' time limit on.'

'Yeah, but according to the paper today they were real happily married.'

'Yeah, well my main worry is, Bill, that if the situation arises that some cunt comes to my place, or fuckin' after you because we are liabilities to these people—we're fuckin' disposable.'

'Yeah.'

'We know what took place . . . the three of us, mate, three fuckin' nothin's to these cunts, whoever they are . . . I've got me missus and two kids to worry about and we don't even know what this cunt looks like.'

'True.'

'If I know who he is, I can spot the cunt and then I've got an even break.'

'Yeah.'

'And if it becomes necessary, I'll kill the cunt in the car. If he happens to be tailin' me from fuckin' anywhere, I'll—'

'But then it gets heavy, mate.'

'Mate, this is fuckin' heavy. How heavy do you want it? The fuckin' sheila was one of the top fuckin' sorts around Manly apparently. That's why they wouldn't tell me who she was . . . and now it's bad fuckin' news, bad problems.'

'So what can we do?'

'Protect ourselves.'

'Yeah, but how?'

'All right. Who's the cunt that's in the business? Who's the cunt that can come after us?'

'Oh fuck, George! I can't say that. Of course that wouldn't be fair. Same as if you'd done it, there's no way I can mention it to anyone, because that's not fair, I mean that's—should be part of the game.'

'Well let me put it this way, Bill. How much do you value your fuckin' arse? How do you know that they're not just playin' along with you for the time bein' until you're not fuckin' required and the heat's died right off, and then all of a sudden you're fuckin' dead in ya carpark or in the fuckin' flat somewhere? You know who this cunt is. Protect us. We've protected you, haven't we? Makes it fuckin' easier for me to be able to sleep at night without havin' to fuckin' worry about some cunt blastin' all me fuckin' windows out and hittin' me with a stray. What about if they grab one of our fuckin' kids at school? You know the fuckin' coppers can't be involved.'

'No, I know.'

'The only thing I can't understand is why didn't he kill the bloke? If it wasn't done by the bloke himself, why didn't he kill him too? This cunt wasn't shooting fuckin' up in the air because he put two straight into her fuckin' nut. Why didn't he hit the bloke?'

'But what if the bloke suddenly rolled?'

'All right, if he rolled I'd've shot him quicker, because I wouldn't want to be discovered,' Canellis said.

'Yeah?'

'I'd want to eliminate the time factor that I'd be able to get away from the place and if that cunt sits up and looks at me, I've either gotta belt the cunt or fuckin' drop him. So why did he leave him alive?'

'Because he's gotta pay the money.'

'Well, if he's gotta pay the money, why didn't he do it his fuckin' self and save himself a quid?'

'Yeah, I s'pose.'

'Is he above suspicion?'

'That's the rumour in the air, George. You know that, don't you?'

'Fuck the rumour, mate. I haven't been near the cunt of a joint and I won't be going there for the next twelve months,' Canellis said.

'Politicians are saying there's no way in the world he could have done it—he's not the type.'

'But what happens if he has fuckin' done it? That's what I'm saying to you, Bill. He don't need us no fuckin' more. Unless you're still workin' for him.'

'I don't know, I don't know. They said there'd be more work, but just what . . .'

'What about if you go on a fuckin' job and you don't come back? Eh?'

'Are you trying to make me feel good or something, George?'

'I'm layin' it on the fuckin' line to ya. What happens if they say "right" and you end up in a fuckin' national park somewhere with your fuckin' head blown off?'

'I hope it's not a question of that, but I couldn't answer.'

'Yeah, but hey, you're not in the fuckin' game, Bill. You're on the outside of it. Now you've come into the fuckin' big league.'

'Thanks.'

'You're welcome, but I'd like to see ya around, not fuckin' goin' in the ground. You'd better have a think about it. I want to know who this cunt is so I can take care of meself. You must know him—you got the money off the cunt.'

'No, I got mine off the middle man.'

'Do you know who the big man is?'

'I've never met him, but—'

'Well, it stands to reason it's gotta be the old man himself—this Andrew cunt—and he's just sent some bastard into bat for him.'

'He's not the one, I can tell you now. He didn't do it.'

'Yeah, well, have a think about it, Bill. It's very imperative that I know who this cunt is because I'm not leaving my arse out on show. I've gotta get home, take me fuckin' mutts out for a run. You seen the cunt, didn't ya?'

'I've never seen him, no. I only know what I know through Warren.'

'Who's fuckin' Warren?'

'Warren's my . . . is . . . is the man that was in-between, that was always doing the organising with me for you.'

'All right. Think about it, mate. It's our arse. All right? I'll leave youse with it. I've gotta get home, OK? Take it easy.'

'Right-o, George.'

Warren. The Snake now had the name on tape. The link to Kalajzich. Better get some surveillance on Elkins he thought.

'Will ya get this all taken off me.' Canellis' angry voice interrupted his train of thought. 'I'm sweatin' like a pig under this. You hear me all right? Did it come out all right? Can you hear me . . . ?'

'. . . Her prime concern was always to be a loving wife and mother.' John Webb, solicitor for the Kalajzich family for many years, read the eulogy, his eyes filling with tears. 'She was characterised by her humility . . . Her hard work and devotion to family ideals have left a very rich memory for us all . . .'

Detective-Sergeant Bob Richardson estimated there were 1500 people present. It was the biggest funeral Manly had ever seen. They spilled out of the doors of the Mary Immaculate Church—the church where Andrew and Megan had married 24 years ago. On Saturday, 1 February, five priests joined in the celebration of a requiem mass for Megan.

It was an outstanding show of mourners: politicians, businessmen, local residents, friends, family and representatives from the Yugoslav community. Police security was tight. They had arranged to escort the cortege through Manly and on to the Northern Suburbs Crematorium, where Megan's body would be cremated. There were also several unmarked cars on the road. Detectives hovered on the edge of the crowd.

Richardson watched from a distance as Kalajzich, dressed in a dark suit, his hair neatly combed and a deep frown etched on his brow, emerged from the church. Tears streamed down his face and he clung to Butch for support. He weaved in and out of the crowd for almost thirty minutes, accepting condolences.

Richardson overheard the New South Wales Sports Minister, Michael Cleary, speaking to a group of reporters: 'What could possibly be achieved by hurting Megan?' Good question, Richardson said to himself. Kalajzich wept as he watched his wife's coffin being placed in the waiting hearse. Then the cortege moved slowly down to the beachfront, the gleaming black car leading the train of vehicles as they filed slowly towards the Manly Pacific hotel. Richardson watched as the flags at the hotel were flown at half-mast and the hearse stopped outside the hotel's marbled foyer for one minute as a mark of respect.

Vandenberg was back at Cronulla. Two days after he returned from Kurri, he went to visit his friend Paul Blake. They were watched by surveillance detectives outside the Cronulla Beach Resort motel. What the detectives did not know about was the transaction going on inside.

'Here, hold on to this for me.' Vandenberg handed Blake the $10 000 he had been carrying in his briefcase.

Vandenberg was a man with nowhere to go. Everything had changed. It was as though his life had no order, as if he had been lifted up and suspended above the real world, real people and their daily lives. Now he had killed someone, he had some money in his pocket, but nothing to spend it on. He rang Orrock in Kurri.

'Let's take Gloria and the girls to Wonderland,' Vandenberg said, enjoying the role of benefactor. If he could not spend the money on himself, he would spend it on the children.

As they headed out west along the F4 freeway, Orrock panicked momentarily when he saw two highway patrol officers flagging him down.

'Your licence please, sir.'

Orrock handed it over. 'What's the problem?'

'Oh, we're just doing a blitz on seatbelts. And who is this?' The police officer indicated the man in the front passenger seat.

'My name is Bill Vandenberg.'

'And where are you heading?'

'We're on our way to Wonderland—a family outing.' Orrock nodded at Gloria and the children in the back seat.

'Everything seems in order, thank you.' The officer waved them on.

The surveillance report came back to Inkster immediately. He smiled when he heard their destination.

The other surveillance detectives had nothing concrete to report. There was still nothing to implicate Kalajzich in the murder plot. Kalajzich and Butch had driven to the airport less than two weeks after Megan's death, where they boarded a flight to Perth. Kalajzich was attending a promotion for Swan Breweries—peculiar behaviour for a man in mourning thought Inkster, but that was all.

Elkins had also been visiting airports. Carey Harvey had gone to Auckland for her sister's wedding and Elkins flew out to join her, booking them a room at the Hyatt in Auckland. He was spending up big. He planned to fly home early on 13 February, the same day the boss was due back from Perth.

SIXTEEN

THE ARRESTS

Bang, bang, bang. The knocks reverberated like an explosion in Vandenberg's dreams. The sound shook him out of bed and sent him fumbling for his trousers in the dark, then running to the door. As he opened it, eyes blinking with fear behind his glasses, a hand grabbed him on the arm.

Seven detectives, one wielding a sledge-hammer, burst through the door of Flat 402, 12 Ithaca Road, Elizabeth Bay. The arrests had to be swift. They had to catch them unaware at all costs. It was 7 am on 14 February. Megan Kalajzich had been dead for eighteen days.

The Snake, keyed up after days of waiting, pulled his quarry's face close to his own. 'We are investigating the murder of Megan Kalajzich.' He almost hissed the words. 'You are suspected of being involved in the commission of the murder.'

In a peculiar way, Vandenberg was momentarily overcome with relief. The waiting was over, he thought. Someone else could sort out this mess.

Inkster loosened his grip and showed him the search warrant. 'This authorises us to enter and search for evidence which may implicate you in the murder.'

'This is a bit much,' Vandenberg said nervously. 'Just let me think for a minute. Can we talk over there in the kitchen?' Inkster could see 'the middle-man' at least was going to cooperate.

The detectives started pulling out drawers in the bedroom, turning out cupboards and rifling through papers. Inkster noticed the walls had recently been painted canary yellow. A ladder was propped up in the hallway.

'Do you have any firearms in the unit?' Inkster asked.

'Yes. There's one on top of my wardrobe—you'll find it anyway,' Vandenberg answered.

Detective-Sergeant Graham Lisle returned to the kitchen carrying the weapon, balanced between four of his fingers: two at the end of the barrel and two on the stock.

'Is this the gun you are referring to?' Inkster asked.

'Yes it is.'

'What can you tell me about that gun?'

'I bought it off a bloke for my own protection. I'll tell you about it later.'

Elkins' instructions flashed through Vandenberg's mind. There was no need to mention any names. Elkins had always told him: 'This is all well set up. We'll never get caught. But in case that should happen, nobody is to put nobody in. We'll all use the Croatians as an excuse. You'll always be looked after.'

'Do you have any knowledge about the murder of Mrs Megan Kalajzich at Fairlight?' Inkster's voice broke Vandenberg's train of thought.

'I can help you out quite a lot, really,' he said. 'You see, there's so much I can tell. But, can we talk about it at the CIB? I don't want to involve Trevor in any of this. He had nothing to do with it.'

'If you are aware of the identification of the man who actually fired the shots at Mrs Kalajzich, I'd prefer that you tell me before we leave the unit,' Inkster said. He had Hagan on stand-by to go after the murderer. He *had* to get the name out of Vandenberg now, before news of his arrest spread.

'You don't have to worry about losing him,' Vandenberg said. 'You see, because you have got him now. It was me who pulled the trigger.'

The Snake was dumbfounded. Surely this man was calling his bluff. Bullshit, he thought. The bloody liar. He looked at the mild-mannered bespectacled figure in front of him.

'Mr Vandenberg,' he began, 'are you admitting to me that you are the person responsible for the murder of Mrs Kalajzich at Fairlight on the 27th of January last?'

'Yes I am.'

'Is this the gun you used in the commission of this offence?'

'No, that's not the one. I threw that one away over at Lane Cove. I can show you where I threw it.'

The detectives stood around listening. They had done their job. The flat was ransacked. Inkster had decided to take Vandenberg to Manly police station. 'I intend asking you questions about the murder of Mrs Kalajzich,' he said.

'It's all over for me now. I did it and that's that. What else can I say?'

'What car did you use?'

'I can show the car on the way out. It's down in the carport.'

'I accidentally discharged the gun and put a couple of bullet holes in the passenger door,' Vandenberg said some five minutes later, standing next to the beige Commodore sedan, pointing to two small holes under the door handle. Inkster examined the marks and told Lisle to take the car to the ballistics unit in the city.

By the time they left the unit, Inkster had in his possession a leather briefcase, a silencer and a Gregory's street directory with blue biro marks on Map 77 at Fairlight Crescent. On the trip to Manly, Inkster didn't say much. He was anxious about the other arrests. He was relying on them to help him get indemnity for Canellis. The Solicitor-General had refused his first application because no-one had been charged. He decided to stop at North Sydney station to check how the other raid had gone.

Inkster still did not believe Vandenberg. It was too easy. He had to be covering for someone else. Just before they reached the station, Inkster popped his question: 'So when you went into the house—you come in from downstairs and when you get up the top of the stairs, you turn left and—'

'No,' Vandenberg, interrupted from the back seat. 'You don't go left, you go right.'

'And when you go into the bedroom, the bed's directly in front of you,' Inkster continued.

'No, the bed's not in front of you. It's on the left, the wardrobe's on the left. And there was a puddle at the bottom of the stairs, on the floor.'

Inkster knew he had his killer.

Inkster didn't trust the police radio. When the car pulled up outside North Sydney station, he went inside to ring Bob Worthington, his boss, now back from leave.

'I have some news for you,' Worthington said as soon as he heard Inkster's voice. Detective Brady, in charge of arresting Orrock had already phoned. 'Mick Brady's just rung through and we know who the murderer is.'

'So do I,' said Inkster. 'I've got him in the car.'

The police cars stopped on the side of the road outside the Northern Suburbs Crematorium. Inkster had asked for an officer from scientific at Chatswood to meet them. He had decided to look for the gun before he took Vandenberg to Manly.

Vandenberg, dressed in a shirt and trousers, was helped out of the car. He raised his handcuffed arms and pointed to a grassy area off the roadway. 'That's where I threw the gun and silencer,' he said.

Inkster organised an 'emu parade'—a search of the area—and Vandenberg was bundled back into the car. At 1.30 pm, police found the silencer in long grass a few hundred metres from Fullers Bridge.

When he first heard the voice at the bottom of his bed, Orrock thought he was dreaming. 'For a start, my name is Detective-Sergeant Brady,' the voice said. 'This is Detective Wilkins. We are both from Manly in Sydney. The other police are from Newcastle and the ballistics section in Sydney'.

'Can you prove it?' Orrock asked, propping himself up.

'Of course. What're the patches for? Are you able to see?'

Orrock pulled them off and wiped some of the ointment out of his eyes. Three men stood at the end of his bed. He looked at his watch. It was 7 am. It had been a long night. The previous day, while visiting his friend at the Holden dealership in Kurri, a welding flash had temporarily blinded him. He had been in considerable pain so, finally, after midnight, Gloria had taken him to Casualty at Kurri Hospital. A resident doctor had given him ointment and eyedrops and had covered his eyes with patches. Orrock went home and eventually dropped off to sleep at about 2 am. And now this.

'Get out of bed. I want to talk to you,' Brady ordered after showing his police badge. 'I've been told that you might be able to help me about the death of Megan Kalajzich in Manly a couple of weeks ago.'

'Who told you that?'

'I can't tell you.'

The police left the bedroom and Orrock dressed. He came through to the kitchen wearing a pair of shorts. 'Wait, not here,' he said. 'I'll talk to you out the back.' Orrock didn't want his family involved.

As they walked down the stairs into the backyard, Orrock felt cold drops of rain on his back.

'What do you know about it?' Brady was blunt and to the point.

'I know about it. I was up here when it happened. I heard about it on the news.'

'Well, you're coming with us. Get some clothes on.'

Detective Wilkins followed Orrock into the bedroom and

watched as he pulled on a T-shirt and pushed his feet into a pair of thongs.

'Can I get a packet of cigarettes out of the cupboard?' Orrock asked.

'Yeah, but hurry up.'

With a detective in front and one behind, Orrock walked to the front door. Outside, he saw a Toyota Landcruiser with two other police in it. Brady saw Orrock looking at them.

'Do you know who they are?'

'No.'

'They're the boys from ballistics. They're looking for spent cartridges.'

'Oh well, instead of them digging up my whole yard, tell them to look in the fernery.'

While Brady spoke to the ballistics men, Orrock turned to Detective Wilkins. 'Where're we going? Am I under arrest?'

'Yes.'

'Well, it's no good going to Kurri police station because it's not open yet. It's Friday.' Orrock was trying to impress them.

During the fifteen minute drive to Maitland police station, Orrock told Brady that Vandenberg was the killer.

At 3.20 pm that afternoon, Elkins walked out of McDonald's in Wood Parade, at Fairlight. He looked up and saw two men in suits approaching. Bluff, just bluff it, he thought. His grip tightened on the paper bag containing his hamburgers. The police were almost a day too late. He and his fiancée, Elizabeth Gillespie, had arranged to leave for a holiday in Hong Kong the following day.

Elkins glanced over at Liz sitting in his new Fairlane. She was watching him, unperturbed. Elkins was always up to some sort of business. Liz was unaware of Elkins' liaison with Carey Harvey and the other women in his life who flitted in and out like butterflies, and Carey Harvey was not aware of Liz. Elkins wondered if Liz noticed one of the men flash his identification badge.

'I'm Detective Hagan and this is Detective Lennon. We're from the homicide squad at the CIB,' Hagan said. He was a quiet, cautious man, with mutton-chop sideburns and glasses. To those who knew him, he had an unexpected, dry sense of humour.

This was the moment Hagan had been waiting for. He and Lennon had sped up the hill to McDonald's from Manly station the moment the surveillance boys rang with news of Elkins' whereabouts.

Hagan mentally noted Elkins' appearance: neatly coiffed hair, smart but casual dress and white shoes. Hagan's eyes glinted behind his spectacles. 'What is your name?'

'Warren Elkins.'

'We are making inquiries into the death of Mrs Kalajzich and I would like to ask you some questions in relation to her death. I want you to come with us to the Manly police station.'

Elkins nodded. This would be easy. But he was not prepared for Hagan's next words.

'You are under arrest in relation to Mrs Kalajzich's death. You are not obliged to say anything unless you wish. Do you understand that?'

Elkins went pale. He looked towards the Fairlane. Elizabeth was still watching.

'Y-y-yes. What about Liz?'

'She'll be looked after by Detective-Sergeant Lisle and Detective Wilding. They have a search warrant to search your unit. Liz can go with them. Is that all right?'

'Yes.' Perhaps this wouldn't be so easy after all.

'Is this your car?' Hagan asked, pointing to the Fairlane.

'Yes.'

'Would you lock it up and leave it here. You can make some arrangements about it later.'

'Yes.'

Elkins sat in a room on the first floor of Manly police station while Hagan repeated the formalities: '. . . and you're not obliged to say anything unless you wish to do so as anything you do say may be used against you in evidence. Do you understand that?'

Elkins had already decided, sitting between two detectives on the trip down the hill to Manly, that he could not afford to be too naive. He opted for the direct approach. They obviously knew something or they would never have organised a search warrant and placed him under arrest. He knew the rules.

'Yes,' he answered. 'But why have I been singled out for this? I didn't pull the trigger.'

'Who did pull the trigger?' Hagan was quick to pick up on the offering.

'I can't tell you. It's just too involved.' He bowed his head and rubbed his hands, giving himself more time to think through his answers. Lying came easily to Elkins, but he had to find out what they knew. It was a game of cat and mouse.

'What's your full name?'

'Warren James Elkins.'

'Where do you live?'

Hagan had returned to formalities. Elkins told him where he worked.

'What are your duties?' Hagan said.

'To see that everything runs smoothly. I am the eyes and ears of the boss, you know.' Elkins spoke with pride.

'Who is your boss?'

'Mr K—,' Elkins began to stutter. 'K—K—Kalajzich.'

Hagan showed no reaction to the name. Coax him gently. 'Who are you directly responsible to?'

'I report to the beverages manager, who's in charge of all the bars. Nick . . . I'm not too sure . . . Nicholas. I only heard his name once.'

'Would you like something to eat or drink?' Hagan asked. He wanted Elkins to relax.

'Yeah, I'll just have some coffee.' Elkins' appetite had disappeared along with the cold hamburger he had deposited in a bin near McDonald's.

'How do you have it?'

'Plenty of milk and two sugars.' Hagan's offsider, Lennon, left the room.

When he came back with the coffee, Hagan pointed to the typewriter sitting on the desk behind him. 'I want to continue to ask some questions about this matter and Detective Lennon will record your answers on the typewriter as the interview takes place. Do you understand that?'

'Do you have to type it down?' The prospect of typewritten words made it seem so final, Elkins thought.

'No, I don't have to.'

'I'd prefer it if you didn't.'

'OK. Detective Lennon is making notes of our conversation. Do you wish to continue to answer my questions?'

'Yes.'

Hagan took him back to his job. 'How long have you known Mr Kalajzich?' He slipped the question in quickly.

'Only about four years.'

'How did you come to meet him?'

'I had a little security run and I grabbed some little kids running around and we looked up his number and we rang him up and I got to know him after that.'

'What is Liz's full name?'

'Elizabeth Gillespie.'

'What is your relationship?'

'I'm permanent with Liz ... well, I haven't decided yet. We have been going together for two years.'

When Hagan had finished with Elkins' background, he left the room. Elkins was biting his fingernails. When Hagan returned shortly afterwards, he asked Elkins to move to a room on the second floor, near the detective's office.

The search of Elkins' unit had turned up three briefcases in his wardrobe.

'How do you get them open?' Hagan asked him.

'The two black ones' combination is one-one-zero, and the grey one ... um ... is five-two-four, I think.' Hagan left the room carrying the briefcases.

A receipt for $404.60 with Vandenberg's name on it was found in the third briefcase.

'Before I ask you any further questions, I would like to search you. Do you understand that?' Hagan asked when he returned.

Elkins stood up. Hagan unclipped an NEC Insta-page attached to Elkins' trousers. Elkins delved into his pocket and pulled out wads of $100 notes bound in elastic bands.

'How much money have you got there?'

'Two thousand and some small notes.'

So far, Elkins seemed to be telling the truth. 'How much do you earn each week?'

'Three-eighty clear from the hotel. Liz and I put our money together. I've always worked two or three jobs. I used to work for Manly council.'

'Your briefcases have been searched and the black ones contain recording equipment. What have you got those for?'

'I bugged some rooms at the hotel for the boss.'

'Do you own the unit at Fairlight?'

'Yeah.'

Hagan went through his finances with him. He had a $70 000 loan from St George Building Society for the unit. His assets included jewellery and his security business. The next question caught Elkins by surprise.

'Do you know a person by the name of Trevor Hayden?'

Elkins knew someone had been talking. When Hagan asked if he had met anyone at Trevor's flat, he volunteered the name straight away. 'Bill Vandenberg.'

The interview was going well. Vandenberg, sitting in a room down the hall, was also beginning to talk and each time Hagan left the room, he was given more information. Orrock had also been brought to Manly police station. The story, unbelievable as it was, was beginning to unfold.

'I've been informed that a guy named Warren, who had a security business, set up the death of Mrs Kalajzich for the husband. This Warren had something to do with the Manly Pacific. What can you tell me about that?' Hagan asked Elkins.

Elkins knew the game was up. The man Hagan had picked up that afternoon was no longer confident and easygoing. 'People are accusing me of doing everything. I–I can't tell you.' He bowed his head, his shoulders trembling.

Hagan pressed on: 'I have been informed that arrangements had been made between Warren and Bill Vandenberg for Mr Kalajzich to be in bed with his wife. After she had been shot, he was to roll off the bed, and then shots were to be fired into the bed where he was lying. What can you tell me about that?'

Elkins remained silent, staring at the floor. He was pale, his eyes large with fear when he looked up. 'Look, guys, I'm frightened to say anything against that person.'

Hagan paused. 'Who are you frightened of?'

'Mr K—K—Kalajzich.'

'Would you like another cup of coffee?'

'Yes, and I would like to think about this.' They left him on his own.

When they returned, any questions about the murder were met with resistance. 'Oh, my God,' Elkins almost sobbed. 'Why did I get involved? I asked Bill to do it for the boss. I can't say any more or I'm dead.' He refused to answer more questions. 'I think I've said enough,' was all he would say.

'You'll be charged with conspiracy to murder Mrs Megan Kalajzich. Do you understand that?'

'Yes.'

Not much that could be used as evidence against Kalajzich, Hagan thought, but still, it was a start. Elkins seemed a pleasant enough fellow; a real pretender with all that jewellery and the slickness of a used-car salesman. Hagan guessed that Elkins would never have been accepted by people with real wealth. An unusual sort of fellow to become involved in a murder—not the aggressive type at all.

In the charge room, Elkins was joined by his solicitor. Hagan read out the charges. Elkins did not reply.

Richardson was sitting in the Manly detectives' office when

the call came through at 6 o'clock that night.

'Hello, detective.' Richardson recognised the voice.

'It's Andrew Kalajzich here. I believe you have made some arrests concerning the murder of my wife.'

Within thirty minutes, Kalajzich was standing at the front counter of the station. Richardson and his offsider Detective Monk met him.

'This is Detective Monk,' Richardson said. 'We're making certain inquiries into the murder of your wife. A number of persons have been interviewed and I now propose to ask you questions about the matter, and also about an attempted murder on your wife on 11th January this year, in the driveway of your home. Whatever you say may be used in evidence. Do you understand that?'

'Yes,' Kalajzich replied. 'My solicitor is on his way down.'

John Webb rushed in a few minutes later. Richardson spoke to him briefly, then left him with Kalajzich.

Richardson returned fifteen minutes later: 'As I've already explained to you, Detective Monk and I are making inquiries into the attempted murder of your wife in the driveway of your home on the 11th January this year—'

'I've advised my client not to say anything,' Webb interrupted. Kalajzich nodded. Richardson had expected as much.

'We are also making inquiries into the murder of your wife at 31 Fairlight Crescent, Fairlight, on 27th January and what you say may be used in evidence. Do you understand that?'

'No. I don't want to say anything.'

Richardson looked at him. 'You will be charged in connection with these matters. Can I speak with you, Mr Webb?'

Richardson showed Webb a search warrant for the hotel. He and Kalajzich read it.

'Do you occupy a suite of the hotel apart from your office?' Richardson asked.

'No, I only occupy my office.'

'I'll go now and arrange for the execution of the warrant,' Richardson said.

Richardson, Webb and an officer from the Corporate Affairs Commission drove to the hotel.

Back at Manly police station, Kalajzich was charged with Megan's murder. Kalajzich posed for the police photographer, his head held high, an expression of distaste on his face. As the whorls from his inked fingers were pressed onto the sheet of paper, he remained silent.

When the arrests were over, the detectives chose the local watering hole, the Hotel Steyne, a landmark in Manly. At 11.30 pm they had time for two beers; the hotel closed at midnight.

'We just couldn't believe it when Bill Vandenberg admitted to the murder,' the Snake joked. 'We must have looked like the clowns at Luna Park with our mouths open.' The men around him laughed.

On the night of the arrests, the Kalajzich story was back in the news. Before the names of the four charged men were released, the newspapers recounted the crime, telling how the bullets narrowly missed Mr Kalajzich and how he had raised the alarm. But the next day the headlines told a different story: 'Multi-millionaire hotel owner conspired to kill his wife' the papers screamed. It was sensational stuff.

The co-conspirators appeared in Manly Local Court on Saturday, 15 February. Kalajzich sat slumped in the dock wearing grey trousers, a blue shirt and an expensive white jumper. They were all refused bail. Vandenberg, Elkins and Orrock were kept in custody at Manly police station and Kalajzich was taken to Long Bay jail, the largest remand centre in New South Wales.

Constable Phillip McGowen moved his fingers gently along the slimy surface of the riverbed. The water was muddy, visibility nil. He had to rely on his hands.

It was 11.30 am on 16 February and he'd been in the water

for several hours. He had already discovered part of a hand gun and another old weapon. The river had been used by people other than Vandenberg to dispose of their weapons. McGowen and his partner were making 'arch searches' along the bottom of the Lane Cove River, starting ten metres south of Fullers Bridge.

Vandenberg, with a blue jumper covering his handcuffs, stood watching men in blue overalls swarm over the banks of the river. He looked a sorry sight, his bald head uncovered, dressed in a cheap sports coat and navy blue pants. Vandenberg initially had lied about the whereabouts of the murder weapon. It was Orrock who told Brady that Vandenberg had thrown it in the river.

At 11.45, McGowen's fingers felt something hard and metallic. He tugged his lifeline, a signal he was coming up. In the murky black depths he couldn't see what he'd found but he was sure it was a gun.

The following day, using ultrasonic cleaning equipment, Detective John Barber from scientific cleaned the weapon. It was a dirty .22 calibre Stirling rifle and when he test-fired it, he found it was in working order although the trigger guard and its screw were missing. When he tested it a second time, the gun discharged accidentally. Hardly a sophisticated weapon, but lethal all the same, thought Barber. The gun had the same calibre bullets as those taken from Megan's body and Kalajzich's pillow.

The television cameras returned to Manly. Police reporter Norm Lipson from Channel 7 arrived at 31 Fairlight Crescent early on 17 February after a tip from one of his contacts. At 9.30 am police, using a metal detector, found what they had been looking for in the hydrangea bushes to the left of the carport. A black metallic silencer with a broken thread was lying among the wandering Jew. It was further proof of Vandenberg's story.

At 10 am that day, the four accused appeared at the Glebe Coroner's Court for a bail application. Kalajzich wasted no time speaking to Elkins as they sat in their shared cell before court started. 'Don't worry, Warren,' he whispered. 'I'll fix up your legal fees and bail. While I'm doing that, when you go back to the jail at the Bay, try to get in touch with Bill and tell him he'll get another twenty grand if he says that we had nothing to do with Megan's death.'

At the bail hearing the magistrate, Peter Norton, was told that Orrock required special treatment for a growth on his heart. Vandenberg told the court he was the main witness against Kalajzich and feared for his life if Kalajzich got bail. He said he was prepared to give evidence for the Crown. 'I have already admitted to the crime. I cannot incriminate myself any more.' Kalajzich was released on $200 000 bail. Orrock and Elkins were both granted conditional bail, but by the end of the day they were still in custody, unable to raise the money.

Inkster had again re-interviewed Vandenberg about the weapon, in front of his brother John, but he had still refused to implicate Orrock and Elkins.

In the cells that evening during another interview with Inkster, Vandenberg changed his mind: 'By the way, Bob, there was no Yugoslavs I dealt with. I only saw Warren Elkins. He was the only person I dealt with. I didn't want to get him into trouble for his small involvement.'

It was the break Inkster had been waiting for. 'I'll discuss the matter with you later,' Inkster said and left.

That same evening, Orrock asked to see Brady and told him he had been threatened by Elkins, who was in the cell across the corridor. Orrock said he had been lying in his cell when he heard some of the conversation between Elkins and a visitor.

'. . . Ten years tops, five years for being first offender with two or three years' remission,' he heard one voice say. Then, shortly afterwards, the visitor left. As the visitor stood outside the cell, Orrock heard: '. . . depending on how he testifies . . .' About ten minutes after the visitor left Elkins had shouted out: 'Orrock, Orrock . . . Shut up and listen to me. If you testify against me, you're a dead man. I've already arranged one.'

Vandenberg was in protective custody in Programs Unit, in a small jail known as the 'dog box'. Within days of being in jail, Elkins arranged to meet Vandenberg at the gate between the dog box and the main jail.

'We want to make sure me and the boss are not involved in any of this,' Elkins told him through the gate. 'You'll have nothing to worry about. And there's twenty grand in it for you if you keep your mouth shut—'

'What are you doing?' A prison officer appeared suddenly. 'You are not allowed to talk through here.'

Elkins spent fourteen days inside. He was then bailed out which gave him easier access to Vandenberg and Kalajzich.

Inkster found out about the bribe offer a few days later. Orrock told him. Inkster decided not to confront Vandenberg yet. Vandenberg still rang him every few days. He never said much except that things were okay. Inkster encouraged the contact.

'Well, as I've told you, Bill, if you ever want to tell me anything about this that you haven't already said, you know I'll be happy to listen,' Inkster reminded him at the end of every call.

Vandenberg felt safe in the dog box. It was small and everyone there needed protection. There was a multiple murderer, a couple of former police officers and a 'rock spider' (child molester). They all got on well enough, and most of them liked Vandenberg. He was always the first up, and by the time the others had come out of their cells, he already had the table set and porridge bubbling on the stove. He would sit and wait for them, chain-smoking, with the tag of a teabag hanging out of his cup. They all thought he was a bit of an 'old woman'. He was almost obsessive about his personal hygiene and they would snigger when they saw him walking around in socks to keep his feet clean.

Some nights he kept them amused with his tales of the repeated bungled murder attempts. Most of them laughed at his theatrics. He also bragged about the $20 000 bribe offer from Elkins. He never showed remorse in those early days, and often his laughter was the loudest.

It was some time before the news of Megan's death filtered through to the local newspapers in Makarska, near Omis on the Adriatic coast. Many locals who knew the Kalajzichs could not believe it, yet here was the story and a photo of the smiling couple.

More than a month later, about 2.15 pm on 19 March, Lydia Iurman picked up the phone at her office in the Bank of Brazil in Martin Place.

'Do you recognise who I am?' the voice at the other end of the phone said in Yugoslav.

She hung up the phone without answering, her hand shaking.

SEVENTEEN

THE COMMITTAL

Her name was Lydia; Marcellina Lydia Iurman. And if Sergeant John Radalj's information was right, her evidence was invaluable. She could help them prove an unhappy marriage and she may have been one reason why Kalajzich had wanted Megan out of the way back in the 1970s.

The police still had no motive for the murder, and Inkster wanted reasons. He wanted to fill in the background, the vacuum that a jury would face when deliberating its verdict. Megan had never owned any shares in the hotel and Kalajzich neither gained nor lost financially from her death. So why did he want her killed?

Inkster knew Bennett Street, Harbord. Number 25 was a comfortable two-storey red brick home with a well-kept garden and lots of trees. A purple carpet of petals from a flowering crepe myrtle covered the front lawn. He straightened his tie and pulled on his jacket before they walked up to the house. Inkster glanced at his watch. 7.30 pm on 18 March. He knocked on the door.

Irma answered. 'Come in,' she said after Radalj had introduced himself and Inkster.

'Lydia,' Irma called down a hallway. 'There's some policemen here to see you.'

Lydia appeared in the doorway. She looked startled. She was an attractive woman, Inkster guessed about five years younger than Megan. She had strong Slavic features: high cheekbones, clear skin and thick light brown hair. She was dressed in casual clothes.

Radalj would do most of the talking. Born in Yugoslavia, Radalj had given Inkster a rare insight into Sydney's northern suburbs Yugoslav community. He had worked with Inkster in Manly years ago and Inkster had turned to Radalj for help in the early days of the investigation.

'We'd just like to have a talk with you. About Andrew Kalajzich,' Radalj said. 'But we don't insist it's a private conversation—your sister can join us if you'd like.' Radalj smiled. He was a burly man of 50 with a deep, friendly voice and an open face that encouraged confidence. He didn't want Lydia to think they were going to intimidate her.

Lydia nodded and Irma invited them to sit at the dining room table. Djuro, Irma's husband, joined them.

Radalj spoke a few words in Croatian to Lydia. She stumbled over a reply, then said: 'I'm afraid you remember more than me.' She smiled back. Radalj felt he was gaining her confidence.

'Miss Iurman —'

'Please, call me Lydia.'

Radalj continued in English: 'Lydia, we have been told you knew Andrew Kalajzich in the 1970s, when you used to work at the fish shop?'

'Yes, that's right.'

'And we're aware that you had more than a close relationship with him.'

'Yes.' Lydia lowered her eyes.

'Well, you must remember that we are not here to prosecute you—you're not being persecuted in any way—but we're told that you had an affair with him and we're obliged to ask you some questions.'

Lydia paused for a few seconds. 'It's happened,' she said quietly, looking down at the table as she spoke. 'It's happened. I knew the relationship would come out when I read in the paper he was charged with murder. I just can't believe it.' She shook her head.

Radalj continued: 'We've been told that you received some letters from him, when you went back to Brazil.'

'Yes, I did,' she said.

'Do you still have the letters, Lydia?'

She paused again. 'Yes. I kept them.' She looked up at Radalj. 'All of them. For sentimental reasons.' The 69 letters were in a shoe box in the top of her wardrobe. She was on the verge of tears.

'We have to ask you if we can have them,' he said softly. Inkster cut in: 'And I have to tell you that we can arrange a search warrant if need be.'

'I don't know,' Lydia said. She was confused, upset. 'I would like to speak to my solicitor.'

'By all means,' Inkster answered. 'Maybe we could arrange to take a statement from you in his presence, tomorrow.'

'I'll see,' she said. 'I'll ring him in the morning.'

Inkster and Radalj said very little on the way back to the station. They were pleased, but both men felt uncomfortable. She had impressed them as being a woman of principle, understandably reluctant to have her private life broadcast. But there was something else about her, a forlorn vulnerability for which they had not been prepared.

'Let's just keep this to ourselves until the morning conference,' said Inkster when they arrived at Manly. 'We'll tell the others then. There's not much more we can do tonight.'

The next day, just before midday, Inkster received the phone call he'd been hoping for. Lydia had agreed to make a statement that afternoon. She was also prepared to give up the letters.

Inkster's eyes blinked open in the dark. *That was no bloody accident. Kalajzich had tried to kill Megan. And the boy too. His own son.* Lying there, staring at his bedroom ceiling, it was all starting to make sense. He recalled Lydia's statement: '. . . a few days after my return to Australia he was involved in a car accident . . . That was September 1973.'

Inkster turned onto his side and squinted at the figures on the bedside clock: 3.10 am—almost three hours since he last woke. He was wide awake, again, his mind racing. He wished he could remember more about the car accident. Commonwealth Parade. Megan had been in the car when it went over the cliff . . . that's right, no-one was injured. Inkster had checked it out, just after the murder. A woman had rung, saying she had some information about the murder: 'Someone tampered with the brakes on her car. You should be looking to see if she's ever been in an accident.'

It wasn't much but Inkster had tapped the name 'Kalajzich' into the police computer traffic records. The 1973 date came up. He would check again, but he was pretty sure it was September. There were no tampered brakes, no-one injured, but . . . it was the same month Lydia had returned. Bits of Kalajzich's letters to Lydia in Brazil drifted through his mind: *. . . all I want to do is break out and I want to do it with you . . . the time has come for action . . . when you are here, I will be with you all the time . . .*

Inkster had spent most of that day talking to Lydia and reading the love letters. Kalajzich had risen from the pages as naive, hopelessly lovestruck and increasingly desperate as he begged Lydia to come back to Australia in 1973. All those broken promises. No wonder Lydia had been so upset. If he had been willing to kill his wife then, why not later?

Inkster closed his eyes again and tried to imagine Megan's terror as the car skidded towards the cliff. Did she realise what he was doing? She had lived for thirteen years knowing her husband had tried to kill her. She *must* have confided in someone. Her mother? First thing he'd do was find the accident file and go back to the scene, tomorrow—no, today, he realised, as he looked at the clock again. He'd track down the police involved . . .

'You know, I've always had my doubts about that one.' Constable Stephen Nicholas now worked in Internal Affairs in the city. Inkster had phoned him early that morning. 'It just didn't seem to add up ... I mean, you know he wasn't even in the car when it went over?'

Inkster remembered Nicholas as a keen and fresh-faced constable. They had both worked at Manly about ten years ago.

'I was scratching my head for months after that,' Nicholas said, 'and I've got to admit I was worried about her, but I didn't really know what I could do. Mrs Kalajzich wouldn't accept my offers of help. She obviously didn't want me to investigate the accident, and she insisted her husband had been driving at only five miles an hour when the car went over the edge.'

Nicholas had doubted that was true. At that speed the car couldn't possibly have climbed the gutter, smashed through the fence, headed up a rise and skidded over a grass verge. No way. And there was the peculiar way Kalajzich had acted after the crash. He wouldn't speak to Nicholas, didn't even speak to his wife, who was white and shaken. And then he had climbed down the cliff to the wreck and got himself hauled up on a stretcher. Nicholas had felt intimidated by Kalajzich. Everybody knew he was a powerful man.

Nicholas had written it off as a standard accident report because nobody had been badly injured: running sheet number 73/3/339.

'Well,' said Inkster slowly, 'I think the "accident" was an attempt on her life. What do you reckon, mate?'

'I agree,' Nicholas said, 'but I don't think he planned it. It would have to have been spontaneous. It was so clumsy. I mean, the tide was out at that time of the night. Otherwise, she and the boy would probably have drowned.'

'I think,' Inkster said, 'you'd better come over and give us a statement, Steve.'

While Inkster waited for Nicholas at Manly police station, he waded through the thickly bound back copies of *The Manly Daily* until he found the headline he was looking for:

'Manly Family Escape Crash With Shaking'. And there was a picture of Kalajzich, all right, being carried up on a stretcher. Inkster shook his head. He picked up the phone and began arranging for aerial and site photos of Commonwealth Parade. Then he rang the council engineers for details of the gradient of the curve where the car had left the road. He'd take a look at the spot with Nicholas as soon as he arrived.

Inkster was puzzled by Megan's behaviour. She must have suspected something but, according to Nicholas, she had tried to protect her husband. Inkster wondered if she was just scared—or perhaps she just refused to admit to herself that Kalajzich had tried to kill her. None of her friends or family they had interviewed so far had ever mentioned the crash. Megan didn't seem to have said anything to anybody.

That afternoon, Radalj came up with more news. Eleven days after the crash, Kalajzich had been admitted to Alanbrook private hospital where he spent a week recovering.

'He was seeing a psychiatrist, a Dr Hill,' Radalj said. 'Apparently he had some sort of a nervous breakdown. But the doctor knew about problems in the marriage, I'm told. It wasn't such a big secret. Some of the family knew about Lydia. Megan certainly did. She and Andrew were having marriage counselling. And the father and Tony knew, too, I think.'

'We'd better track down this Dr Hill. I'll organise a warrant for the records of Kalajzich's admission.'

Kalajzich returned to work a fortnight after Megan's murder but, as the court proceedings began, he dropped his role as general manager. His hotel had been dubbed 'The Murderer's Arms', although many of his staff stayed on despite the murder charge against their boss. He moved out of his office into a smaller one next door and appointed Merrill Barker to act as general manager. Later still, he moved down to the back of the lobby to an even smaller office known as the lobby shop. Marlene continued in her role as executive assistant and they saw each other daily.

One day in April, the security guard, James Taylor walked

through Kalajzich's open office door reading a report. As he looked up, he saw Kalajzich and Marlene embracing on the other side of his desk. Taylor backed out quickly and closed the door. It was the second time he had stumbled on them hugging in Kalajzich's office. The first time they had been kissing and they broke away as soon as he walked in. That had been embarrassing enough. And now this.

This time Taylor waited a few minutes outside and then began fumbling noisily with the door handle. When he walked in they were standing a metre apart, both watching the door.

'Here's the security report,' Taylor said, eyes on the desk.

The courtroom at the Coroner's Court in Glebe, was packed. It was 7 July 1986, day one of the committal hearing. Kalajzich sat behind the bar table, his chair slightly away from the others, with Elkins on his left, and Orrock and Vandenberg close together on his right.

Megan's mother, May Carmichael, sat in the public gallery. Andrew Kalajzich senior sat next to her. Kalajzich jotted down notes as the police prosecutor, Bernie Niven, opened the case before the magistrate, Mr Greg Glass.

Niven told the court that Vandenberg had admitted shooting Megan twice in the head and being paid $15 000 for the job. The four accused men had entered into a conspiracy to murder Mrs Kalajzich between December 1984 and January 1986, he said.

One of the first witnesses was Constable Delores Lassen who told the court how Kalajzich had knelt beside the body of his wife and sobbed, saying, 'What bastard would want to kill her?'

Tony Kalajzich gave evidence that his family had become so scared after the murder he had installed security locks and lights in his apartment. Inkster had taken out a warrant for the notes taken by Kalajzich's psychatrist in the 70s. When Dr Hill was called to the stand, he read excerpts from the notes he had taken.

On the second day, Marlene Watson was called to the stand.

She kept her eyes fixed on Kalajzich's barrister, Chester Porter, QC, while he asked her about her relationship with Kalajzich.

'Did you ever have a personal relationship with him?'

She spoke clearly and convincingly. 'I considered him a very close friend of mine.'

She denied ever having an affair with him: 'Those are the sort of rumours that go around with a secretary and a boss,' she said.

Inkster's surprise witness was to appear two days later. He had not notified the defence that she was appearing. He wanted to see Kalajzich's reaction when she was called.

Inkster drove Lydia to the back entrance of the courthouse. They arrived early, planning to walk up through the forensic science entrance, but, just as they pulled up, Inkster saw the car behind them. It was Kalajzich and Porter, unusually early. Inkster saw the look of shock on Kalajzich's face and smiled. Kalajzich had ten minutes to explain to his barrister who this woman was.

When Lydia was called to the stand she was as credible as Marlene. She told the court how Kalajzich had promised to marry her in 1976, but that he had stood her up on the day.

'I saw him in 1982, I can't remember what month. I had to go to Dee Why to clean up the flat that we'd bought, and he came there and we talked. We talked about general things . . . the hotel, what he expected it to be, his dealings, and I talked about my things—money exchange, how the rates were going and his kids at school, nothing else.'

'On that occasion,' asked Niven, 'were there any relations between you two? Sexual relations?'

'Yes, it happened, yes . . . it just happened,' she said quietly.

When Carey Harvey first entered the witness box giving evidence for the prosecution, she refused to answer questions. When she did give evidence, she changed her story, denying many of the answers she had given police in her original statements.

Sergeant Niven then cross-examined her as a hostile witness. She now strongly defended Elkins, telling the court that she had lied to police in her statements because at the time she was carrying a grudge against Elkins.

'I had returned from New Zealand and discovered that he was due to fly out to Hong Kong the next day with another woman,' she said.

She told the court she was seeing Elkins again and had lunched with him at the Opera House, and that the previous week he had come to her home when she asked him to fix her washing machine.

It was not until much later during the trial that Carey Harvey's change of story was explained. Elkins admitted at the trial he had asked Carey Harvey to marry him two weeks before the committal hearing. He said he knew that a wife could not be forced to give evidence against her husband.

Elkins' emotions during the committal hearing fluctuated. His mother died suddenly from a heart attack in the middle of proceedings. He was sure he had killed her because of the stress she had been placed under. The burden of her death was an extra weight for him to carry.

In the end none of the defendants chose to give evidence, reserving their defence.

The hearing lasted three weeks. Finally, on 25 July, Greg Glass announced his decision. His words stirred the court-room:

'It is my opinion that the case against Kalajzich is based on suspicion—perhaps in the eyes of many a strong suspicion—presumptive evidence, conjecture and speculation. Three people were in the room that night ... Two of those people are available to give evidence before the inquiry but because of their position at law they were under no obligation to answer questions at this tribunal.'

Glass said Vandenberg's statement admitting firing the fatal shots was not admissible evidence against Kalajzich.

'For the case against Mr Kalajzich to go further, it is incumbent on the prosecution to produce evidence that he has committed the offence. I do not believe the prosecution has done so.'

Porter had done his job, thought Kalajzich. The charges against him had been dismissed even though Elkins, Vandenberg and Orrock were committed for trial on a date to be fixed.

Kalajzich, looking drawn but relieved pushed past the waiting media. Later that week, his mother spoke out for him. The 'horrible lies' had hurt the close-knit family, she said: 'We have all been hurt by them, especially Andrew. We all try and speak to him about it but he is still very upset and doesn't like to talk. I will always be beside him because I have known all along that he was innocent . . .' She added: 'Even if I thought he was guilty I am the same as any other mother and I would have stuck by him.'

Inkster, Richardson, Hagan and Niven retreated to Manly police station to review the evidence. They were bitterly disappointed. Inkster was sure Glass had not fully appreciated the evidence of the crime scene.

During the next few days, he discussed the case with the prosecutor, Allan Saunders, QC, who had been appointed for the trial. Saunders decided to ask the Attorney-General to consider an ex-officio indictment against Kalajzich.

Kalajzich also knew it was far from over, despite the magistrate's decision. Webb, his solicitor, had told him it was possible he could still be recharged. Vandenberg was his biggest worry. He had to be kept quiet. The night after he was discharged, he rang Elkins. They arranged to meet the following day.

Elkins saw the Jaguar approaching from the other end of the street. He had parked his new BMW a few doors down from Manly police station where he had just reported, as required by his bail conditions. He flicked his headlights once. Kalajzich signalled back and Elkins pulled out, did a U-turn and followed him to some tennis courts nearby.

'You've got to make sure he won't talk, Waz.'

'I've tried,' said Elkins. 'I told him about the twenty thousand.'

'Well, go back and convince him. We've got to destroy any credibility he's got, or buy him off. Tell him there's *forty* thousand for him if he makes a statement saying I'm not involved—and a unit in Perth when he gets out. He can ring up, you can tape the call, and I can give it to John Webb. But we have to be careful. If John ever found out I was involved in this, he'd drop me like a hot pancake.'

Kalajzich gave Elkins $500 for expenses. He told him there would be more—lots more—if everything came off. Elkins was nervous. His time in jail had scared him, but he was still impressed by Kalajzich's power. He would be able to get him out of this.

During the next few weeks they met, always after dark, at several spots around Manly: Fairlight cemetery, the gasworks, a toilet block near the local girls' high school, to discuss Elkins' progression—or lack of it—with Vandenberg.

On 20 August, Elkins went back out to Long Bay. He asked to visit his old cell-mate, Steve Moorehous. Vandenberg, he knew, was a cleaner in the visitors' section.

As he sat waiting for Moorehous, he beckoned Vandenberg over to his table. 'There's big money in this for you Bill,' he said. 'All you have to do is make a statement saying the boss isn't involved. He says he'll give you forty grand all up and a unit in Perth when you get out. All you do is ring up and I tape the call. He said he'll give you ten grand up front if you agree.'

'Will he pay the money now?' Vandenberg asked.

'Yeah. In cash, up front.'

Vandenberg could use the money. Not for himself, but for his niece, Patricia McDonald, and her husband, Graham. They now visited him every week because his brother John was in Holland. Before he left, John had impressed on the McDonalds how important it was to keep up Vandenberg's spirits.

Each weekend they made the 60-kilometre trek from their

home at Doonside in far western Sydney. Vandenberg knew their mortgage repayments were behind and they had been having trouble meeting their bills now they had a baby.

'OK,' he told Elkins, 'I'll do it. I'll give you an address to take the money to. It's Doonside, where my niece lives. I'll ring her and tell her it's coming tomorrow.'

That night, 22 August, Elkins rang the McDonalds and told them he had something belonging to Vandenberg. 'My name is Sid. I'm a friend of Bill's,' he said. 'I've left a little foil package by the car in your driveway. If you go out now, you'll find it. I'll wait.'

Graham McDonald retrieved the package and came back to the phone.

'Open it,' Elkins said.

McDonald had never seen so much money—several bundles of $100 bills. 'Do you want me to count it?' he asked.

'No. There's ten thousand dollars,' Elkins replied. 'Just make sure Bill gets it.' He hung up.

The McDonalds were astonished and puzzled. Graham took the following day, Friday, off work. They wrapped up the money and took it out to Long Bay.

'It's money owed to me, and I want you to have it,' Vandenberg told them. 'It's of no use to me now.'

The McDonalds could not believe it. They told him they couldn't possibly accept it, arguing with him for almost an hour, insisting he bank it for later, when he was released.

'No, I don't need it,' Vandenberg was adamant. 'It's for you, I want you to have it.'

Finally, they gave in. Vandenberg agreed to keep $500, which they banked in his account at the jail. He would buy a colour television set with it. He already had a TV, but he wanted a second.

The McDonalds told Vandenberg he was like Santa Claus. After they paid the mortgage, car registration and Bankcard bills, they took their first holiday and spent five days in Queensland.

Two days after the money was delivered, Elkins had still not heard from Vandenberg. He sent him a message through Moorehous.

'They're waiting for you to keep your end of the deal,' Moorehous reminded him.

On the afternoon of 24 August, Vandenberg rang. Elkins switched on his tape recorder.

'How are you, Warren?' he asked.

'Good, mate. Why did you set me up with this conspiracy shit?'

'Look, Warren, I had a lot of problems, you know how it is. You get all the blokes, the heavies, that force you.'

'Right.'

'It was never meant to go that way, you know.'

'Was Andrew Kalajzich involved?'

'No, no, not really, mate. It was much deeper than that . . .'

'So, who did you get . . .'

'I didn't have much choice . . . You know, you've been a good friend for a long time, a good while, you know. I've respected you, but . . . once you get them heavies, you don't really get much choice.'

'Right . . . so, what you were telling me—you had to say that I was involved and also Andrew Kalajzich?'

'No, never, you're not. But you've got to understand, I was in a position, you know.'

'Right, right . . .'

Elkins made three copies of the tape and took them to Kalajzich. A few hours later, Kalajzich called. He was planning a trip to Yugoslavia later that month and he wanted this sorted out.

'What's this you've delivered to me? It's nothing to do with what I was talking about.'

Elkins wasn't really surprised. He knew the tape was unconvincing. And it had cost $10 000. Elkins and Kalajzich met again that night at the cemetery.

'I want something in writing,' Kalajzich said. 'That tape is fucking useless. Tell Vandenberg to make a statement.'

But the statement never came. Elkins continued to apply the pressure through Moorehous.

'I've got it,' Vandenberg would tell Moorehous. 'It's in my cell, but I've got to think about my own position. I want a couple of days to think about things.'

'You've already been paid—just remember that,' Moorehous said.

But Vandenberg had no intention of writing a statement. He was becoming more brazen, less scared of Kalajzich. He was in protective custody. They could sweat on the outside.

Kalajzich had booked his flight for 27 August. He met Elkins the night before he left.

'I want that statement, Waz,' he told Elkins. 'Offer Vandenberg anything he wants.'

'There he is.' Steve Barrett spotted Kalajzich checking in at the JAT airlines counter. 'In the yellow jumper. Go.'

Barrett, the police reporter for Channel 9, pushed his camera crew through the crowds milling around the check-in area of Sydney airport. He had a scoop. He could see this piece leading the 6 pm television news bulletin.

Kalajzich was checking in at the first-class counter for his midday flight. He saw the camera crews and Barrett approaching, and turned the other way. But the camera's spotlight singled him out. Heads turned.

Barrett strode up to the counter: 'Mr Kalajzich, Steve Barrett from—'

'Go away. I've got nothing to say.' Kalajzich looked over his shoulder, dismissing him with a wave of his hand. But Barrett was used to this treatment in the years he had been a police reporter.

'Can you tell us where you're going and if you're coming back to Australia?' he persevered.

Kalajzich ignored him. He continued filling out his boarding form.

'Look, you might as well speak to me—because your wife certainly can't,' Barrett said.

Kalajzich reacted all right. He raised his arm as if he was about to hit the television reporter, but stopped himself. The cameraman continued filming: all good footage for Barrett's story.

'If you don't leave me alone I'll call the police,' he snarled angrily.

'No need to,' Barrett replied with a smirk. 'They're already here.'

Kalajzich was furious. He tried to storm off, shielding his face from the prying camera, but the crew and Barrett followed.

Michele, Kalajzich's daughter, watched the spectacle from a nearby seat where she sat rocking her baby, Mathew, in a pram. Her husband, Jim Economides, did his best to keep the camera away from his father-in-law as the crew chased them into a duty-free shop.

Economides pleaded with Barrett: 'He's had enough. Can't you leave him alone?' The cameras stopped on Economides in front of a stand of duty-free videotapes.

'Will he be coming back to Australia?' Barrett asked.

'Yes.'

'When?'

'I don't know when.' Economides walked off.

Richardson and Inkster watched it all from a distance. They'd been tailing Kalajzich since he arrived at the airport at 11 am.

There was nothing Inkster could do to stop Kalajzich leaving the country. He was a free man. And there was no extradition treaty between Australia and Yugoslavia.

Richardson waited until all the passengers were on board, sitting in the purple and turquoise interior of the Boeing 747 Jumbo. An Australian federal police officer led him through the back door of the plane. He walked down the aisle and through the curtain leading into first-class. Kalajzich was sitting on the left reading a newspaper, his reading glasses balanced on his nose. Richardson stood beside him. Aware of someone's presence, Kalajzich looked up. As he saw

Richardson, his head jolted back in surprise, sending the reading glasses sailing into his lap.

Not a word was spoken. Richardson looked down at Kalajzich for a few moments, his face expressionless, then walked away.

Three days after Kalajzich left the country, Moorehous again approached Vandenberg.

'Why don't you get moved out of the dog box?' he suggested. 'Get a transfer to 12 Wing, where I am. I'll look after you.'

Vandenberg was tempted. He felt like a change. That afternoon, he applied to be moved but was annoyed when he was refused. He was told it was for his own safety. Vandenberg felt 'they' were being difficult.

From Yugoslavia Kalajzich made long and frequent calls to the Manly Pacific Hotel. He was also inquiring about running his hotel business from Omis: checking computer compatibility and cost. Inkster was worried. He began looking at their options if a warrant was issued for his arrest.

Rumours that Kalajzich could be recharged began to surface early in September. Over the next few weeks, newspapers canvassed the possibility with headlines such as: 'Government Officers Review Kalajzich Case', 'Manly Murder Acquittal is Under Review', 'Kalajzich May Still Go To Trial'.

Later that month, the local Liberal MP, Terry Metherell, acting for a concerned constituent, asked the Attorney-General to lay fresh murder charges. Meanwhile, Allan Saunders was still analysing evidence from the committal.

On 15 October, Kalajzich flew back to Australia. He had been back in the country for two days and was already making headlines in the local paper.

On 17 October he read about his case in *The Manly Daily*.

KALAJZICH: NO DECISION YET
The Crown law office is still considering a private request

to file a bill of indictment against Manly millionaire Andrew Kalajzich ... A spokesman for the NSW Attorney-General said no decision had been made yet, it will be some time ...'

Kalajzich wasn't pleased. He wanted Vandenberg's statement. He rang Elkins and told him to meet him that night at the Manly Bowling Club. Elkins kept the appointment but still did not have the statement.

'You tell him that I want that letter,' Kalajzich ordered Elkins. 'You go back out there and remind him we've already shown him goodwill and paid him ten thousand dollars. He gets another ten once he's done the statement and twenty more when the trial's finished.'

But Vandenberg would not comply. He simply said he wasn't ready.

Kalajzich's face was cold and unemotional as Elkins told him he had failed again.

'I should have got rid of you, too, Waz.'

EIGHTEEN

P2 LIFE

Kalajzich had been back in Australia only a week when his position as a commissioner of the New South Wales Tourism Commission enabled him to escape for a weekend in the country.

It was the New South Wales Tourism annual conference in Armidale. Marlene attended as a delegate. They booked into different motels but dined together in the restaurant at the Cattlemen's Motor Inn. After the conference, they shared the same flight back to Sydney. It was respite from the rumblings of disquiet waiting for him back in the city.

There was a long list of messages and a pile of unopened mail waiting on Inkster's desk when he walked back into his office on 1 December after two weeks' holiday. It had been just the tonic he'd needed. He felt refreshed, even though he had spent the fortnight at home. He looked through his messages: '14.11.86. 8.45 am Bill Vandenberg rang. Wants you to contact him when you return from leave.'

It was the message he had been waiting for. Vandenberg

wanted to talk, he was sure of it. He picked up the phone and dialled Long Bay jail.

'Bob, I want to have a talk with you,' Vandenberg said. 'I want to clear the air. There's a few things you should know about. Can you come out and see me?'

Vandenberg, finally, had had enough of Moorehous pressuring him for a statement. He had told him the deal was off two days ago but that had had no effect.

'Of course I can, Bill,' Inkster said. 'I'll get permission to take you to Maroubra police station. It'll be a better place to talk. I'll clear it with the jail this afternoon. Would that be OK with you?'

'Yes,' said Vandenberg, 'there's quite a lot I want to tell you.'

'Phone call for you, Bill. In the main office.'

The prison officer stuck his head around the doorway. Vandenberg was sitting at the table playing cards with a few other prisoners. It was mid-morning. He was filling in time until Inkster arrived.

'OK,' he said, 'coming.'

As soon as he walked into the office Vandenberg knew there was no phone call. Wally McCaskell, from the jail's Internal Investigation Unit, told him to take a seat. Several other senior officers were also in the room.

McCaskell began: 'We've got some pretty disturbing news, Bill . . .'

Inkster had been on the phone to Maroubra when McCaskell rang. 'Hi, Bob. My name's McCaskell. I'm the deputy superintendent from the IIU. I have some news for you. We've just uncovered a plot to murder Vandenberg in the prison.'

'You're joking? I was just on my way over to see him. Did you know about that?'

'Yes. He's here in my office now. We've just told him. You'd better talk to him.'

'I can't believe it, Bob,' Vandenberg said. There was fear in his voice.

Arrangements were made to transfer Vandenberg out of Long Bay that afternoon. He didn't even have a chance to collect his things from his cell. Within two hours he had been placed in high security segregation at Parklea jail at Blacktown.

Early the next day a police escort brought him to Castle Hill police station. He was a frightened man. Richardson and Inkster met him there. For the next five hours he told them everything he knew about Kalajzich, Elkins, Canellis and the plot to kill Megan. He made a statement and signed it, saying he wanted to plead guilty and give evidence for the Crown.

The murder plot was enough to make Vandenberg tell all.

Two weeks later, on 17 December, Elkins walked through the front door of Manly police station at 9.20 pm. He was reporting for bail, as he was required to do three times a week.

Inkster was waiting for him. He took Elkins through to the detectives' room again and told him he was under arrest. He would be charged with conspiring to pervert the course of justice and conspiring to murder Vandenberg. Inkster knew Elkins wanted to talk, but he could see he was crippled by fear.

The following afternoon there was another major breakthrough. Coincidentally, an ex-officio indictment for Kalajzich's arrest on a charge of murder had been filed, and a warrant was issued for his arrest. The indictment had been granted without the new evidence from Vandenberg.

That night, Inkster arrived at Kalajzich's parents' house in Oyama Avenue about 8 pm. Michele answered the front door. Inkster did not need to introduce himself. She recognised him and moved aside. Kalajzich had not long been home from work and was standing inside the door. He was still wearing his suit trousers and a white business shirt. His face was drawn and pale.

'I have a warrant for your arrest,' Inkster said.

Michele looked at her father. Kalajzich took the warrant from Inkster and read it:

To the Commissioner of Police for the State of New South Wales and to all Police officers in the said state ... that

ANDREW PETER KALAJZICH

on the twenty-seventh day of January, in the year of Our Lord one thousand nine hundred and eighty-six at Fairlight in the State of New South Wales did murder Megan Kalajzich.

These are therefore to command you in her Majesty's name forthwith to apprehend the said ANDREW PETER KALAJZICH ... to be dealt with according to law ...

'I want to call my solicitor,' Kalajzich said.

Kalajzich made a brief appearance the following day in the New South Wales Supreme Court. Reporters jostled for seats in the crowded room. As Kalajzich appeared before the judge, two kilometres away Moorehous and two other prisoners—Tom Domican and Peter Drummond—were brought into Central Local Court. They were charged with attempting to pervert the course of justice and conspiring to murder Vandenberg.

Kalajzich was released on $200 000 bail. He left the court with his solicitor and refused, as usual, to speak to the press. Domican and Drummond were taken back to Long Bay jail. Vandenberg's location remained a secret.

On 31 December, Elkins decided to talk. He wanted immunity from prosecution and had applied to the Attorney-General.

Two weeks later, Inkster interviewed him at Manly police station. Elkins started by giving him the tape-recording of the phone call he made with Vandenberg. At 2.30 pm they sat down to make a formal record of interview. Eight hours later, Inkster offered to suspend it.

'No,' said Elkins, 'I want to finish it. I have to get it off my chest.'

At 4 am the next morning, Inkster finally stopped the interview. A week later, Richardson and he finished it in the bare, desolatory segregation unit at Parklea jail where Elkins, now in custody, was also being held.

Acting on fresh information from Elkins, Inkster applied for a second warrant to search the manager's office at the Manly Pacific hotel. Inside the office Detective Ray Constable crawled around on his hands and knees, carefully tracing a finger over the aluminium skirting board.

'This looks like it, Bob,' he said to Inkster, pointing to the pitted marks.

'See, there's still some particles here, in the channelling,' he said, looking through a magnifying glass.

If Elkins' information was correct, the indentation on the skirting board was just behind the desk where the gun had been tested.

Constable began photographing the skirting board and collecting the tiny paper particles in glass phials. He and Inkster then removed a section of the skirting board and took it with them for further testing.

On 7 March Kalajzich failed in another application for bail.

After hearing what he described as the 'somewhat chilling' synopsis of the Crown case, Justice Maxwell said he had the same fears as police: that Kalajzich might not appear at court, or might interfere with witnesses.

Kalajzich's lawyers argued that Elkins' evidence was highly suspect, circumstantial and shaky, with the 'rank smell of a set-up'. But at the end of the day, the Crown won. No-one was better prepared, they said, to give evidence against Kalajzich than Elkins. Justice Maxwell agreed.

Kalajzich had been arrested within a month of Marlene's return from an overseas holiday. February had passed quickly. They had spent as much time as they could with each other. She knew it might be a long time before they were together again.

Parklea Jail
27th April 1987

Dear Bob,

I don't really know what you people expect from someone in the jail system and I realise that I am a prisoner but I do expect that we should be looked after to some extent and never to this day have I asked for more that I am entitled to . . .

I have no reason to feel safe here as we are locked away from not only the rest of the world but also from other prisoners. We don't have anything to do here but play with ourselves. We are not in any way given any privileges for being locked away like animals yet the danger is on more that one occasion been brought into us and I may as well take the risk of being knocked in the main jail and if that did happen then at least I would be out of my misery.

When I came here in December you said I would be here for a few weeks and that is now a couple of days off five months and then I read a statement by Mr Akister [then Minister for Corrective Services] and he has not made up his mind about what he is going to do with police informers or if he is going to build a new jail or rebuild some old ones so God knows how long you intend on keeping me in this bloody madhouse . . .

For Christ sake don't blame me for losing faith in you . . . only last week you informed Warren that you would be here to see us and you didn't turn up and I have told him that if you turn up next week do not expect to talk to me for as far as I am concerned we are not even thought about, but when it suits you I am supposed to jump . . . I have been ever helpfull [sic] to you or for that matter to any officer or inmate but no-one has ever been prepared to do the same for me and I am afraid I am at the end and no-one cares for me and I truly am at the stage that I don't care for anyone else anymore . . .

Yours,
Bill Vandenberg.

Inkster was used to receiving his bleak, sad letters, but this one was worrying. Vandenberg and Elkins were due to plead guilty in two weeks' time and Vandenberg was becoming increasingly anxious.

Inkster had not had the time to visit him in Parklea. The new Special Purposes Prison at Long Bay was due to open the following week and Vandenberg would be the first prisoner in the Witness Protection Unit (WPU). Inkster had now been working full-time on the Kalajzich brief for fifteen months. He had spent most of March and April digesting Elkins' evidence and preparing for the trial.

On 22 May 1987, Elkins was sentenced to ten years with a non-parole period of five years for conspiring to murder Megan Kalajzich. With remissions, he would be out in two, maybe three years. Six days later, Justice Maxwell sentenced Vandenberg to life:

> Franciscus Wilhelmus Vandenberg, on the first charge of conspiracy to murder, I sentence you to penal servitude for ten years. On the second charge of attempt to discharge a loaded gun with intent to murder, I sentence you to penal servitude for twelve years ... On the third charge, that of murder, I sentence you to penal servitude for life ...

Vandenberg did not raise his head during the entire proceedings. Handcuffed, he was led from the court and taken back to Long Bay.

Two days after Vandenberg was sentenced, extra charges were laid against Orrock and Kalajzich. Aside from the existing conspiracy to murder charge, both men now also faced murder and attempted murder charges. The June trial date was delayed until the fresh charges could be heard at a committal hearing.

The second committal hearing began on 19 October and lasted three days. Vandenberg and Elkins both gave evidence for the prosecution. After hearing the new evidence, the magistrate, Greg Glass, was satisfied that both men had a case to answer on the new charges and he committed them for trial.

223

Witness Protection Unit (WPU) Work Report.
Dep Supt Garry Jones. 6.7.87.
Subject: P2. Vandenberg. Life.

P2 has deteriorated and taken it upon himself to do a
one man protest. He doesn't want to accept any bonus
earnings because he feels he didn't earn them. He says he
doesn't want to crawl to authorities . . .

Orrock was still on bail and he and his family were making
frequent visits to Vandenberg. The authorities had no objec-
tion as it helped lift Vandenberg's spirits. Orrock had found a
job driving trucks. It wasn't much, but it gave him a bit of
money until the trial. Vandenberg always looked forward to
seeing him. Orrock would listen to his complaints about the
'thick-headed staff' and the daily gripes of jail life. Vandenberg
felt responsible for Orrock's fate and always told him so.

While at Parklea, Vandenberg had become infatuated with
another, younger inmate, Lesley Murphy, who was serving life
for the brutal murder and rape of Sydney nurse Anita Cobby.
After Vandenberg moved to Long Bay they often wrote to
each other. Murphy usually would write asking him for money
and Vandenberg complied.

To Mr W. McCaskell. 7.7.87.
From Prisoner 5002 P2 Life.
Re: Transfer.

Dear Sir,
    It's my desire . . . that if I was going to be placed
anywhere, I'd be placed in Parklea 5 wing where Lesley
Murphy was . . . I don't wish to place myself at risk but I
also realise that if something went wrong with every
prisoner I couldn't hold the Dept of Corrective Services
responsible. I would also like $60 transferred from my
account to Lesley Murphy as soon as possible . . .

Sergeant Trevor Alt from the police department's Physical
Evidence Section enjoyed his forty-minute train trip to work
from his home in Yagoona in Sydney's western suburbs to

Sydney Town Hall. The trip gave him time to read, although his choice of literature was curious.

In March, Inkster had given him the paper fragments from the telephone book found impregnated in the skirting board in Kalajzich's office at the Manly Pacific. Alt had to try to prove that the fragments, which he carried with him in glass phials on the train, matched any of the letters in the 1985 phone book. It was one aspect of Elkins' story which might be verified.

Some of the fragments only contained part of a letter but Alt narrowed the fragments down to the A–K section of the phone book. Alt became obsessed with the hunt for those letters. It was better than a crossword. Puzzled commuters would stare as he brought out the phone book from his carry bag to read on the train. When he got home at night, he would pull the phone book out again and continue to search for the elusive letters.

Eventually he worked out that some of the letters in the fragments had come from a suburb, Canley Vale. He then had to search for every Canley Vale address in the A–K phone book to find which combination matched the fragments. Then in September, after several weeks, he found a match, then compared them to the entries in the 1984 and 1986 phone books. They did not match. Elkins had to be telling the truth. Bullets had definitely been fired through a 1985 A–K phone book.

He had further proof from tests already conducted on the fragments. He discovered that they contained lead.

WPU Report. 29.10.87.
Re: Prisoner 5002. P2 Life.

Recommendations: During discussions with the Committee P2 showed he was greatly agitated. Bill is also very upset about the lack of educational facilities available in the unit. The Committee felt that he should have a break from the unit for a period of up to two weeks to help stabilise his mood. The Goulburn High Security Unit is suggested.

Comments: I feel a break from the WPU would do him the world of good.

Supt D. S. Farrell.

Officer Report Form.
To: Supt Farrell from PO Barry Tanzer.
Re: Unusual action by prisoner P2. 13.11.87.

Sir,
At approximately 7.30 am I walked into cell 20 where prisoner 5002 P2 was sitting on a chair crying. I asked him if he was all right and he said he was. I went to the wing office. About five minutes later I saw prisoner P2 come out of his cell and throw a plastic garbage bag on to the floor. He came into the wing office and said he wanted to talk about anything at all because he was feeling very down.

He said he had to throw his garbage bag out of the cell before he used it on himself. I talked to him for about five minutes until Officer Smith came and took him out of the wing to see a psychologist.

Vandenberg took to writing letters of complaint to jail officials. He said his nerves were shattered, he could not sleep and he wanted to see a psychiatrist. The only treatment he could get was medication. 'I have never in my life been a pill popper and I don't intend to become one . . .' he said.

In November, he requested a visit to Les Murphy, who was now being held in another part of Long Bay. McCaskell felt a one-hour visit would be beneficial but the Superintendent refused the request, saying it would be 'opening the floodgates for similar requests'.

Shortly afterwards, in December, Vandenberg cancelled a visit with his psychiatrist. 'It is one week since I had my last sleeping draught. With my present problems the last thing I think I need is a psychiatrist.'

NINETEEN

THE TRIAL

Kalajzich sat at one of the old round wooden tables in the visiting section of Long Bay's Remand Centre. Like all the other prisoners sitting at the numbered tables, he was wearing white overalls—compulsory dress for inmates during visits.

It was 12 January 1988, a date he had been looking forward to. He was waiting for the letters.

Karin Lohning, 26, a senior prison officer, also knew the letters were coming. She was with the Internal Investigation Unit (IIU), and one of her duties was to watch out for prisoners or visitors passing drugs or other prohibited items. IIU officers had the power to make spot searches of visitors before visits, and inmates after visits. Today, they had been told, Kalajzich was about to receive some illegal documents.

Lohning looked like a regular prison officer. She watched Kalajzich from behind the superintendent's desk while another of her colleagues, Pat Farrell, walked around between the tables. On the table in front of Kalajzich was a pink manilla folder which he would flick open occasionally.

Shortly after 11 am, Kalajzich smiled as he saw his visitors coming through the gate. There was his friend of many years,

Bob Kelly, and two other visitors searching for him among the inmates. They made their way to his table. Kelly sat down and the other two went off to buy coffee.

After almost a year of incarceration, her letters were what Kalajzich lived for. It was the same dependence he had felt for Lydia's letters so long ago.

He enjoyed the little notes Marlene put inside the pages of the magazines she sent. She was always worried about doing the right thing, whether to send him a parcel and a letter once a week, or whether she should make it every second week.

Lohning caught Farrell's eye and motioned towards Kalajzich's table as Kelly slid several folded pages of white paper under the pink folder. Kalajzich pulled the folder towards him and put the pages inside. He glanced at the pages furtively before he did so. As his other visitors returned he closed the folder, but even as they sat chatting, he kept flicking the folder open and glancing down at the words before him.

It was time to act. Lohning and Farrell signalled to another officer on duty, Assistant Superintendent David Stalker. All three moved towards table 14.

'My name is Farrell.' Kalajzich looked up. 'I am from the Internal Investigation Unit of the Corrective Services Department. About six minutes ago, I saw this visitor—he indicated Bob Kelly—place some papers on the table under the folder. Could I have those papers, please?'

'I don't know what the problem is,' Kalajzich said haughtily. 'The papers are for a land deal. This man is my insurance broker and he brings in papers all the time for me to look at.'

'What have we done wrong?' asked Kelly. 'It's not as if we're dealing with drugs.' He opened his jacket and brought out a blue envelope which he opened in front of them. 'I'm always bringing in papers for Mr Kalajzich and I always bring any papers out again.'

'Sir,' said Farrell, 'under section 38 of the Prisons Act, you are still trafficking.' He turned to Kalajzich. 'Will you now give me the papers, please?'

Kalajzich handed him the six pages. Farrell looked at them

briefly. Two pages were dated 4 January 1988, the others, 11 January. Farrell looked back at the four people sitting in front of him.

'This visit is terminated,' he said. 'Would you please leave the visiting area.'

Farrell escorted the three visitors to a nearby office where he took their names and addresses.

'I will be submitting a report to my superintendent for any recommendation he may make as to prosecution for trafficking,' Farrell said.

At 10 pm that night, two prison officers from the Malabar Emergency Unit raided Kalajzich's cell.

'Leave the cell,' one officer ordered. They stripped the cell, throwing everything out on the landing. They found several 'illegal items'—glasses, a knife, some departmental envelopes with names and addresses typed on them, magazines and personal papers. They put them in a box, and the following day the IIU handed them over to Inkster.

Inkster also asked to see Kalajzich's telephone record card of calls made from jail. Remand prisoners at Long Bay were allowed three paid local phone calls a week, and all calls were recorded—date, time, duration and number. Several times Kalajzich had written 'Michele' as the person he was calling, but Inkster recognised the number: it was Marlene Watson's.

Marlene had spent the first few days of 1988 alone. On New Year's Eve she had gone to a formal dinner party for twelve at a friend's house.

Kalajzich had sent flowers to her office at the hotel on New Year's Eve, but she had taken that day off work. By the time she got them on Monday morning, they had wilted.

Kalajzich spent New Year's Eve watching the Barry Manilow show on television, reminiscing over the songs that reminded him of Marlene.

At the beginning of the New Year, she put on rubber gloves, dug out some disinfectant and started cleaning her flat. It was therapeutic and gave her something to concentrate on.

Now, it was a matter of waiting for the trial. She must not allow herself to think that he might be found guilty. There were other painful aspects that worried her—his daughter, Michele, was refusing to have any contact with her. And she was beginning to feel redundant at work. The new manager was employing a resident manager who was to be second-in-charge and Marlene was sure she would end up as the housekeeper.

But what Marlene found hardest to cope with in her life was that she could not visit Kalajzich. It was too risky. She was bitter when his friends talked to her about their visits to the jail. They thought their words would comfort her and put her mind at rest, but all she wanted to do was see him and she was not allowed. Occasionally, he was able to make a phone call. And there was always a letter. She would shred the evidence.

On 4 January she sat at the electric typewriter. No endearment at the top of the letter, no names, only initials.

4 January

I have been thinking about this a lot lately. I wonder how I will see you after things are over (pray God it will be your way). Will I be able to see you straight away or will I have to wait my turn? Will we have an opportunity to rejoice together? They are all strange thoughts and I get really emotional when I think about it. I know all I want to do is run up to you and hug you and kiss you and love you to death and never leave your side again. I guess it won't be as simple as that. I try not to work it out too much. I keep telling myself to let everything work itself out and I'm sure it will. I just wish I had your strength at the moment.

She told him news of the hotel, of how so many of the old staff were leaving:

I just don't know who's genuine and who isn't. I know one thing darling. I know where my heart lies and I just want you back to rub my feet and my back and my head and my whoops ... I had better stop here. My thoughts are getting carried away ...

She wrote more a few days later:

*Oh darling ... I must settle down again and start giving
myself more space ... I have been buying a few books for
myself lately. I think I will spend the next couple of months
catching up on some reading, and studying up on my
antiques. I get so excited when I read about the antique
places and fairs in England. I think your idea of being
chauffeur-driven around to all the places we want to see is
a brilliant idea, I really do. It would be such fun and I
could have you all to myself in the back seat. I can't wait
to explore new places and new things with you. I wish the
next few months were gone. The sooner we know our future
lives, the better ...*

*It is now 12.15, I am going to bed. Will be waiting to
hear from you Friday. Sleep well and take care.*
Your cornflower blue.

She enjoyed his letters. 'If I had never met him and only got
to know him through his letters, I still would have fallen head
over heels in love with him,' she told her closest friends.

She helped in other ways, preparing a list for John Webb of
people who might appear as character witnesses at the trial.

Family and friends stood by Kalajzich, refusing to accept he
had committed such a cold-blooded crime. As the trial
approached, they tried to plan ahead, taking early holidays so
as to be available when the time came.

Kalajzich found himself thinking of Cottage Point, how to
renovate two other old properties he had bought there—
perhaps he could put in a tennis court. He asked Marlene to
take photographs for him. Would she want to do up Cottage
Point first or go on a world trip? It was the sort of wistful
daydreaming they liked to indulge in, the same sort of daydreaming he had once shared with Lydia.

Marlene wrote of Cottage Point, of a recent trip there with
her godson, Nigel, and two hotel employees, Joan the housekeeper and Fido, both friends of Kalajzich:

*It was such a beautiful morning. We picked up some cheese
and bread and a few other things and then came back to
Manly. We got back at about 11.30 which gave us time to
get changed and organised ... We all went in Fido's car
and the drive down was beautiful.*

Poor Joan was so worn out and so grateful to be looked after. She had staff let her down the day before and she worked right through, turning down beds etc until 10, anyway we let her get it all out of her system and by the time we got down there she'd forgotten all about work . . . We had quite a feast between the three of us. It's surprising how much you can do in a day if you get up early.

It was perfect down there, the water was high tide and your little beach was all intact and the water was crystal clear. It didn't take us long to unwind. One minute after arriving there, Joyce [the caretaker's wife] was there to see us, in fact, she almost never left us . . . Fido and Nigel did some fishing. (Remember our last day there when you spent nearly all day fixing up your fishing lines.) The mullet were jumping out of the water but they only caught a little one. Nigel had a ball.

The place looks good, the house is a little untidy though, (the kids don't leave it like we do. Joyce said that she found the shed door open after Andrew's last visit). But then I guess you and I are different to most people. I am glad that we have the same habits and likes and dislikes, I don't believe in that old saying that opposites attract (what we think is untidy is probably very tidy to some people). They have definitely been using the bed but I think I mentioned that last time. I have lots of pangs and some sad little moments on my own but in all the experience of being there brought me so very close to you, darling, and I just can't wait for you to be free again and to enjoy all the simple things with me that we speak about and treasure so much. No-one can take those things away from us and no matter what happens in our lives, those memories are ones that I will cherish forever and know that I will never be able to replace them unless it's with you again.

I took a film of photographs and will forward them to you later in the week and try and mark on the back exactly where they are. I took quite a few from the water. Joyce's husband took Nigel and myself out on the boat whilst I took them. I hope they turn out and they will help you with all your planning . . .

Marlene also inspected the two other properties Kalajzich owned in Cottage Point. They both needed work, she told him; they were not the sort of places she could imagine living in. She picked some flowers from the garden and decided to dry them and put them in the pages of the next magazines she sent to him.

By the time she returned from Cottage Point, she was exhausted. It was one of those humid nights in January and she found it difficult to sleep. She sat, tyepwriter balanced half on a chair and half on her knees, typing another letter.

> *From what people tell me when they have spoken to you, is that you want to do them both up. I presume for your family to use. I think it's pretty hard to communicate on this matter at this stage. I dare not let myself get carried away on what we should do. I'm afraid of building up my hopes too much because my mind cannot take too many more setbacks. But you ask me am I there for you in your plans for there and the answer is 'Yes'. I want to be included in all of your future plans. Just try and leave me out now. I've waited this long—a few more months won't make any difference to my life now although the waiting is really getting to me . . .*
>
> *There was a movie on last night called Come Back. I don't suppose you saw it. The theme song was particularly moving and I jotted down some of the words which were: 'Love is forever until there is no tomorrow.' That is how I feel about you darling and I will not give up until I know there is no tomorrow.*
>
> *. . . It really grieves me when I hear of all these people coming to see you who really don't mean anything to you . . . I'm not too keen about the four girls coming on their own without me. But what can I do? I find it very difficult to rise above these things and pretend it has no effect on me and I politely tell them to give you my best wishes . . .*

It was after 11 pm. Time for her hot milk.

> *Darling. No matter what happens, I have to get out of Manly. I'm beginning to hate it here. I love my little unit still because of what it means to me, but it also keeps me sad darling. We have to close this chapter and start afresh somewhere . . . I will get through the next couple of months with you. I just hope there is someone to help me through the trial weeks. They will be the most difficult. I sometimes*

think it is better for me to go away then, but I know that I will want to be as close to you as I can even though I can't do anything ... I do love you so.

Gosh darling, if our letters were to fall into the wrong hands, it would be fatal, so please destroy as soon as you have read them. We have come this far and I am careful with whom I talk with so please don't worry in this regard ...

When Inkster entered Marlene Watson's North Steyne unit with a search warrant on 13 February 1988, he didn't take long to find the electric Nakajima typewriter. He also took possession of some typing paper, the carbon and correcting ribbons.

It was another job for Detective Alt. He compared Inkster's finds with the letters. He found some of the text from the letters still on the carbon ribbon.

Marlene had dissolved into tears as soon as Inkster appeared at the door. As he searched the unit, she wept uncontrollably. Inkster had been relentless in his pursuit, but for once he ignored his maxim: 'Don't tell me, show me'. He did not have the heart to ask her if she was prepared to make another written statement or to ask her any penetrating questions.

After all the waiting, the beginning of the trial was an anti-climax, the swearing-in of the jury consuming most of the first day.

Darlinghurst Courthouse, in the heart of Taylor Square, is a grand old sandstone building. Huge pillars flank the vestibule outside Courtroom 5 at the centre of the complex. The three robed and wigged protagonists who assembled there on 7 March 1988 were veterans of the arcane rituals practised within.

On the bench sat Justice Victor Maxwell, 66 and approaching retirement. He had a round, pleasant face with a crimson flush on his plump cheeks. Gout forced him to use a walking stick these days, a condition he could not have imagined in 1940 when he held the 120 and 220 yard Australian junior hurdles records. From behind his spectacles, Maxwell had been presiding over criminal trials for fourteen years, after a distinguished career at the New South Wales Bar. He had been a major with the Australian Army Legal Corps and had been President of the War Crimes Tribunal in Rabaul in 1945. He had a reputation as a fair sentencer, and he kept a tight rein on his court.

Facing Maxwell and to his left stood Allan Saunders, Queen's Counsel, a crusty old-style barrister and the State's deputy senior Crown prosecutor. He was a small man who carried the frowsty air of the many stale courtrooms he had inhabited and the many cigarettes he had smoked. His nickname was 'Slipper', after his reputation for 'sinking the slipper in'. With his wig often a little awry and his hands thrust deep into his pockets, he had a habit of relentlessly pounding a witness, slowly tying up their evidence in contradictions. He rarely looked directly at a defendant or a defence witness he was questioning. He cross-examined with the air of someone a little bored with the process of justice. And when the witness replied, his distracted gaze suggested to the jury that he had heard these lies many times before. Saunders prided himself on his pre-trial preparation and his knowledge of the evidence, which he studied with terrier-like tenacity.

His opponent at the bar table, Chester Porter, QC, was an even match though a contrast in appearance and style. He was known as 'The Smiling Funnelweb' because of his ability to disarm his victims with affable chat while drawing them deep into his web. He was a thin man of average height with a worn-looking wig. His voice was distinguished by a speech impediment, but the difficulty he had in pronouncing the letter 'r' lent him charm, accentuating his eloquent oratory.

By the time of Kalajzich's trial, Porter had a series of high-profile wins to his credit. For a time during the mid-1980s, it seemed he never lost a case and the phrase 'Chester Porter walks on water' was coined. Successful cases included those involving Lindy Chamberlain, the mother who claimed a dingo killed her baby; a district court judge, John Foord, accused of conspiring to pervert the course of justice; and Roger Rogerson, then a police officer who faced several criminal charges.

Porter knew this case would be hard to defend. The facts suggested his client did it.

The swearing-in of the jury was a tedious process, with each side scrutinising the 'talent' as those called up for jury duty filed into court. One elderly lady, who did not want to be selected, beckoned conspiratorially to Maxwell, and lowered her voice to a whisper, confiding: 'You see, your honour, it's the hot flushes . . .'

'I understand,' Maxwell said, breaking into one of his unpredictable beams. 'I suffer from that myself.'

On day two, the trial ground to a halt. Only eleven jurors had taken their place on the panel: the twelfth had sent a medical certificate. Of those who turned up, one said she was too nervous to continue and another said he knew one of Kalajzich's relatives. As if that wasn't enough, a fourth came to court with a letter from her employer asking to be excused.

Maxwell empanelled a new jury but the following day two women jurors told him that their jobs were threatened. One said that her employer would not keep her job open for the eight weeks the trial was expected to run. The second said her employer had told her to 'pay a fine and get off the jury'.

Maxwell, was furious. This was an offence under Section 69 of the Jury Act, he told the court, carrying a jail sentence of six months or a $1000 fine. The Court of Appeal would be hearing of this, he said.

Finally, forty minutes late, on Wednesday 9 March, the trial began. Maxwell refused a request from Orrock's lawyer, Julian Van Aalst, for a separate trial.

The defendants were an incongruous pair. Kalajzich, the successful businessman in a dark, tailored suit, followed the proceedings intently, writing industriously as if he was sitting at the bar table rather than in the dock. Orrock, nervous and with the hang-dog look of an all-time loser, was dressed in a pale suit which somehow emphasised his scrawny appearance.

Most of the time he sat staring at his lap. The two men were to sit together for the next twelve weeks. As if to emphasise their separateness, they rarely exchanged so much as a glance. Kalajzich made a point of rising and sitting a few seconds after his co-accused.

The six men and six women jurors listened as Saunders opened the Crown case, telling them what was alleged and what he would try to prove.

'It would be difficult to imagine a more soul-destroying event than that your partner should be murdered as she slept beside you,' said Saunders. 'But, far from being a soul-destroying experience on the part of Mr Kalajzich, the death of his wife was engineered by him . . .'

Saunders said there was an agreement between a number of people to murder Megan, and Kalajzich had arranged for his wife's killer to enter his house through a door which had been left unlocked.

Vandenberg would give evidence that, acting on Kalajzich's instructions, he shot Megan Kalajzich twice in the cheek and fired two shots into her husband's pillow while Kalajzich was in the room, he said.

The Crown would also show that Vandenberg had been paid an extra $10 000 while he was in prison to deny the involvement of Kalajzich and Elkins, in the killing. In all, Saunders said, the Crown would call 90 witnesses, three of them key players in the murder conspiracy.

Holding up a cut-down .22 calibre rifle, Saunders told the jury that the murder weapon would be fired in the court.

'We are all accustomed to what happens on television when people fire guns with silencers and I can assure you, that is not what it's like,' Saunders said as he displayed the weapon to them, bereft of its wooden stock. The dark, rusty metal looked strangely sinister—more like a poker than a gun.

The witnesses began as soon as Saunders finished his two day address. One of the first to be called was Dr Godfrey Oettle, from the New South Wales Forensic Medicine Division. He told the court how he had examined the two bullet wounds on Megan's face during the post-mortem examination. Blood had been found in her ear passage and right lung. She would have been unconscious almost immediately. 'I would have thought she would have died very quickly,' he said.

Porter objected to the jury viewing a close-up colour photograph of Megan's corpse. He said it was 'unduly horrific and added nothing to the narrative'. Justice Maxwell agreed, but allowed more than 100 other colour and black and white photographs of the murder scene, and the Kalajzich house, into evidence.

On day four of the trial, the rifle was fired. Detective Barber placed a pillow, supported by two sandbags, into an alcove at the side of the court usually reserved for probation officers. It was the first time a gun had been fired in a New South Wales courtroom. Maxwell and the jurors stood to make sure they had a clear view as Barber fired four shots—two with a silencer and two without—into the pillow. Several jurors flinched as the explosions rang through the courtroom.

Inkster was one of the first witnesses. Saunders took him methodically through his evidence. Porter then began cross-examination.

He asked Inkster about newspaper articles, published shortly after the murder, stating that police were working on the theory that Megan was murdered by a professional killer. He was leading up to Kalajzich's defence.

'It will be our case,' Porter told the court, 'that the prisoner Vandenberg did not in fact carry out this murder and it was in fact done by a professional killer. It bears all the hallmarks of a professional killer. Vandenberg is, in fact, an amateur.'

The day Vandenberg was due to give evidence, Tuesday, 12 April, the courtroom was packed. Journalists and artists from every media outlet in Sydney crammed into the press box. Here was a most unexpected, self-confessed murderer—a hunched and red-haired version of Billy McMahon. Dressed in a three-piece suit, Vandenberg was led by four court officers to the witness stand.

In his cultured, gentle voice, Vandenberg described the series of events which led him to the murder. It was hard to believe he was speaking about the brutal killing of Megan Kalajzich. He told of the attempt on her life on 11 January and his bungled attempts to kill her. 'All I can say is that each time something went wrong,' he explained.

On 27 January, he had walked into the Kalajzichs' bedroom. The couple lay with their backs to each other. Megan appeared to be asleep, he said.

'I just walked over to the bed and pulled the trigger; aimed and pulled the trigger. Mr Kalajzich rolled off the bed as per arrangement, and I just held the gun towards the pillow and pulled the trigger twice and walked straight out again.'

Under cross-examination by Orrock's counsel, Van Aalst, on his second day of evidence, Vandenberg said he had never been interested in weapons. He had never owned a gun and without his glasses, he could barely see one he was holding. 'I don't think I am a violent man,' he said. He was a 'hopeless shot' and admitted he had great difficulty hitting a target in Orrock's backyard. In fact, he had never fired a gun until ten days before he shot Megan.

Porter watched him curiously. He had cross-examined many criminals in his years at the bar, but he had never come across one like this man. Vandenberg seemed to be enjoying the attention of the centre stage. Porter was sure he was incapable of committing the murder and he set about to prove it. His gruelling cross-examination lasted several days, but Vandenberg refused to budge.

'No, sir,' Vandenberg replied calmly when Porter alleged he was not responsible. And when Porter suggested Vandenberg was trying to claim credit for the murder for reasons best known to himself, Vandenberg disagreed. 'You have already tried that before,' he reminded him. It seemed to Porter that Vandenberg was playing an elaborate game, laying decoys for him during his cross-examination which had nothing to do with his own preservation. On the occasions when Porter discovered he had been misled, Vandenberg would simply smile as if to reward him for his efforts. He denied that he had chosen a second assassin, whose identity was known only to him.

On his fifth and last day in the witness box, Vandenberg denied that anyone else had committed the murder. 'It was me,' he said. 'I don't know why I was stupid enough to get involved but I was.'

Vandenberg was a magnetic witness. It was hard to believe what he was saying. Jenny Cooke, chief court reporter for *The Sydney Morning Herald*, found that listening to him did little to remove the farcical nature of the whole court case. It was like Keystone Cops, she wrote. It would have been laughable except that Megan Kalajzich had been murdered. Jon Cleary, the Australian novelist who had dropped in for a few days to research his next book, found himself becoming a regular spectator.

On day sixteen, 30 March, Elkins was called. He looked anxious as he sat in the box with Saunders taking him slowly through his evidence. Maxwell suggested Elkins refer to Kalajzich as 'AK' because of his obvious difficulty in pronouncing his name.

Elkins outlined the murder conspiracy and how Kalajzich had ordered him to find a hitman. Porter was on the attack as soon as his cross-examination started, accusing Elkins of organising Megan's death for his own purposes, without Kalajzich's knowledge.

'That's not true,' Elkins replied, adding that he was not the architect of the murder. 'I was just conveying what AK told me to do.'

'You were the instrument of murder,' Porter suggested.

'Yes,' he replied.

Elkins said his motivation had been fear.

When Porter began asking him about his immunity from prosecution, Elkins became indignant. 'The only reason I am here is for my own peace of mind. I have to live with this for the rest of my life.'

Each day he was in the box, Elkins' new wife came to court

to support him. Belinda Crowley, English, blonde and neatly dressed, had married Elkins in November 1986. They had met when Elkins came round to install a burglar alarm at her flat. His previous engagement to Elizabeth Gillespie had been short-lived. He admitted that he had proposed marriage to Carey Harvey knowing that, by law, a wife is not compelled to give evidence against her husband.

Other witnesses included an extremely hostile Brian Stokes, the first 'hitman' Elkins had contracted at the Cross. He was now a prisoner appealing against his conviction on an unrelated charge.

'I don't know what I'm doing here and I don't want to be here. I'm not saying nothing,' he told the court. He answered 'no' to every question Saunders—whom he referred to as 'China'—asked him, and finally, he said: 'I'm not saying anything. Can't you get that through your head?'

Porter also tried. As to why he had never turned up at Manly wharf, Stokes said: 'Take me out of Kings Cross and I'm lost.'

Trevor Hayden followed Stokes and told the court that Elkins had offered him $1000 to 'disappear' before the first committal hearing in July 1986.

When witness 71, George Canellis, alias 'Black George' and Noel Sherry, strode confidently to the box on 19 April, an air of excitement rippled through the courtroom. Canellis swaggered gracefully across the room, his head held high. He wore a new, rather expensive checked sports jacket and his trousers had been beautifully pressed.

No-one would have guessed at his earlier bout of nervousness as he lay on the floor of a Mazda van on his way to court. Richardson drove him to the court every morning, picking him up from a secret location on the Central Coast and smuggling him in and out of the building. Canellis was paranoid about being photographed or even seen, and he would quiz Richardson whenever he stopped the van suddenly, or slowed down. Canellis did not want his face in the newspapers or on television. Every morning he slipped past the waiting media.

'Take your pick,' Canellis replied when he was asked which of his three names he should be addressed by.

Van Aalst had encountered Canellis in court on another occasion in Newcastle. He asked Canellis if he remembered him. 'No, but I remember your smartarse questions,' Canellis replied.

Van Aalst suggested that perhaps Canellis had 'muffed' the murder attempt.

'No. If I had gone down to assault that woman I would have killed her then, not at a later date. I would not have left that woman standing there. Is that understood?'

He was asked why he had not gone through with the murder of Megan Kalajzich: 'She was class . . . not a shitkicker in the street,' he said, '. . . and that's what made it stink. I just dropped out of it.'

Maxwell cleared his throat in an exasperated fashion. 'Could you please find another descriptive adjective, Mr Canellis?'

In Canellis' words, the whole thing was a 'balls-up'. 'It didn't sit right,' he told the court. 'She was a very attractive woman, well-groomed and everything, and I don't get involved in what I class as a domestic. They don't work out. They come undone . . .'

Even Porter was impressed with Canellis' detailed knowledge of firearms, even if he wasn't convinced Canellis was always telling the truth. When shown the gun, Canellis had handled it with practised ease, caressing the barrel and explaining its workings in great detail.

Jon Cleary decided Canellis was a James Cagney-type gangster, a leopard in a suit. 'A casting director's dream for a hitman,' he remarked to one journalist.

Kalajzich sat in court each day listening and scribbling notes, his face expressionless as the weeks dragged on. Sometimes at night, he studied his notes in his cell, or filled his time writing letters to loyal friends.

Sunday 17 April 1988
Long Bay Jail

Dear ... (he wrote to one friend)

Life has changed greatly for many of us over the past couple of years and I often think of that period in our lives when we were able to discuss, to debate, even argue without losing our sense of friendship and camaraderie. We all wanted to achieve the one common goal and make Manly something we would all be proud of.

I am doubly sad that my communications with the area have been severed in this manner for a reason which still eludes me, for the necessity of Megan's passing in such tragic circumstances ...

It appears as if this trial will never end with another four to five weeks to go but it will go quickly and God willing I will be able to rejoin my family and friends ...

Andrew

Gradually, the Crown worked its way through the witnesses. By lunchtime on 26 April, the eighth week of the trial, it had finished presenting its case. That afternoon, just before 3.30 pm, Andrew Peter Kalajzich, dressed in a dark blue business suit, entered the witness box.

Porter addressed the jury, saying Kalajzich's evidence was 'perhaps the most important'. He had decided not to call many character witnesses. He did not want any surprises. Kalajzich, he told the jury, might be nervous but he should be given a fair go. Kalajzich had no motive to murder his wife. What's more, until February 1986, he had not even known Kerry Orrock existed.

'I lost my greatest partner,' Kalajzich told the court quietly. He described how Megan had been involved in the hotel's public relations, sales and marketing, which meant she travelled overseas twice a year while he stayed home 'to mind the shop'.

Their shared routine included breakfast, the occasional lunch together and dining together every Friday and Saturday night as well as weekly family dinners with their children. Theirs was a 'very happy, fulfilling and busy marriage', he said.

243

As for Marlene Watson, he had a platonic but close working relationship with her until after his wife's death. They had become 'much fonder towards each other' in early 1987 before he was taken into custody. They had been physically intimate once, and later, she had visited him in jail. They wrote letters and spoke on the phone. She was in love with him, he believed, but he wasn't sure whether he was in love with her despite being very fond of her. Asked if he wanted to marry her, he said: 'I don't know . . . being in the environment I have been for the last thirteen months one's outlook on life is quite different now . . .'

Kalajzich admitted destroying several letters Marlene Watson had sent him. This was not because they would pre-date his attachment to her, to a time before his wife's murder, he added.

Asked whether he had arranged the death of his wife, Kalajzich replied: 'Most definitely not.'

His voice quavered as he told how he had returned to kneel at his wife's side after she had been shot, to reassure her 'everything would be all right'.

'. . . I was horrified to see blood pouring freely out of Megan . . . I could start to feel her hands getting a bit stiff . . .'

He also admitted it was his voice in the taped conversations with Elkins, recorded after the committal hearing, that the crown had in its possession. Elkins and Kalajzich had been taped discussing money and meeting arrangements after the commital. The police had discovered the taped conversations on Kalajzich's answering machine. But discussing money with Elkins was not unusual, Kalajzich said. He often gave Elkins money when he ran out of cash. As for the $20 000 mentioned in one of the tapes, that was money he was going to pay Vandenberg to encourage him to tell the truth.

When confronted by Saunders with a detailed record of his financial transactions around the time of the murder, Kalajzich explained that withdrawals from the hotel account were used to pay for renovations to the house at Cottage Point, fees for hotel interior designer, staff bonuses and spending money for his wife.

When asked about one large withdrawal in late November 1985—from the joint account he shared with Megan—he said this account was only used by her. 'She'd wanted to purchase a fur coat. It was our anniversary on the first of December,' Kalajzich said. 'I think I actually gave her $10 000 ...'

'On November 30, 1985, you took out $10 000 in cash?'

'Yes.'

'On December 11, 1985, a further $10 000 in cash?'

'Yes.'

'What was done with that $20 000?'

'Somewhere in that period, I paid for my interior designer for work he had done at the hotel ...' No, he had not been issued with a receipt he said.

Kalajzich had mostly withdrawn small amounts of up to $1000 from the hotel safe. But there was one withdrawal in January 1986 for more than $25 000.

When Kalajzich was asked about that he said: 'I had withdrawn those sums of money to have on hand. I had in that period in late December/January ... given my wife somewhere between $8000–10 000. I had provided money for my parents when they had arrived home from Yugoslavia. I had given my sister $8000 ...'

Orrock followed Kalajzich into the witness box the next Monday, week nine of the trial. But, rather than give evidence which could be cross-examined, he opted to make an unsworn statement to the jury from the dock.

He began by telling the court that he knew nothing of his friend Bill Vandenberg's plan to commit murder until several days after it had happened.

'But I didn't believe it at the time and I still don't—that Bill is capable of murder,' he said.

Orrock had known Vandenberg for twenty years. Orrock's wife, Gloria, who was close to Vandenberg, had asked Vandenberg whether he had committed the murder. 'He couldn't answer her,' Orrock reported. 'A couple of times since Bill had been locked up I said to Bill: "Did you do it?" and he said: "I have admitted to it". Someone saying that they have admitted to it and someone doing it, to me, is two entirely different things.'

Orrock admitted buying a gun from Canellis for $100 and accepting payment for it from Vandenberg when he handed it over to him. 'But, if I had known Bill was going to murder someone with it he would not have got it for $250 000,' he said.

For eighty minutes, Orrock struggled through his statement, and ended by urging the jury to find him not guilty of the charges against him.

There was something pathetic about his tale. Helping a mate—who had shot up his son's aviary—had cost him everything.

The closing addresses began early in May. Saunders accused the defence of making 'extraordinary' and 'desperate' propositions. The planning of Megan Kalajzich's murder had been dealt with as casually as an enquiry about the price of a pound of butter, he began.

'The very circumstances of the case were suspicious. Here is a woman killed in bed and her husband lying beside her escapes injury . . . You had to have come down in the last shower to believe what has been put in the witness box by the accused.'

Porter, in turn, called Elkins and Vandenberg 'admitted liars and scoundrels'. Vandenberg, he said, was 'one of the most inexplicable characters in Australian criminal law.' He had shown no fear or remorse in the witness box, but had enjoyed his 'great moment' in playing a key role in the trial. Above all, Porter urged the jury to consider that Kalajzich had no motive.

The jury remained unaware of Kalajzich's relationship with Lydia. The letters were considered too remote in time to be a possible motive in Megan's murder so Saunders did not tender them in court. As for Marlene, there was only evidence that she had a relationship with Kalajzich after Megan's death. Marlene was subpoenaed at the trial but Saunders had decided it might be detrimental to call her. He reserved the right to cross-examine Kalajzich on the content of her letters, which were never seen by the jury.

When Saunders asked Kalajzich if he had ever heard of 'cornflower blue', he said he thought it was a gemstone. When asked if he had ever called Marlene by that name, he acknowledged that he had. If he had lied, Saunders could have produced the letters.

The jurors retired at 11 am on 25 May 1988, the 49th day of the trial. During their five-hour deliberation, they asked three questions of Maxwell. At 4 pm, shortly before the court was due to close, they re-entered the courtroom and took their seats in the jury box. The verdict was apparent even before the foreman stood to deliver the verdicts. One of the women jurors began weeping and continued to weep as the verdicts were read. Tony and Sue Kalajzich walked into the courtroom just before the foreman stood.

Solemn-faced he turned towards Maxwell as he was asked for his verdict on the first charge.

'Guilty,' he said five more times as the judge's associate read out each of the three charges against both men.

Maxwell asked if either man had anything to say.

'I am not guilty of these charges. I have nothing further to say,' Kalajzich said.

Orrock said nothing. He had admitted in his record of interview with Detective Brady that he knew the gun he gave Vandenberg was to be used in a murder. For that he would suffer the same fate as Kalajzich.

The Snake, who was also in the court, stood with the rest of the spectators as the courtroom was adjourned. 'No,' he told one reporter, 'we felt no jubilation at the result. I would like to express sorrow for the members of the Kalajzich family.'

Olga Alagich, Kalajzich's sister, arrived after the verdicts and was told the result, outside.

Two days later, Orrock and Kalajzich again stood side by side in the dock as Maxwell sentenced them both to life: '. . . the macabre situation of a husband going to bed bedside his sleeping wife, awaiting the entry of her assassin, to say the least, almost beggars description,' he said. 'His pursuit of the murder of the deceased was persistent and determined.'

Maxwell said he had heard nothing from Porter that could satisfy him that there were mitigating circumstances on Kalajzich's part.

'I should add that despite my preliminary thoughts, I am unable, in the case of the prisoner Orrock, to find that there is any material before me, which likewise, could satisfy me that . . . his blameworthiness for the murder is significantly diminished by mitigating circumstances.'

The sentences would be aimed 'at demonstrating the seriousness of crimes such as these and the court's attitude to them'.

Kalajzich listened with his head bowed. When the court rose, he leant across the back of the dock. The family were sitting in the front row of the public gallery. 'It's OK,' his daughter Michele said, close to tears, as she approached her father. Olga, Tony and his wife, Sue, left their seats to speak to him. Butch was not in court.

Kalajzich and Orrock still did not look at each other. Journalists in the press box whispered comments about the severity of Orrock's sentence. They felt sorry for him. His life sentence was something no-one in court had expected.

As Kalajzich and Orrock descended the steep stairs to the cells, Kalajzich raised his left hand to wave goodbye to his relatives.

It was almost a year to the day since Elkins and Vandenberg had been sentenced.

Outside the walls of the court, in the peak-hour trafic of Darlinghurst, the television cameramen had been patiently waiting outside the courthouse grounds on the footpath behind the heavy iron gates. Finally, Tony and Sue Kalajzich emerged from the court. As soon as they saw the waiting media, Sue ducked behind a pillar, her hands over her eyes. She was crying and Tony comforted her. A photographer captured their grief with a telescopic lens.

As they walked across the pathway to the gates, they were

besieged by more than forty members of the media.

'We will still back him all the way,' Tony Kalajzich affirmed. He had a friendlier, more approachable face than his brother. Sue was still distressed and waved reporters away.

'Yes, we will be lodging an appeal,' Porter told the media as he strode from the court.

TWENTY

THE HANGING

Kalajzich had no appetite for the regulation plate of porridge, two slices of toast and carton of milk. It was 28 May 1988, his 48th birthday. That morning, he opened his eyes in 4 Wing of the maximum security section of Long Bay—the start of his life sentence.

In his thirteen months on remand, Kalajzich had procured the privileged position of librarian, which gave him access to books on the law. He would now study the laws of appeal. Elkins, in another part of the jail, was working as a cook.

Vandenberg was only a few hundred metres away in the Witness Protection Unit. His section smacked of newness and sterility. It was so isolated, the inmates, confined to their cells, often did not even know who was in the cell next door.

Vandenberg, being the workaholic he was, turned the arid sandy soil near the basketball courts into a garden.

Although death had crossed his path many times in the past two years, when the plot to kill him was unhatched, he was surprised. In a strange way, he was not scared. Not the way that he had been before all this business started. He remembered the fear which led to him buying a gun for his own protection when he thought his enemies included Canellis, Kalajzich and Elkins.

That fear had passed. He had handled a gun. He had killed someone. He had done something they had never done. Now they could be scared of him. 'The Man', as he referred to Kalajzich, had no power now.

He often thought of death these days. He was tempted to 'knock himself', to be the final arbiter of his existence.

Suicide was not new to his family. One of his brothers had gassed himself in a car.

Vandenberg had been given the sought-after job of sweeper/handyman. Later, he became the gardener, bringing life to the garden he tended rather than redistributing dust. Every day, dressed in a khaki shirt, dark blue trousers, white Dunlop Volleys and a baseball cap, he would turn the soil in the vegetable garden with a fork. He and another prisoner, 'Rocky' Cartwright, used to joke that they were growing marijuana. They told prison officers they were going to buy a racehorse and an aeroplane, and crop-dust the garden from the air.

On top of the ten-metre high red brick walls, the prison officer on duty in the dome-shaped tower watched as Vandenberg, walking between the beds, watered the tomatoes and carrots. Outside the walls, out of Vandenberg's sight, the traffic on Anzac Parade bustled along through the beachside suburb of Malabar.

Vandenberg was a popular inmate. When he 'had a downer', the prison officers would give him more work. His worst punishment was idleness. Now he was in the Witness Protection Unit, he saw himself as a 'witness' rather than a prisoner. Whenever he was transported, Vandenberg would complain about having to wear handcuffs. He had put on weight, which did not please him. He would pinch the small roll of fat around his middle distastefully.

His vulnerability was not lost on prison authorities, who watched him, waiting for any sign that he might harm himself. Apart from Rocky Cartwright, his friends included a former police officer, Max Gudgeon.

Pressure from the pending trial had taken its toll on Vandenberg. On 2 May, as the prisoners returned to their cells after dinner, Vandenberg was stopped by the supervisor, Assistant Superintendent Jenkins.

'You can't take that food back to the wing,' Jenkins said.

'What d'you mean I can't,' Vandenberg replied. 'Don't you know Max is fucking sick?'

'Mr Farrell has an order on the noticeboard that food isn't to be taken to the wing,' Jenkins countered.

Vandenberg, shaking with rage, smashed the two plates on the floor, spreading custard and bananas everywhere.

'You are a fucking idiot,' he screamed at Jenkins. 'You should be locked up.'

The other prisoners looked on. Jenkins said nothing.

'He wouldn't know if he had a fuck if he didn't ask his missus,' Vandenberg yelled. Jenkins opened the wing door and the prisoners filed silently through. Vandenberg followed, leaving the debris behind, still abusing Jenkins.

He accepted the punishment when it came: two days' cell confinement.

As the trial had progressed, Vandenberg's behaviour worsened. On 20 May, he refused to be searched or handcuffed while being escorted to the Internal Investigations Unit.

The day before Orrock and Kalajzich were sentenced, Vandenberg awoke distressed and stayed that way over breakfast. 'Concerned he might react violently toward any officer or himself,' one prison officer observed in his report.

Vandenberg was taken off the work roster. In the past he had been given more work when he was depressed. Now, authorities thought work would make him suicidal. Vandenberg took to writing letters and making complaints to prison authorities. When he was in one of his moods, he would write to Inkster or anyone who would listen.

Dear Sir, I have a serious complaint to make about the thick headedness of the staff in this place. The psychiatrist came in early this morning but couldn't see me until 9.30 due to me being locked up ... I was not able to see him myself. It gets bad when you are refused medical attention just to satisfy warped minds . . .

Despite believing he was prepared, Vandenberg was shattered when Orrock was sentenced to life. His mood was not helped by other prisoners gossiping about the case: 'I don't reckon Vandenberg looks like a hitman—more like a wimp,' one had said.

On the Saturday after the sentencing, his brother, John, and John's wife, Mary, came to see him. John Vandenberg, with his oiled black hair and smiling, sad eyes, decided to spend the day with Bill. John was used to the huddled position his brother adopted when depressed.

'Why did he get life?' Vandenberg kept asking the rhetorical question. 'Out of everybody, his part in all of this was because of me. And now he will spend the rest of his life in jail . . .'

There was nothing to say.

'I blame myself. I have destroyed his life and what about Gloria and the kids?'

Later that day, Orrock's girlfriend, Lesley Farrell, visited. She stood in front of Vandenberg, who looked up at her imploringly.

'He's going to get a divorce from Gloria,' she said, cutting Vandenberg to the quick. 'He wants you to know that he doesn't mind doing twenty years if you did the murder, but he doesn't want to sit there for somebody else.'

Vandenberg paled and looked away. The girl left, her words hanging in the air. Vandenberg got up. He wanted to go back to his cell to write.

At around midnight, the prison officer on duty Keith Paton saw Vandenberg writing at his bench when he checked his cell. At least he was occupied. Satisfied, he continued his rounds.

Vandenberg wrote more that night than he had managed the entire time he was in jail, writing separate letters to his family and friends. The he began one final letter: 'My family and the WPU should surely be entitled to a copy of this immediately . . .'

Writing was cathartic. He also found comfort in religion. They had promised him a priest, Father Terry McDonald. It was strange how he felt drawn to the Roman Catholic faith— he, whose only concession to religion was to whistle the Lord's Prayer in the shower. Seven months ago, he had seen a priest for the first time. Now he wanted to see one again. But, as usual, bureaucracy had got in the way.

'I felt I could have poured my complete heart out to him without restricting the man. So the final pieces would have fallen in place for Bob as to why a respectable man came to get himself involved in such a disastrous mess . . .' he wrote.

'My pills are now starting to work . . . and I'm just waiting for Mr Paton to make his hourly check then I will wish you good in the future and for all in here . . .'

He was glad he'd had a 'practice run' three weeks ago: a Rohypnol and Valium sandwich. He knew exactly how the drugs would affect him.

Strange how Keith Paton was on duty that night too. Vandenberg remembered the prison officer's face when he had told him he had taken ten sleeping tablets he had stored up. Vandenberg had already decided to place his own towel between his legs to minimise the mess.

Because of what I already know about dying this way, I have tried to make it as clean as possible for the people finding me. I hope that little part might be appreciated . . .

When I got sentenced to life by Justice Maxwell it hurt bad but I never once cursed the police, the prosecutor, nor the judge because I took a life . . .

I destroyed the life, not only of the woman, but just as much her daughter and son as well as her mother. All of them are the innocent victims of my terrible crime . . . My actions are done with a heavy heart but I find myself incapable of living with myself . . .

What I have done tonight should still be lawful as I think I've taken a life and deserve to lose mine.

> *I do wish to thank Bob Inkster and Kerry Flood—police officers—for their honesty in this whole matter and, as was proven in this case, because of their total honesty that nothing was based on verbals but all on facts with an awful lot of patience . . .*
>
> *They only ever asked me to search my conscience for the truth so as to make it easier to live with myself. In the long run that's what I did, but unfortunately also found that my downfall.*
>
> *I hate me for what I've done . . . I hope I have at least left a reasonable mark . . . with the authorities not to mark me down as a ratbag. But if I was to be classed as some kind of ratbag, I hope it's only because I took this way out . . .*

After writing six pages, Vandenberg was exhausted. His head was swimming from the effects of the tranquillisers. Paton had done his final check. Vandenberg knew it was now or never. 'Please don't let them treat me as a crim if I'm dead,' he wrote in the last few paragraphs. 'I should return to the very bosom of my family as I served my time very hard, but unable to go any further.'

It was Anthony, his nephew, of whom he now thought, the boy who had to face the end of his life at the age of 21. He was the only person who meant something to him.

It was 1.50 am when Paton checked the cell again. As Vandenberg had predicted, it was Paton who was left to discover his body.

Inmate 5002 P2 was hanging from a rail inside his cupboard, a noose made from torn strips of prison sheets around his neck. His body was still warm.

The rostered medical sister was called. She rang Dr Peter Paisley, the prison medical officer, who examined Vandenberg's body and pronounced life extinct.

Then the cell was photographed by the crime scene unit and an examination was made. The letters were discovered and taken to be analysed by handwriting experts. Maroubra, the closest police station, was informed and a prison officer made a report of the incident.

Post-trauma counselling was set up for some of Vandenberg's closest friends.

Vandenberg's suicide sent ripples throughout the Witness Protection Unit. Everyone was affected.

Inkster was cleaning out his aluminium fishing boat at South-West Rocks on the north coast. He had been catching flathead with an old mate, John O'Neil, a sheep farmer from Yass.

That morning, Inkster had hooked the boat onto the back of his Land Rover and towed it down to the creek. At 6.30 am, the two men had headed out to sea.

As he stood in his gumboots, shortly before 11 am, swilling the cold water out of the bottom of the boat, he looked up as two men came down the beach towards him. It was Kerry Flood his offsider and another police officer, Roger Hardy.

'Did you hear about Vandenberg?' Flood asked.

'No. What happened?'

'He necked himself.'

'Bullshit ...' Inkster knew it was inevitable, but now he couldn't believe it.

'Haven't you heard it on the news or the radio?' Flood asked.

'We've been out fishing all morning,' Inkster replied. He paused in shock.

'Come over to the hotel if you don't believe me. You'll get a paper over there,' Flood said.

They all walked up from the beach and across the road into the hotel, and waited for the 11 am news bulletin.

Inkster listened to the newsreader, then switched into official mode. Still wearing his gumboots, he plodded into the one-man police station to use the phone.

'Better get rid of those flathead,' Inkster said, emerging from the station. But as he walked back to the boat, flanked by the other three men, he felt a little deflated. Funny man that Vandenberg, the strangest criminal he had ever come across.

Vandenberg's death had little effect on prisoner 133975. Kalajzich was more concerned with the possibility of losing his appeal a prospect which gnawed at his stomach each day as he woke in his cell. The thought of spending the rest of his life in this foreign and miserable place filled him with an overwhelming despair. The verdict was a vicious blow but underneath his anguish a combative spirit flickered—the thought of a challenge and emerging victorious against all odds. He continued writing to his supporters, who still stood by him and visited him in jail.

27 July 1988

Dear . . . [he wrote to one friend]

To be found guilty of having slain Megan and to know I'll spend the rest of my life in this wretched and miserable environment is a heavy weight to carry knowing I haven't done anything to bring this about.

Our whole lives were dedicated to helping others and in any so called success I may have had was brought about by honest hard work.

I promise you I will never accept this defeat but will use all my resources and energy to find the truth. I will not allow myself to be put down for being where I am now, but I am trying to understand why this has happened and how it has changed the course of what I was pursuing as my destiny. I now see this challenge taken up by my children and I hope to regain my spirit . . .

Andrew

It was a matter of waiting until almost a year later in March 1989 that the Court of Criminal Appeal dismissed his appeal against his conviction. Now he had only one avenue left—the High Court of Australia in Canberra. Orrock also lost his appeal. Chester Porter told him there was a 90 per cent chance his appeal would be upheld by the High Court and Kalajzich hired a former top-ranking police officer to investigate his case. He told his family and friends that he had been 'a victim of a conspiracy', although the perpetrators had yet to surface.

He was working as a clerk in the prison's print shop, starting at 7.30 am, processing all incoming jobs including pricing and quoting, checking artwork and altering forms which arrived from government departments. A recent change of state government meant a change in the logo on all of the letterheads, so there was plenty of work. He also prepared the wage sheets each week, stock cards and production schedules.

He was paid $17 a week plus a bonus payment, the maximum allowed to be paid to prisoners. More importantly, he had his own office which was smoke-free. Work helped time to pass quickly.

In the evenings he read, or watched television on his own set. He had requested a computer so that he could finish a computer programming course he had started at TAFE but this was denied.

John Thomas, his accountant, was a regular visitor, and Kalajzich always found time to spend on his business, following the property market closely. Now was the time to make some investments, The Manly Pacific had been sold on May 26 1988 for $33 million.

Despite organising his life as efficiently as possible, and Porter's optimism, Kalajzich remained pessimistic about his chance of success in a High Court appeal. He disciplined himself to always expect the worse. His new life brought other diversions. He tried dabbling in water colours, toying with the idea of making some money out of his creations, but he was not artistic enough.

Weekend visits for two to four hours on Saturdays and Sundays, depending on the weather conditions, were the highlight of his week. Here were people from the real world, the world he had left behind. He could smell the 'outside' on their clothes and see it in their eyes. He continued to write to those who visited him regularly:

'. . . My battle has gone into another phase and I will do everything in my power to have myself released from here. Maybe in my life I deserve to be punished but God is my judge of that not any man. I have done nothing wilfully to hurt anyone and most of all I don't deserve to be here.

'In twenty-five years of marriage I never raised my voice to either Megan or my children and I can never conceive or condone such violence which has occurred against us all because in some way all of us have had to endure some pain from this tragedy.

Please take care of yourselves and maybe, just maybe, I will get to see you again one day.'

POSTSCRIPT

Andrew Kalajzich In May 1991 Kalajzich, jail classification A2 (security risk), was transferred to Four Wing at Lithgow maximum security prison where he is still serving his life sentence. The High Court of Australia refused Kalajzich special leave to appeal against the New South Wales Court of Criminal Appeal decision upholding his conviction in November 1990.

In March 1990 Channel Nine news reported that Kalajzich had lost his fortune in poor business investments, and one newspaper article stated that Kalajzich had spent more than $1 million on legal and investigative fees in an effort to overturn his conviction. During that year Kalajzich began selling his real estate. He put his prime Sydney business asset, a fourteen-storey office block in Market Street overlooking Darling Harbour up for sale for $28 million.

On 7 September 1990 Kalajzich's company, Britcorp, sold Beneficial House, a seven-storey city office block in George Street, for $20.5 million—$7 million less than the asking price. Kalajzich had bought the building for $15 million in May 1987.

Late in 1990 a *Sydney Morning Herald* journalist was contacted by a 'friend' of Kalajzich, who said he had a letter from Kalajzich stating that 'one man' had destroyed him financially. He also said in the letter that he had had to forfeit his substantial deposit on a Neutral Bay apartment he had planned to live in following his release.

On 8 March 1991 Kalajzich was forced to list for sale his luxury waterfront property and two houses at Cottage Point. One was sold in November for $500,000. He told a friend that he had sold the properties reluctantly, because it was where he had placed Megan's ashes.

Warren Elkins In October 1989 Elkins was released on parole from Long Bay jail after serving less than five years of a ten year sentence. He was released with a new identity under the Witness Protection Program.

Bill Vandenberg On 7 December 1988 a coroner's inquest found Vandenberg took his own life in his cell on 30 May 1988. The Coroner, Kevin Waller, found Vandenberg had hanged himself because of remorse for his crime. From evidence given at the inquest, Vandenberg emerged as a hardworking and community-spirited man who became overwhelmed by his crime and its effects.

Waller said there had been nothing but praise for police and prison authorities who had allowed Vandenberg unlimited visits and phone calls to alleviate his depression.

On 31 March 1989 Tom Domican and Peter Drummond were sentenced to fourteen years for plotting to kill Vandenberg in jail, and soliciting another prisoner, Fred Many, to carry out the murder. The Court of Criminal Appeal later quashed the convictions of Domican and Drummond. A fresh trial which started on 4 May, 1991 was deferred on request of the Crown which said it was investigating 'serious concerns' about its case and that it was not in a position to determine whether the prosecution would proceed.

Kerry Orrock On 18 July 1989 Orrock was found unconscious in his Parklea prison cell after attempting suicide by overdosing on sleeping tablets. Orrock, then 38, failed to appear for the 7.30 am muster. An empty bottle of sleeping tablets was found beside the bed.

Detective-Inspector Bob Inkster received the Australian Police Medal in the honours list on Australia Day 26 January 1991, the fifth anniversary of Megan Kalajzich's death. It was an award was for distinguished service to the NSW Police Force.

Sergeant Trevor Alt left the New South Wales Police Force in 1990 and is now working for the Department of Immigration. In 1989 he received a Police Commissioner's commendation for outstanding police work.

Detective-Inspector Mike Hagan also received an Australian Police Medal in the same honour's list as Inkster.

Allan Saunders, QC, was appointed to the District Court bench in February 1991.

The Kalajzich family On 3 February 1991 Andrew and Olga Kalajzich senior who were returning to Yugoslavia to live, put their waterfront townhouse in Oyama Avenue, Manly, on the market. It failed to reach the reserve price of $680 000 at auction.

May Carmichael On 26 May 1991 she made her 64th visit to her son-in-law Andrew Kalajzich in Lithgow jail.

Chester Porter, QC, who ceased working for Kalajzich after the second appeal to the High Court has a two-metre high portrait of himself dominating an entire wall of his Phillip Street chambers. The portrait was painted by Kalajzich's old cell-mate, Phil Player.

Legal proceedings After failing in his High Court appeal, Andrew Kalajzich is still pursuing a judicial inquiry which, if enough evidence came to light, could result in his matter re-opening along the lines of the McLeod-Lindsay case. Alexander McLeod-Lindsay's conviction for the attempted murder of his wife was overturned after he had served nine years of a fifteen year-sentence. It is the only legal avenue now available to Kalajzich.

In July 1991 the Independent Commission Against Corruption (ICAC) heard allegations that Steve Hahn and John Gordon, Kalajzich's solicitor and barrister, requested Bracey and McNab, his investigators, to conduct Corporate Affairs searches of companies, checks on telephone calls, and immigration and criminal records (not then publicly available). ICAC was investigating allegations that police and public servants routinely sold confidential government information to private investigators.

Hahn and Gordon denied they had engaged in any illegal activity in seeking that information. Hahn said that Bracey, who stopped working for Kalajzich in May 1990, had departed 'with some bitterness'.

EPILOGUE

'Tis strange—but true; for truth is always strange;
Stranger than fiction; if it could be told,
How much would novels gain by the exchange!

Lord Byron, *Don Juan XIV*

In his closing address, Chester Porter, QC, invited the jury to decide whether the 'two scoundrels', Vandenberg and Elkins, were telling the truth. There was no motive for this murder, he said.

Was Vandenberg the one who pulled the trigger? He was a self-confessed killer, but since Megan Kalajzich's murder five years ago, there are some who still say he did not do it.

Chester Porter, insisted the groupings of the bullet wounds—their accuracy and position on Megan's face—were indicative of the work of a professional killer—not Vandenberg.

John Vandenberg does not believe his brother's confession. 'He was never capable of killing her. He did it to protect someone else,' he says.

George Canellis at the trial: 'I just couldn't see him doing it.' And later: 'Vandenberg's hands would have been shaking so much he could never have aimed accurately.'

Kerry Orrock, Vandenberg's friend of twenty years, has always maintained that Vandenberg did not do it.

Vandenberg himself said that with his poor eyesight and

inexperience, he was not confident handling a gun. Ten days before the murder, he had never fired a gun. In the unedited version of a television interview he recorded with Channel Nine's Steve Barrett, shortly before he hanged himself, Vandenberg was asked about specific movements in the bedroom. When Barrett asked what happened as he approached the bed, Vandenberg replied nervously: 'I cannot talk about that' and refused to answer any other questions about it.

One of the few people who gained financially from Megan's death was Paul Blake, a convicted armed robber and friend of Vandenberg who ended up with $10 000—two-thirds of Vandenberg's pay-off for the murder. During their initial investigations into the murder, Blake was interviewed by Detective Brady, mainly to corroborate Vandenberg's story. They were apparently satisfied that they did not need to investigate further. Police knew where to find Blake during the committal proceedings and he was prepared to give evidence. His statement was tendered. But when the trial started they could not find him.

After he was convicted, Kalajzich hired his own investigators, who followed the same trail. Two of his investigators spoke to Blake and seven people said they played cricket with Blake in Wagga on the day of the murder. There were no flights that day or night from Wagga to Sydney.

Having investigated the Blake possibility, the Kalajzich camp turned elsewhere in pursuit of a killer.

In May 1989 two Sydney private investigators, John Bracey and Duncan McNab, were retained by Kalajzich's legal team at a cost of $100 an hour—about $15 000 a month. They conducted a series of interviews with Orrock at Parklea jail.

The following is a summary of notes made by McNab after a conversation he claims to have had with Orrock on 16 December 1989, Orrock, according to McNab, refused to allow any notes to be taken during their conversation.

Orrock: You said you need something big?
McNab: Yes.

> Orrock: Well, try this. Bill Vandenberg didn't do the murder . . . I killed Megan Kalajzich, I was supposed to kill Andrew as well, but I missed.
>
> McNab: How?
>
> Orrock: Bill was standing at the sliding door from the balcony. I shot her first, and just as I was about to shoot him, Bill tried to open the door a bit more but it squeaked and distracted me. I got such a surprise that I missed, and turned the gun on Bill before I realised.
>
> McNab: What did you do then?
>
> Orrock: I went to Bill but he was a mess. So I dragged him through the room and down the steps. We went out through the rumpus room, and Bill slipped a bit on the wet floor.
>
> McNab: Why did you go that way?
>
> Orrock: I didn't think I could get Bill back over the balcony, the state he was in.

Orrock reportedly said he had shot Megan before Kalajzich because 'women scream'. Orrock also allegedly told the investigators that there was another party involved, a man of 'possibly European extraction' who, along with Elkins, was a middleman in a contract killing for an unnamed third party. Orrock was to use an AR7 rifle with a silencer. The European and Elkins supposedly appeared at the Crest hotel when Orrock was staying there. They brought the weapon and discussed how to do the murder. According to Orrock the European also appeared at Fairlight Crescent on the night of the murder. Orrock was hired as the hitman and his brief was to kill Kalajzich as well as his wife. McNab and Bracey also claim that Orrock told them he had 'some twenty killings to his credit'.

McNab and Bracey claimed Orrock confessed to assaulting Megan on 11 January, saying that he hit her 'lightly' on the back of the head with a police baton. He said he had been expecting—right up to the point of hitting her—that his target would be a man, despite the fact that Megan was dressed for dinner and wearing high heels.

McNab said Orrock also told them that Vandenberg had written three letters detailing everyone who was involved in the murder. Blake, Orrock and John Vandenberg had possession of those letters.

McNab and Bracey say they are convinced Orrock is the real killer. They say they took their findings to Kalajzich's new legal team—barrister John Gordon and solicitor Stephen Hahn—who they said dismissed the theory. Then, on 14 May 1990, Bracey said he took a summary of his findings and theories to Kalajzich in Parklea jail.

He told Kalajzich that Gordon did not believe Orrock because Gordon was convinced Orrock was fabricating a confession to get Kalajzich out of jail, hoping he would be paid $1 million. Bracey said Gordon believed Canellis was the killer. That Orrock was working for anyone other than Kalajzich seems unlikely. After his many bungled attempts at the murder, Vandenberg may have confided in Orrock, his best friend, that he could not do it. Orrock came down to Sydney to stay at the Crest hotel, booked in under his own name, to offer Vandenberg moral support. Realising his friend was incapable of killing anyone, Orrock, after many hours of discussion, could have offered to do the job for him. Vandenberg who already knew the layout of the house may have accompanied Orrock on the night of the murder. Vandenberg may have told Orrock that they would never be caught, having been assured by Elkins that it would be blamed on Croatians.

After his arrest, while waiting at Maitland police station to be taken to Sydney for further questioning, Orrock was told that Vandenberg had confessed to the murder. It is possible Vandenberg decided to 'take the rap' for his old friend, not knowing that Orrock would be convicted for life for his role in the conspiracy by supplying the murder weapon.

The theory that Orrock did the killing could explain Vandenberg's cryptic references in his suicide note that Bob Inkster never really knew the full story and that, had he been able to speak to a priest, Vandenberg could have given a full confession. Vandenberg also stated in a letter to the priest Inkster in December, before he committed suicide: 'A man could have a heart seizure or anything else go wrong with him without having said the things he wanted to.'

When asked by the authors about the comments in the suicide note, Inkster said they referred to Vandenberg's homosexuality, which Vandenberg had never discussed with him.

Another theory for the killing was that Kalajzich was being framed with his wife's murder so he would be forced to sell the Manly Pacific hotel at a greatly reduced price. Another rumour suggested Elkins was acting for an Asian connection or a notorious underworld figure. So far, neither of these rumours has been proved.

Whatever the truth, the identity of the killer of Megan Kalajzich has been buried with Vandenberg. There are only two other people who may know more. One is Orrock, who up until the time of publication had said nothing further about his involvement and had attempted suicide once. The other is Kalajzich himself.

Now, four years after the murder, the Director of Public Prosecutions has been informed that Kalajzich would be lodging an application for a judicial inquiry but at the time this book went to press that application was yet to be lodged.